T·H·E
COMPLETE
FISH ON THE GRILL

BARBARA GRUNES
and PHYLLIS MAGIDA

CB

CONTEMPORARY
BOOKS

CHICAGO

Library of Congress Cataloging-in-Publication Data

Grunes, Barbara.
    The complete fish on the grill : more than 200 easy and delectable
recipes / Barbara Grunes and Phyllis Magida.
        p.   cm.
    Portions of this book were previously published as: Fish on the
grill, Shellfish on the grill, and Gourmet fish on the grill.
    Includes index.
    ISBN 0-8092-3618-4 (paper)
    1. Cookery (Fish)   2. Cookery (Shellfish)   3. Barbecue cookery.
I. Magida, Phyllis.   II. Title.
TX747.G8347   1994
641.6'92—dc20   94-5201
                                                             CIP

Cover photograph by C. C. Cain Photography

Line Art by Princess Louise El

Portions of the material in this book were published previously
in *Fish on the Grill*, *Shellfish on the Grill*, and *Gourmet Fish on
the Grill*, all by Barbara Grunes and Phyllis Magida.

Copyright © 1994 by Barbara Grunes and Phyllis Magida
All rights reserved
Published by Contemporary Books, Inc.
Two Prudential Plaza, Chicago, Illinois 60601-6790
Manufactured in the United States of America
International Standard Book Number: 0-8092-3618-4
10   9   8   7   6   5   4   3   2   1

We dedicate this book both to our readers and to all cooks and eaters who love fresh, healthy food made in the best way possible—on the backyard, back porch, or outdoor balcony grill.

PART I
THE FUNDAMENTALS

PART II
THE RECIPES

INTRODUCTION

Fresh grilled fish is the food of today—it's speedy and easy to make; it's healthy, sophisticated, and delicious!

Before turning to the recipe section, take a few moments to read the information in Part I. There you'll find some fish and shellfish grilling fundamentals, including fuel selection and tips for grilling shellfish successfully. Part I also provides charts listing the various kinds of seafood and nutritional information for each, information on buying fresh fish, and general tips on serving amounts, cooking times, and substitutions. If you need instructions on how to get the shellfish out of their shells, refer to the information in "Cleaning Various Shellfish," where each type of shellfish has its own section, presented alphabetically. Also see "Special Strategies, Tips, Ideas, and Recipes" in Part I for suggestions on extra fast fish preparation in addition to some basic recipes for sauces and a marinade. Ways to use leftover fish, suggested grilled vegetable accompaniments, and hints for entertaining are also presented in "Special Strategies. . . ."

Part II includes recipes for a variety of seafood ranging from the popular and more familiar salmon, sole, and shrimp to the less familiar snails and rockfish. These recipes have been chosen with several considerations in mind. First, we wanted to use different varieties of fish so we could explore the textural possibilities. The fish used in our recipes range from the very delicate, such as sole, to the sturdier varieties like swordfish. We also wanted to explore the different cuts of fish. Like pasta, which many people insist changes flavor and texture with its shape (i.e., manicotti is said to have a different quality than linguine), we think that a fillet of fish has a different quality than a fish steak, that fish chunks on a skewer differ greatly from fish grilled whole.

The recipes here reflect the healthy and exciting innovation prevalent in cooking today. You'll find these recipes both flavorful and light, with influences ranging from Cajun to Californian, from Thai through Southwestern American. We combed the globe to find recipes and flavors that are interesting, unusual, and fast and easy to prepare. Then we adapted them to suit the tastes of Americans and to call for ingredients available in this country. In addition, we think we've succeeded in bringing you the best that many cuisines have to offer for entertaining. Remember, though, that when you are entertaining and serving something unfamiliar, to include something familiar, such as a bowl of hot barbecue sauce or another familiar sauce; you'll discover that there is always at least one guest who has trouble with any food that is new.

And, of course, we wanted to include recipes that would give you a choice of time spent in preparation. While most of the recipes in this book are not at all time-consuming (one of the advantages of grilled fish) for entertaining or even just for the days when you have the afternoon available, we have included longer, more complicated recipes, like Shrimp Tandoori, where the shrimp marinate for some time before being cooked.

We designed the recipes to be flexible. For example, you'll note that we suggest margarine as an alternative to butter in many recipes. Also, for many recipes we have included specific suggested substitutions for the fish called for, which are in addition to the substitutions noted at the beginning of each fish section. Try our recipes as written, and then go ahead and experiment! Create and enjoy, as we did in developing this book for you.

Happy Grilling,
Phyllis Magida and Barbara Grunes

PART I
THE FUNDAMENTALS

A COMPENDIUM OF FISH FACTS

*

HOW TO BUY FISH

This is the most important technique you can master.

Go to a fish market with the largest possible turnover, then make frien[ds]
with your fishmonger. Ask him for the freshest possible fish. If you want to
cook fresh trout, but the grouper is fresher, buy the grouper and change your
recipe plans. Freshness is more important than anything else in buying fish.

To choose a fresh whole fish, look for crystal-clear, bright eyes and gills
that show a little bit of red underneath. If the eyes are cloudy, or if the gills
are brown or darker underneath, the fish is too old. Also, the skin should
look fresh and glistening; if it has begun to turn gray or fade, the fish is old.
With your finger, push a small dent into the side of the fish. If the fish is
fresh, the flesh will be elastic and firm enough to spring back, filling up the
dent. If the dent remains, the fish is too old. Lastly, open the fish up and
smell the inside, where the intestines have been removed. If the fish is fresh,
it will have no odor beyond the faint smell of seaweed.

Fish steaks and fillets should feel firm and moist to the touch, not spongy
or dry. The flesh should have a translucent, clear look and not be at all milky
and white. If possible, ask the fishmonger to cut the fish steaks to order from
a fish you have chosen. Fillets should be firm, translucent, and not white—
whiteness is a sign of age. Run your finger over the surface of the fillet. If
you get a slimy, sticky mucus on your finger, the fish is old.

Fresh fish are available at a number of places: supermarkets, specialty
fish shops, and fish farms (where you catch your own). Look first at the fish
caught in your area—they are probably cheaper and fresher than imported
varieties. In the past, fish and shellfish were always shipped frozen. This is
only sometimes true today, and frozen does not necessarily mean tasteless. Ask
your fishmonger to advise you.

When possible, buy fish with the head, the tail, and the backbone intact.

tail will seal in the juices, and the

which is important when cooking a large

_sh to Buy per Person

sh to allow per person. Although most
meal, we have upped the servings for
ncooked fish, which weighs more than
new in this country, and since your
to serve them slightly larger portions
mounts of animal protein, and you
re skimping on the entree. (4) We

H TO BUY
_UN, PER SERVING

_y small individual 1-lb. fish per person. Figure 1 lb. or slightly less per person when portions are part of a larger fish (3–3½ lb. stuffed fish will serve 3–4 people amply).

Fish Fillets	7 oz. per person
Fish Steaks	7 oz. per person
Fish Kabobs	7 oz. per person

Most of our recipes developed specifically for entertaining serve eight, and they can easily be cut in half to serve four. In these, we call for 3 pounds of fish—roughly 6 ounces of raw fish per person, which will end up as 4½–5 ounces cooked, which should be more than enough.

FISH SPECIES

Fish come naturally in many guises: fatty, moderate, or lean; freshwater (more small, tiny bones) or saltwater (fewer small, annoying bones); cool-water fish (with richer flavor caused by higher fat content) and warm-water fish; and don't forget the textural differences, ranging from tender, delicately melting types to fish so firm and chewy that you'll feel as though you're eating beef.

The chart on pages 5–7 includes fat content, texture, and calories per

100 grams (about 3½ oz., raw) of the wide variety of fish you'll find in this book. Calorie and fat content charts are based on USDA figures. Textural comments are made by authors and refer to cooked texture. When a fish is designated fatty, this means it contains over 10 percent fat; when a fish is designated moderate, it has 6–10 percent fat; when a fish is designated lean, this means it has less than 5 percent fat. While all fish species are relatively low in fat, for those on very low-fat, low-calorie diets, serve the portions designated in the preceding chart but choose one of the lean species listed. In general, fish are not high in cholesterol.

When you're beginning to experiment with fish, you may want to substitute a fish of similar flavor and texture in a recipe. Almost every fish is interchangeable in our recipes. Kabobs are the exception; soft-fleshed fish will not stay on the skewer. The chart below shows which types are similar to others, as well as nutritional information.

FAT CONTENT, TEXTURE, FLAVOR AND CALORIES IN FISH SPECIES

FISH	FAT CONTENT	TEXTURE & FLAVOR	CALORIES per 100 g	SUBSTITUTIONS
Bass, black sea	low	med. firm mild	100	red sea bass, striped sea bass, grouper, halibut, mahi mahi, rockfish, snapper, tilefish, monkfish, porgy
Bass, red sea	low	med. firm mild	90	same as black sea bass
Bass, striped	low	med. firm mild	90	red sea bass, black sea bass, grouper, halibut, orange roughy, ocean perch, rockfish, tilefish
Bluefish	mod. high	delicate distinctive	110	mackerel, kingfish, whitefish, lake trout, rainbow trout
Buffalofish	high	med. distinctive	215	red sea bass, black sea bass, snapper, yellowtail, butterfish
Catfish freshwater	mod. high	med. firm sweet	115	orange roughy, ocean perch, small rockfish, walleye pike
Cod	low	delicate mild	75	scrod (the same as cod), haddock, pollack, lingcod, black cod, flounder

FISH	FAT CONTENT	TEXTURE & FLAVOR	CALORIES per 100 g	SUBSTITUTIONS
Grouper	low	firm mild	95	black sea bass, red sea bass, snapper, halibut, walleye pike, tautog, tilefish
Halibut	mod. high	med. firm sweet	110	black sea bass, red sea bass, snapper, mahi mahi, yellowtail, tilefish
Mackerel	high	med. distinctive	175	bluefish, rainbow trout, brook trout, whitefish, lake trout, yellowtail, sea trout
Mahimahi	mod. low	med. firm mild	90	black sea bass, red sea bass, snapper, ono, salmon, yellowtail, sea trout
Ono	med.	firm mild	120	swordfish, shark, kingfish, rockfish, snapper, grouper, yellowtail, pompano
Orange Roughy	low	med. very mild	75	sole, catfish, scrod (cod), haddock, pollack, small rockfish, ocean perch, turbot, flounder, tilapia
Ocean Perch	mod. high	med. mild	105	walleye pike, orange roughy, flounder, turbot, small rockfish, tilapia, sea trout
Pompano	high	med. mildly distinct	165	ono, yellowtail, kingfish, swordfish, bluefish, mackerel
Redfish	low	med. firm mild	90	same as black sea bass
Rockfish	low	med. firm mild	90	snapper, grouper, catfish, ocean perch, sea bass, tilefish, monkfish, sea trout
Salmon Atlantic	high	med. firm mildly distinct	220	all salmon can be substituted for one another. lake trout, whitefish, rainbow trout, brook trout
Salmon Chinook	high	med. firm mildly distinct	185	same as Atlantic Salmon
Salmon Sockeye	high	med. firm mildly distinct	155	same as Atlantic Salmon

FISH	FAT CONTENT	TEXTURE & FLAVOR	CALORIES per 100 g	SUB
Scrod	low	delicate mild	75	same as cod
Shark	mod. low	firm mildly distinct	85	swordfish, ono (marlin
Sole	low	delicate sweet	85	orange roughy, ocean p flounder, turbot, tilapia
Snapper, red	mod. low	med. firm mild	110	same as black sea bass
Swordfish	mod. high	firm mildly distinct	125	ono (wahoo), shark, tuna, marlin
Trout, brook	mod. high	med. mildly distinct	110	rainbow trout, lake trout, salmon, walleye pike, whitefish, crappie, sunfish, haddock, pollack
Trout, rainbow	high	med. mildly distinct	130	same as brook trout
Trout, lake	high	med. mildly distinct	165	same as brook trout
Tuna, bluefin	high	firm mildly distinct	160	swordfish, shark, ono (wahoo), any other tuna, marlin
Tuna, yellowfin	mod. high	firm mildly distinct	125	same as bluefin tuna
Yellowtail Pacific coast	mod. low	med. firm mild	100	snapper, grouper, kingfish, ono (wahoo), pompano, rockfish, tautog
Walleye pike	low	med. firm mildly distinct	90	flounder, rainbow trout, brook trout, ocean perch, catfish, lake perch, crappie, sunfish, tilapia
Whitefish, lake	high	delicate mildly distinct	165	same as brook trout

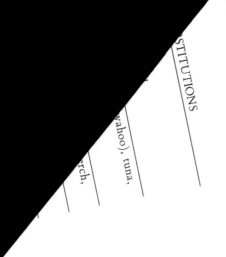

STITUTIONS

wahoo), tuna,

rch,

TO STORE FISH

ing it home. But if you must store the fish
with water and setting it in the freezer.
e pan to freeze, rinse the fish in cold,
er towels. Rewrap it in clean waxed
bag and secure it with a twister seal. Set
and the fish with the plastic wrap;

e the pan from the freezer. Place the
t in the refrigerator overnight. It will
se it.

FACTS

kinds of aquatic life by their
ive them both structural support and
against enemies. This armor ranges in
easy-to-remove shrimp shells to the oyster and blue crab
which are difficult to open.

Shellfish are divided into two classes: crustaceans and mollusks. For
culinary purposes, the distinction is simply that the crustaceans (except for
the hard-shell crab varieties) have softer shells and the mollusks harder shells.

Technically, crustaceans are sea animals with hard-crusted bodies that are
segmented and joined together by flexible membranes. Crustaceans include
American lobsters, crabs, crayfish, shrimp, and spiny lobsters.

Mollusks are more complicated. They're defined as aquatic animals
characterized by a calcareous (hard) shell of one or two pieces, enclosing a
soft body. What makes them complicated is the fact that they're divided into
two classes: univalves (having one valve or shell) and bivalves (having two
halves or shells). The univalves we use in this book include conch and snails;
squid, too, is a univalve, in which the shell was once present but has been
outgrown. The bivalves we use here include clams, mussels, oysters, and
scallops.

Whether crustacean or mollusk, bivalve or univalve, the important thing
to remember is that all shellfish are accessible, no matter how complicated or
hard their shells. Directions on opening shellfish appear later in Part I.

The shellfish species chart provides comments on cooked texture.

TEXTURE AND FLAVOR IN SHELLFISH SPECIES

SHELLFISH	TEXTURE & FLAVOR
Clams	firm distinctive
Crab	med. firm mildly distinct
Lobster	firm mildly distinct
Mussels	med. mildly distinct
Oysters	med. distinctive
Scallops	med. mild
Shrimp	med. firm mildly distinct

The charts that follow provide nutritional information on some of the shellfish species represented in this book. Latest research indicates that the cholesterol levels of shellfish are negligible to moderate at most. Because shellfish are lower in fat that most fin fish, there is less of this protective substance than in higher-fat seafoods such as salmon and mackerel. Various studies have shown that omega-3 fatty acids work many ways in the body to help prevent heart disease and cancer. Except for imitation crab (*surimi* blend), all shellfish are suitable for use on sodium-restricted diets if sodium is not added in food preparation or in sauces.

CALORIES, PROTEIN, AND FAT IN SHELLFISH
(3½-OZ. RAW SHELLED PORTION)

SHELLFISH	CALORIES	PRO (g)	FAT (g)
Clams	80	11.0	1.5
Crab, Dungeness	81	17.3	1.3
Crab (imitation), *Surimi* Blend	90	13.4	0.1
Crab, King	75	15.2	0.8
Lobster (1 pound, in shell)	90	16.9	1.9
Lobster, Spiny	74	8.2	1.6
Mussels	75	12.2	1.6

SHELLFISH	CALORIES	PRO (g)	FAT (g)
Oysters	70	14.2	1.2
Scallops	82	15.3	0.2
Shrimp	90	18.8	0.8
Squid	85	16.4	0.9

CHOLESTEROL LEVELS, OMEGA-3 FATTY ACIDS, AND SODIUM LEVELS OF SHELLFISH (3½-OZ. RAW SHELLED PORTION)

SHELLFISH	CHOLESTEROL (mg)	OMEGA-3 FATTY ACIDS (g)	SODIUM (mg)
Abalone	85	—	—
Clams	34	Trace	80
Crab, Blue	78	—	—
Crab, Dungeness	59	0.3	266
Crab (imitation), *Surimi* Blend	50	—	600
Crab, King	42	—	70
Crayfish	139	—	—
Lobster	70–95	0.2	210*
Mussels	80	0.5	80
Oysters, Eastern	55	0.6	75
Scallops	33	0.2	160
Shrimp	152	0.3	140
Squid	233	0.3	160

*1 pound, in shell

CLEANING VARIOUS SHELLFISH
Removing Conch from Its Shell

Removing the live conch from its shell is difficult and unpleasant. A hole must be made in the top of the shell at the third spiral with a hammer; this exposes the muscle that attaches the shell to the body. This muscle must then be cut so that the conch can drop out of its shell. The foot portion should be cut away from the rest of the animal and must then be skinned, pounded, and cut into slices, strips, or chunks.

Another method: We recommend buying it already prepared and frozen, if possible. Once it has been tenderized, conch meat needs only a few moments on the grill on each side. We suggest dipping it in a protective coating before grilling, such as the egg white and bread crumbs we call for in the conch recipe in this book.

Shucking Clams

Tool: clam knife. (Note: This is not an oyster knife; a clam knife is a straight-sided knife with a blunt, rounded four-inch blade and a two-inch handle.)

Pick up a clam with one hand and stand it upright, hinge side down, on a pot holder. Hold it tightly with your hand while you insert the clam knife blade between the shells directly opposite the hinge. Once the knife is inserted, begin twisting it and prying open the shells. This may take a couple of minutes.

Another method: Beg your fishmonger to open them for you a short time before you are due to use them in the recipe or substitute canned clams.

A note on clam freshness: Clams are fresh when their shells remain tightly closed. Like oysters, if they are slightly open and do not close tightly once they are touched, they should be discarded. Next, clams should be given the following test: place them in a large container filled with water and see if they float; most of them will sink to the bottom, but if any do float, they should be discarded. Discard also any clams that have broken shells.

Removing Meat from the Crab Shell After Grilling

Many varieties of crab can be grilled, and the procedure for extracting the meat is basically the same for all of them. Therefore, we've chosen to give directions for the blue crab, one of the hardest-shell varieties. If you wish to remove shells from other varieties of crab, just use these instructions as a guide.

Tools: lobster pick, lobster cracker or mallet.

Once the crab has been grilled, pick it up and look at the underside, locating the apron flap. This is the portion of the shell that grows where the apron would be if the crab were wearing one. Pry off the apron flap, using either your thumb or a knife point. Underneath the apron flap, you will find light green gills on either side of the body. Scrape these out; then scrape out the dark gray digestive organs, which are located in the center of the crab. If you find some orange roe—which means the crab is a female—discard it. Lobster roe is delicious; crab roe is not.

Now turn the crab over and use your thumb or the point of a knife to lift off the top body part of the shell. Then break off the large claws and set them aside. Pick up the crab in both hands and break it in half in the center so the body meat is accessible. Remove the body meat using your fingers or a pick; you can also use a knife. Break off the small legs and throw away unless the crab is so large that the meat in the small legs can be extracted as if you're sipping lemonade through a straw.

To open the large claws on the blue crab, you'll need a lobster cracker or mallet. To use a lobster cracker, insert the claw into the cracker as you would put a nut into a nutcracker. Press down hard. You will probably need to do this in several places on the claw. When the shell is sufficiently broken, pick off the shell pieces. Or, if desired, hit the claw with a mallet. Then use your fingers or the blade of a knife to remove the shell pieces.

Cooking Crayfish

For cooking purposes, this variety of crustacean should be considered a small lobster, since it is covered with a similar shell and resembles a lobster. Crayfish are usually anywhere between three and eight inches in length. Ask the fishmonger to prepare these animals for grilling just as you would ask him to prepare lobsters. Then take them home, refrigerate, and cook them within two hours. Grill crayfish in their shells, using a grill basket if possible, or skewer them.

Removing Crayfish Shells

After grilling, pick up the crayfish, holding the tail in one hand and the head in the other. Twist your hands in opposite directions and pull the crayfish apart. Hold the body to your lips, drawing in the juices as if you were sucking on a straw. Then pry the tail open with your fingers to extract the meat, using your thumb as a lever.

Preparing Lobsters for Grilling

We strongly urge you to have the fishmonger do all the preparation of the lobster for the grill, since his manner is both quick and painless to the lobster. Once you've picked up the prepared lobster, take it home quickly and refrigerate, then grill it within a couple of hours. Lobsters can be put whole on the grill, once the fishmonger has prepared them.

Or you can ask your fishmonger to do the following pregrilling preparation: Split the lobster lengthwise, cutting through the top shell and meat, but not cutting through the bottom shell. Then, open the lobster to butterfly it and remove and discard the stomach and white intestinal vein.

If you have had experience with preparing lobsters and feel that you can do it yourself, buy them live (you may store them in the refrigerator for one or two days). Place the lobster on its back, protect your hands with a towel, and with a very sharp, strong knife, make a deep slit from thorax to tail, cutting the lobster in half lengthwise without cutting through the bottom shell. Open the lobster to butterfly it and remove and discard the stomach and white intestinal vein. Green tomalley and roe can be left in place.

Removing the Shell from Whole Grilled Lobster
Tools: lobster cracker, lobster pick.

Pick the lobster up in one hand and locate a claw—one of the big arms that resemble big red boxing gloves. Use your other hand to twist this claw from the body. Then twist off the second claw in the same manner. Pick up the lobster cracker (the tool that resembles a nutcracker) in your right hand, insert one of the lobster claws into it, and press down hard until the shell breaks. Use the lobster cracker on various sections of the claw until the shell is sufficiently broken. Then remove as much of the shell as possible with your fingers and eat the meat. Repeat with the remaining claw.

Next, pick up the whole lobster, holding the tail in one hand and the body/head section in the other, and crack the lobster in half so that you end up with one section in each hand. Lay the tail section down and hold the body/head section belly side up. Stick your right thumb between the meat and the shell bottom and lift, using your fingers to pull the meat out of the shell. Break off the tiny claw-legs still connected to the body meat you've removed and reserve them for a moment. Then remove the second, softer undershell, called the *belly shell*.

Next, discard the black vein that runs the length of the body meat. You should also discard the small sac at the base of the lobster's head called the *sand sac*. Everything else—including the tomalley (drab green-colored liver)— is safe to eat. You may even find some coral-colored roe (eggs), if your lobster is female. Both the tomalley and the roe are delicious.

Finally, pick up the tail section in one hand. Use the other hand to bend the tail section back and break the flippers off the end. Insert a lobster fork into the hole you've made and push gently; the tail meat will come out the other end. When it does, remove the black vein that runs the length of the tail and discard.

To eat the small claw legs, put the open end of each into your mouth, and suck out the meat as if using a straw.

Preparing Lobster Tails for Grilling

Simply use a sharp knife or kitchen shears to cut away the top membrane, then use the knife to loosen the lobster meat from the shell, taking care to leave the shell partially connected.

Monkfish—Poor Man's Lobster

Examine monkfish fillets carefully, making sure they are thoroughly skinned. Look particularly at the ridge area down the center. If any skin remains in this ridge it will make the fish tough.

When cooking monkfish, if one end is much thicker than the other, butterfly that section only to ensure more even cooking. Do this before putting it in the marinade.

Cleaning Mussels

If you cannot find farm-raised mussels, you'll need to clean the mussels.

Tools: wire brush, small sharp knife, bucket, flour or cornmeal.

Scrub the mussel shells with a wire brush, then use a small sharp knife to remove any barnacles. Pull out all seaweed fibers (the beard) sticking out of the shell. Next, put the mussels in a bucket of cold water with a handful of cornmeal or flour. After a while, the mussels will begin to gurgle and bubble. Let them sit in this water one to two hours. Remove them from the pot and rinse them under cold running tap water. If you skip this step after you've allowed them to soak, the mussels will feel slick to the touch. Then pull out any additional fibers that may be sticking out of the shell.

Opening Mussels Before Grilling

Simply steam them above simmering water, broth, or court bouillon for 3 minutes. Discard any unopened mussels.

Shucking Oysters

Tool: oyster knife (a narrow, short, thick-bladed knife in a wooden handle).

After you wash the oyster shell under running water, locate the weakest point in the shell. To do this, look hard at the flat shell, which is the top one. You will see rings—similar to a spiral—which are formed as the oyster grows. Study the spiral for a moment to locate the place where the rings stopped growing. This will be opposite and a little to the left of the hinge. This is the weakest part of the oyster shell.

As soon as you've found it, lay the oyster on a pot holder with the hinge facing to the left. Grab the oyster and pot holder together securely; your fingers will be under the pot holder, and your thumb should be touching the top of the oyster shell to hold it securely. Insert the point of your oyster knife at the weakest point in the shell. Pry the shell open. It will be a little hard to open, but it can be done. If the shell opens too easily, without any resistance, discard the oyster. Difficulty in opening it means the muscle is still functioning. Run the oyster knife around the shell to loosen the muscle from the hinge. Then remove oysters and use as directed.

You might also want to open fresh oysters, remove them from their shells, and skewer them for grilling. To do this, you'll need to protect the oysters by breading them lightly before grilling.

A note on oyster freshness: Oysters are fresh when their shells remain tightly closed, indicating the animal inside is alive. If the shells are open and do not close quickly when you handle them, they should be discarded.

Shelling and Cleaning Shrimp

Shrimp can be shelled before or after cooking. To shell shrimp, simply tear open the shell on the inside of the curve, where it is the softest, then peel off the remainder. Although it is perfectly safe to eat shrimp without removing the black sand vein located along the curved back (and sometimes along the front) of the shrimp, we prefer the nicety of serving them cleaned. Simply make a shallow cut down the back of the peeled shrimp and wash the black vein out under cold running tap water. If you wish to cook the shrimp in their shells—which protects them on the grill—you may split the shells down the back and remove the vein without removing the shell.

Skewering Shrimp: The Serpentine Method

The serpentine or interlocking method of skewering shrimp is guaranteed to generate comments from your guests. This method can be used when you are grilling plain shrimp or when you want to marinate them beforehand; simply skewer the shrimp in this fashion, then lay them in the marinade, turning occasionally, before grilling. These instructions are based on using medium to large shrimp, shelled and deveined.

Tools: Oriental wooden barbecue skewers (one skewer for every six shrimp).

1. Working with two shrimp at a time, and holding skewer upright, thread the tail of shrimp #1 onto skewer with head curling up on the left side of skewer.
2. Thread tail of shrimp #2 on skewer with head curling up on the right side of skewer.
3. Thread head of shrimp #1 on skewer.
4. Thread head of shrimp #2 on skewer.
5. Push shrimp heads and tails together tightly, then push both interlocked shrimp to the bottom of the skewer.
6. Repeat with next two shrimp; then repeat again with remaining two shrimp. You will end up with three sets of interlocked shrimp. If there is room, arrange an additional set of interlocked shrimp on skewers.
7. Marinate and grill or grill immediately. Serve one or two skewers to each guest, depending on shrimp size.

Cleaning Baby or Medium-Sized Squid

Separate the mantle (body) from the tentacles. To do this, hold the body in one hand and use the other hand to hold the tentacles just above the eyes. Gently pull the two sections apart. To clean the body portion, remove the transparent sword-shaped quill called the *pen*. This rudimentary bone is located in the back of the body. You'll be able to feel this tiny bone when you hold the body. Make a small cut at the top of the bony portion, then squeeze or pull the quill out and discard.

Next, take a spoon or use your finger and insert it into the mantle, scooping out any remaining matter. Rinse the body under cold running water and then peel off the outer membrane. The meat underneath will be snow white in color. Finally, pull the fins away from the body.

If you wish to use the tentacles in any of the stuffed squid recipes, clean them as follows: Cut the eye section away from the arms and discard the eyes. In the center of the tentacles, at the base, you'll feel a small, hard bone. This is the beak. Squeeze it out by applying pressure with both thumbs. When the tentacle portion is cleaned, chop it finely and brown it in a little butter; then add it to the stuffing you've made.

THE TOOLS: GRILLS, FUELS, AND MORE

In regular indoor cooking, you have to know your oven and your pots and pans. The same holds true in grilling; you have to know your grill, your tools, and your fuel. This section will help you familiarize yourself with these elements of grilling.

Minimally you will need only the simplest equipment: a grill, some fuel, a way to start the fire, and, of course, a piece of fish. Maximally, you can have every type of skewer and basket. You are limited only by your imagination.

GRILLS

There are basically three types of grills, although many variations and attachments appear regularly on the market. All of these are applicable and workable for grilling fish, but none are any better than any other, providing you know how to use your grill.

The Basic Brazier

The simplest brazier type consists basically of a pan with raised sides to hold the fire and a grill over the fire to hold the food. It has no cover to hold in the smoke and no vents to help control the heat. Sometimes it sits on legs; sometimes it's laid flat on the ground. It is manually heated with charcoal, never gas or electricity. This type of grill sometimes costs very little in drugstores and supermarkets. It is very satisfactory for all fish (and most other foods). It is not recommended for whole birds and roasts—foods that need longer, slower cooking.

Another type of grill consists of a brazier with a hood. The hood may be merely a shield from the wind and rain, or

18

it can be more elaborate, containing vents to help regulate the heat (shutting off the air helps keep the fire under control), which circulates around the food in a manner similar to the heat circulation in an oven. A cover also increases the amount of smoke circulating around the food, resulting in food with a smokier flavor. It hastens cooking, too, since heat is reflected off the inside surface of the cover.

Round grills with round covers are called *barbecue kettles*. Rectangular grills with rectangular covers (sometimes they have wheels) are often called *grill wagons*. Covered grills most often use charcoal for fuel, though many outdoor cooks today substitute aromatic hardwood chunks or add hardwood to a charcoal base.

A more elaborate type of brazier with a hood is heated by gas or electricity. The heating element is often surrounded by a permanent bed of lava rock or contains a plate to catch the drippings. These grills can be either freestanding or installed permanently in the backyard or on a patio (and, in some cases, in a well-ventilated kitchen or fireplace). When the fat from the food drips onto the bed of volcanic rock, it sizzles and sends up smoke, which helps flavor the food. Some manufacturers of gas and electric grills feel that the smoke from the sizzling fat is wholly responsible for the characteristic barbecue flavor. Our feeling, however, is that the sizzling fat smoke makes up only part of the grilled flavor, that the best grilled food results from a combination of sizzling fat smoke and charcoal and/or wood smoke.

The Hibachi

One ethnic grill, called a Japanese hibachi, has become very popular in this country. These cunning little cookers have no legs, which means they can be set up right on the outdoor table where you will be eating. Hibachis are also at their best when set up on fire escapes, back stairs, and rooftops, since they can be easily withdrawn when faced with complaining landlords or neighbors. It's in the nature of the hibachi that it is very small—too small, unfortunately, to make a grilled dinner for four; but it will accommodate two or three adequately. Hibachis can often be quite expensive.

The water smoker, a third type of grill, functions differently from the regular charcoal grill. Food put in it to smoke is usually left for several hours—unlike the grilled recipes we suggest in this book, which take only minutes to cook. Water smokers, which consist of a firebox, a pan of water, a grill, and a cover, are at their best when smoking large pieces of food, such as pheasant, duck, turkey, large cuts of meat, and, of course, whole fish. It also accommodates fish steaks or fillets nicely. This grill is perfect for the large fish you catch yourself, bring home, and put on the smoker the same day.

When purchasing a grill, consider the area where you will be cooking. If you have a small balcony, you will need a small grill. With a larger space you have more options. But if you are keen on cooking a whole fish, you may have to juggle the size of the grill with the size of the fish you want to cook.

Grilling, whether fish or meat, is probably one of the oldest cooking methods. Grill manufacturers have had a lot of time to perfect the equipment and we recommend all types of grills.

FUEL

Charcoal

There are two basic kinds of charcoal: pure hardwood charcoal, which is sold in lump form, and charcoal that has been compressed into briquet form. Pure hardwood charcoal is made by burning hardwood until it's dry and porous. Pure hardwood charcoal is always marked as such on the box (sometimes with the name of the wood or woods also indicated) and is more expensive than briquets. The smoke that comes from pure hardwood charcoal has a slightly more savory, woody scent and is superior to that from briquets.

Briquets may be labeled simply *briquets, charcoal briquets, compressed wood charcoal,* or something similar. They may be made entirely of charred pieces of wood, or the wood may be compressed mechanically with charred paper and/or sawdust, all of which is held together with some kind of artificial mastic such as a petroleum product. Unfortunately, there is no standard of identity for briquets, so the quality of the smoke they produce when burning varies widely. The best briquets contain very little mastic—just enough to hold them together—and, in the bag, smell faintly of burnt wood. Avoid those that, in the bag, have an artificial odor such as motor oil; these may give off the same odor when they burn. The smoke that comes from burning the best of the impure hardwood briquets is pleasant and acceptable.

In terms of flavor, when grilling a fish fillet or fish steak, some people insist it doesn't really matter whether you use pure hardwood charcoal or other kinds of briquets (provided they're of good quality) since fish pieces cook so quickly that they absorb only a small amount of smoky flavor. Of course, if you're cooking a large, whole fish in a smoker or covered grill for a long period of time, you may want to use the pure stuff, since a whole fish takes longer cooking time and so absorbs more smoky flavor.

But for the sake of purity, many people choose pure hardwood charcoal. After all, they reason, a fresh piece of fish is pure and natural, and grilling is a pure and natural cooking method, so why adulterate the finished product by using impure charcoal? For most of us, good-quality briquets are very acceptable, but if you have a particularly sensitive palate, you'll want to use the pure hardwood stuff.

Aromatics

Whether you use a pure hardwood charcoal or plain briquets, you can intensify the smoky flavor of your fish by throwing various kinds of aromatics onto your hot coals before cooking. Most aromatics are available in the form of fruitwood or hardwood cuttings and include mesquite, hickory, oak, apple, maple, and cherry wood chips. Each wood gives its own flavor to the smoke, and you may want to experiment with some of them or mix and match.

Hickory, for example, has a strong, identifiable flavor and a pungent aroma; oak is similar to hickory, but slightly less pungent and a little sweeter. Cherry and other fruitwoods such as apple produce a particularly sweet-smelling smoke and so are effective with more delicately flavored fish.

Another wood that recently has gained popularity in America is mesquite, which is available both in hardwood charcoal form and in chip form. At this moment, many restaurants all over America are advertising their "swordfish over mesquite," using either the charcoal or a handful of the chips. Thicker, sturdier kinds of fish, such as shark and swordfish, are enhanced by mesquite smoke.

Other common aromatics used in America include stalks of fresh herbs such as thyme, tarragon, basil, fennel, bay leaves, rosemary, sage, and juniper twigs, which can be sprinkled over the hot coals right before setting the fish on the grill. (Some buffs tie stalks of fresh herbs into a small bunch, then use this as a basting brush during cooking.) In China, barbecuers throw tea leaves or pieces of orange peel onto the hot coals. And in France, they might substitute grapevine cuttings or a handful of garlic cloves.

Some barbecue buffs enjoy dispensing with charcoal entirely and using just aromatic hardwoods or corncobs as fuel. This is fine for pork or beef. But we do not recommend this with fish because the delicate flavor of the fish would be overpowered by the strong, assertive fragrances of the smoke given off by some hardwoods alone.

Wood chips should be soaked for several minutes (follow package directions) before throwing them onto the hot coals, as this will prolong their smoking life. If the chips float when you put them into the pan of water, simply lay a plate over the top to submerge them.

Aromatic woods, charcoal, and other fuels are so widespread that most are available at supermarkets, specialty shops, some hardware shops, and even department stores and pharmacies all over the country. Once you bring your fuel home, store it in a moisture-free area, away from your furnace or heaters.

Electricity and Gas

If you have an electric or gas grill, you can (and should) throw aromatics onto the bed of lava rock or onto the bottom of the grill. (Remember, we said earlier that the smoke produced by the burning fat of the cooking food is only part of the deliciousness of grilling fish; the other part is produced by the smoke from the fuel.) If you do this, though, be sure to turn your grill upside down to shake out the ash at the end of the barbecue season.

MISCELLANEOUS EQUIPMENT

You don't need special equipment for grilling. You can get away with a grill, some charcoal, some starter, a wire brush for cleaning the grill, and a few tools found around any kitchen: a fork, a spatula (the kind used for flipping pancakes), a pastry brush, and a regular pair of kitchen tongs (the kind that were formerly used to handle sterilized baby bottles).

But if you decide to buy special equipment, then we recommend certain types—ones we have found to work very efficiently. A *long-handled fork*, for example, is not only efficient, it keeps you from burning yourself. And instead of buying a pastry brush, we recommend a *large paint brush* (good quality so the hairs don't come out). A real painter's paint brush is larger, thicker (it will hold more basting butter or sauce), and more efficient than a pastry brush.

Although many *long-handled spatulas*, designed especially for grilling, are available, we recommend those with wide blades. Otherwise, you're better off with a regular kitchen spatula. If you decide to buy *tongs*, buy spring-loaded, stainless-steel tongs. Because they're spring-loaded, they're easier to handle than the ordinary found-around-the-house variety.

Less common pieces of equipment include *skewers*—both metal and bamboo—for shish kabob and *fish baskets*. Metal skewers can be any length, but avoid those with wooden handles. They look pretty when you buy them, but after a couple of uses the wood finish chars and scorches. Four 10-inch-long all-metal skewers will serve you very well. Eight would be better. If you add an additional eight 20-inch skewers, you'll have all you'll ever need. Whatever size you buy, be sure the skewers are not round. If they are round, the fish chunks will slip when you turn the skewer. Each skewer should have four flat sides.

Bamboo skewers are 8- to 10-inch-long, narrow bamboo sticks used in the Orient for making skewered foods and are available in Oriental food marts in this country. Bamboo skewers must be soaked in water 30 minutes prior to using to prevent scorching on the grill.

Fish baskets—wire baskets with covers, which adjust to the fish's thickness, attached to long handles—come in a variety of sizes and shapes. Some are rectangular, some are shaped like a fish. The ones we recommend are rectangular and will hold fish fillets, fish steaks, or whole fish. Fish baskets are useful in turning fish. Secured in a basket, the fish will not flop around when it is turned. Baskets can be quite expensive—as high as $20 or more. But if you shop carefully, you should be able to find one for under $12.

Grill Rack

One particularly effective piece of equipment for grilling both fish and shellfish is a stainless steel wire rack. It fits directly on the grill and is so close-meshed that it provides maximum support for delicate seafood while allowing juices to drip through. Even a bay scallop won't fall through. The grill rack measures 11″ × 11″ and will fit on almost any size grill. It can be oiled lightly before each use to prevent fish from sticking to it. Fish fillets turn more easily on this grill, and spatulas are easily used. One of the ends is folded up to a 1-inch height to function as a spatula stop edge. A second type of grill rack, recently put on the market, has two handles and an ultra-heavy-duty frame and measures 12″ × 16″.

The grill rack is available in many hardware shops and supermarkets, as well as in gourmet cookware shops.

You will, of course, be purchasing something with which to start your fire. You can use an *electric starter* (which requires an electric outlet), a *small chimney*, a *paraffin starter* (a piece of compressed wood or paper with a paraffin base), or the commercial *liquid chemical lighter* available everywhere. But before choosing your starter, be sure to check its aroma. Some chemical starters have an incredibly strong odor that lasts.

HOW TO COOK FISH ON THE GRILL

Grilling fish, although quick and easy, does demand a certain amount of attention. Fish overcooks easily—too easily. If you direct your attention from the grill for just a moment or two, you may find yourself with a dry-on-the-inside, charred-on-the-outside piece of fish. Although we have given the grilling times as accurately as possible in the recipes, remember that grills vary, the distance between the charcoal briquets and the grating varies, charcoals vary, and the heat varies too, since you can't set the temperature on a charcoal grill as you can with an oven. Add to this the fact that thickness varies from fish to fish and that the temperature of the fish, whether fresh from the refrigerator or at room temperature, varies too, as does the weather. All of these things are going to affect your charcoal grilling of fish. So our advice to all fish-on-the-grill cooks is to *pay attention* for the few minutes the fish is on the grill. If you do, your results are all but guaranteed.

DIRECT vs. INDIRECT HEAT

Once you've chosen your grill, your fuel, and your recipe, decide whether you want to cook your fish by the direct heat or the indirect heat method. In the direct method, the fish is cooked directly over the heat. The ashy white charcoal is spread out over the bottom of the grill in an even layer, and the fish is then laid on the grill over the direct heat. An advantage of the direct cooking method is that the fish cooks very quickly. Disadvantages include having to take extra precautions and care so that the fish won't burn and expecting only a minimum of smoky flavor to permeate the fish flesh because of the shortened cooking time.

In the indirect method, the ashy white charcoal is divided into two small banks on either side of the grill. The fish is laid in the center of the grill, away from the direct heat of the charcoal. (Some people lay a pan in the center of the kettle bottom to catch the drippings.) The fish is then cooked—

25

partly by the heat, partly by the hot smoke. If you cover the grill, the smoky flavor will be intensified. The advantages of the indirect method include slow cooking so that you don't have to watch the fish quite so carefully plus maximum exposure to the flavorful smoke. Disadvantages include a slightly longer cooking time and the necessity for a cover so that the fish will absorb maximum smoke fragrance.

STARTING A FIRE

Once you've decided on your grilling method, you may line the grill with heavy-duty foil, if desired; this makes for easier cleanup but is not necessary. If you poke a few holes in the foil and cover the grill for the few moments it takes to cook the fish, the fish will still absorb the delicious smoky flavor. And this ensures easy, intact removal.

Another alternative: you may wish to use a special piece of equipment called a *fish basket* (see the previous chapter, "The Tools: Grills, Fuels, and More").

Start the fire 45 minutes to an hour before you plan to grill so that when you are ready to begin cooking, the charcoal will be covered with a thick layer of grayish-white ash. Pile the briquets into a pyramid in the center of the grill. An average-size kettle (18–22 inches) needs only 30–35 briquets if you are using the direct cooking method. If you're using the indirect method, you may want to add an extra 5–10 briquets. Light the charcoal using one of the methods described in the preceding chapter.

All recipes in this book were tested by the direct method of grilling. If you want to use the indirect method, add a few minutes to your calculated cooking time. The times given for each recipe, again, are approximate. Grilling time will vary with each experience, but once you've learned to judge the fish's doneness using the chart and instructions on page 28, you should have no trouble calculating times.

How long you'll have to wait before the fire is ready for cooking depends on a number of factors, but you'll know it's ready when the charcoal is covered with a fine layer of white ash. At this point, the ashy charcoal will produce a steady, even heat—perfect for grilling. It is the direct infrared radiation from the coals that is supposed to do the major part of the cooking; never a direct flame. If you cook anything, but particularly fish, over flaming coals, you will have trouble preventing it from burning.

Spread out the briquets to accommodate your cooking method. Then carefully brush a little shortening or oil on the grating (don't use butter—it burns too quickly). This step is imperative; fish is delicate and may stick to the grill when you try to turn or remove it. And be sure your grill is clean. Fish has a tendency to stick to a dirty grill.

COOKING THE FISH

Remove the fish from the refrigerator. It is important that the fish be very cold when put on the greased grating. The cold will slow the cooking time and allow the fish to absorb as much of the smoky flavor as possible. Do not salt the fish before cooking. Salting draws some of the moisture out of the flesh and toughens it.

Set a pan of water near the grill and watch the charcoal carefully during cooking. If it flares up into a direct flame, immediately sprinkle water over it to quench the flames. Incidentally, there's some indication that doing this produces a steam that helps keep the fish moist.

Fish flesh sticks to metal, so don't forget to oil your fish well on both sides, to oil the grill, to oil the inside of the grill basket, and to insert lemon or lime slices at a few places between the fish and the grill when feasible.

To figure out the approximate grilling time for a fish steak, a thick fish fillet, a whole stuffed fish, or a kabob, measure the fish at the thickest point (right behind the head) and allow 10 minutes of direct grilling time for each inch of thickness. When using the indirect method, allow 15–18 minutes per inch. Remember, however, that this rule is qualified by the temperature of the air and the fish, by the heat of the grill, and by the distance between the coals and the food. So *watch your fish carefully*—from one minute after you put it on the grill until it's done. When the fish is almost done, you will get the best results if you stand there and give it your full attention for the last few minutes. Use the chart that appears second in this section as a guide to cooking times.

Ready or Not?

We cannot stress enough the importance of paying attention to the fish while it cooks. You don't have to hover over the grill constantly, but check the fish regularly. A well-cooked piece of fish looks opaque. The texture is right when the fish begins to flake when tested with a fork. If it is already flaky, it is overdone. Fish, like steak, continues to cook for a moment or two after it's taken from the grill.

Lay the fish on the greased grating. If you're cooking a fillet, be sure to lay it skin-side down on the grill. The skin, incidentally, helps protect the flesh from burning and drying out.

Check a whole fish for doneness by examining the thickest part—right in back of the head. Another test for a whole fish is to leave the side fins on and, when you think the fish is done, test it by gently pulling on a fin. If it comes off with only a gentle pull, it's done. You could also insert an instant read thermometer into the thickest part of the whole fish. It should read about 135°F. If it reads higher, take the fish off the grill immediately. Whatever you do, be aware of the fact that you have a delicate, easily overcooked piece of deliciousness on your grill. Watch it accordingly.

Don't turn your fillets. They can cook fully just by having one side exposed to the fuel and probably will fall apart if you try to turn them. Fish steaks and whole fish can be turned, but care should be exercised.

The chart that immediately follows can be used as a quick guide. It is based on the direct cooking method. If you use the indirect method, increase the cooking time 2–4 minutes. For a more complete breakdown, see the chart that appears later in this chapter.

HOW LONG ON THE GRILL

Small Whole Fish	6–9 minutes on each side
Large Whole Fish	11–20 minutes on each side (or even longer occasionally, if fish is thicker or stuffed)
Fillets	4–8 minutes on each side (or longer occasionally, when fillet is very thick). Turn only if flesh is firm and thick enough to do so.
Steaks (1 inch thick)	5 minutes on each side for a total of 10 minutes. If fish is thicker, increase cooking time according to thickness (10 minutes per inch).
Kabobs	Most kabobs are cut 1 to 1½ inches thick and will take about 9 to 15 minutes. Cook them 3 minutes on each side, then turn. Continue cooking and turning until they're done.

FISH AND SHELLFISH GRILLING CHART

Louie Green, our very knowledgeable fish consultant, created a special chart for us—one we've never seen before in any fish book—that suggests, among other things, cooking times for different varieties of fish to be cooked on the grill. Grilling is one of his favorite methods of seafood preparation.

This chart (see pages 29–34) includes most of the seafood included in this book, except for seafood that is already cooked when purchased. The fish and shellfish in this chart are to be cooked on a preheated grill about 5 to 7 inches from coals that have partly turned to ash.

FISH ON THE GRILL

FISH	SIZE VARIANCE	TEXTURE & FLAVOR	MARKET FORM	COOKING TIME IN MINUTES	COMMENTS
Bluefish	¾–15 lbs.	Oily, fat, dark, firm	Whole, steak, fillet	Steak—about 6 Fillet—about 4	Excellent on grill. Mild yet distinct texture and flavor. *See Legend: 2*
Catfish	10 oz.–4 lbs.	Fat, firm, mild	Whole, steak, fillet	Steak—about 5 Fillet—about 3	Most catfish are farm-raised, making for good value and excellent quality. *See Legend: 2*
Cod Family: Cod (Scrod), Haddock, Pollack	1½–15 lbs.	Lean, firm, flaky	Whole, steak, fillet	Steak—about 6 Fillet—about 3	If skin is off, should be put on vegetables or citrus or wrapped in foil. *See Legend: 2, 3*
Flatfish Family: Sole (Grey, Lemon), Flounder (Blackback, Fluke)	½–8 lbs.	Lean, crisp, delicate	Whole, steak, fillet	Steak—about 6 Fillet—about 2	Thicker steaks/fillets can go directly on grill. *See Legend: 3*

FISH	SIZE VARIANCE	TEXTURE & FLAVOR	MARKET FORM	COOKING TIME IN MINUTES	COMMENTS
Grouper	3–30 lbs.	Fat, firm, coarse	Steak, fillet	Steak—about 10 Fillet—about 6	Very versatile fish. Can go directly on grill; can be skewered. *See Legend:* 1, 4
Halibut	10–250 lbs.	Medium fat, firm, coarse	Steak, fillet	Steak—about 8 Fillet—about 6	Fabulous grilled. Serve hot or chilled. *See Legend:* 1, 2, 3, 4
Lake Trout	3–15 lbs.	Fat, flaky	Whole, steak, fillet	Steak—about 8 Fillet—about 4	Very tasty. As good as salmon, but less expensive. *See Legend:* 2, 3
Mackerel: Boston, Spanish, Kingfish, Ono	¾–40 lbs.	Fat, oily	Whole, steak, fillet	Steak—about 8 Fillet—about 4	Nice grilling fish. Dark-fleshed, tasty. *See Legend:* 1, 2, 3, 4
Mahimahi (Dolphinfish)	4–25 lbs.	Fat, coarse	Fillet	Fillet—about 4	Excellent grilled as simply as possible. Delicate taste. *See Legend:* 1
Monkfish	3–20 lbs.	Lean, light texture	Fillet	Fillet—about 6	Sometimes sold as "Poor Man's Lobster." *See Legend:* 1, 4
Orange Roughy	2–6 lbs.	Lean, light texture	Fillet	Fillet—about 4	Almost always skinless; can be very delicate. *See Legend:* 3

FISH	SIZE VARIANCE	TEXTURE & FLAVOR	MARKET FORM	COOKING TIME IN MINUTES	COMMENTS
Pompano	¾–3 lbs.	Fat, flaky, mild	Whole, fillet	Fillet—about 3	Very light, delicate fish. *See Legend:* 3
Redfish	2–20 lbs.	Fat, flaky	Fillet	Fillet—about 4	Very popular in Cajun dishes; needs seasoning. *See Legend:* 2, 3
Red Snapper: American, Caribbean, Yelloweye, Yellowtail, Silky, Mutton, Mangrove	¾–20 lbs.	Fat, rich, flaky	Whole, fillet	Fillet—about 4	One of the largest families of fish. Varieties are pretty much interchangeable. *See Legend:* 2, 3
Rockfish: West Coast Snapper	3–6 lbs.	Fat, flaky	Fillet	Fillet—about 3	Can be substituted for Red Snapper. *See Legend:* 3
Salmon: Silver, Sockeye, King, Chum	Farm-Raised, 8 oz; Wild, up to 20 lbs.	Fat, rich, flaky	Whole, steak, fillet	Steak—about 8 Fillet—about 4	One of the most popular fish anywhere. Year-round supply. *See Legend:* 1, 2, 3, 4
Sea Bass: Black, Striped, etc.	15–20 lbs.	Fat, white meat, flaky	Whole, steak, fillet	Steak—about 6 Fillet—about 4	Sea Bass refers to a large number of fish. Many varieties may be substituted. *See Legend:* 1, 2
Shad	2–10 lbs.	Fat, oily	Whole, fillet	Fillet—about 4	Very bony! *See Legend:* 3

FISH	SIZE VARIANCE	TEXTURE & FLAVOR	MARKET FORM	COOKING TIME IN MINUTES	COMMENTS
Shark	4–200 lbs.	Lean, firm	Steak, fillet	Steak—about 8 Fillet—about 4	Meaty, mild taste. Great marinated. *See Legend:* 1, 4
Smelt	$\frac{1}{20}$–$\frac{1}{4}$ lb.	Crisp, lean	Whole	Whole—about 3	*See Legend:* 3, 4
Swordfish	20–200 lbs.	Fat, rich, firm	Steak	Steak—about 8	The King of the Grill. Cooks like meat. These steaks are boneless. *See Legend:* 1, 4
Tuna	10–500 lbs.	Oily, fat, rich	Steak, fillet	Steak—about 5 Fillet—about 3	Outstanding on the grill. Very tricky. Must be cooked like rare steak. Steaks are boneless. *See Legend:* 1, 4
Turbot	3–15 lbs.	Lean, rich, delicate	Fillet	Fillet—about 3	Like Orange Roughy; always skinless. Very delicate. *See Legend:* 3
Whitefish: Lake Superior, Canadian	1½–10 lbs.	Fat, rich, flaky	Whole, steak, fillet	Steak—about 8 Fillet—about 4	Delicious on the grill. Can be delicate. *See Legend:* 1, 4

LEGEND:
1. Can be put directly on grill and handled like meat.
2. Larger, thicker pieces can be put directly on grill.
3. Delicate; should be put on bed of vegetables, herbs, or citrus slices and not turned.
4. Can be skewered.

PLEASE NOTE:
- Cooking times are approximate.
- We have not given cooking times for whole fish as whole fish vary greatly in size.
- Cooking times for fillets are for those boneless fillets placed on citrus slices or vegetables and not turned over. (Fillets are never turned over unless they are more than 1 inch thick.)
- Cooking times for steaks are given for 1-inch thick steaks.

SHELLFISH ON THE GRILL

SHELLFISH	SIZE VARIANCE	TEXTURE	COOKING TIME IN MINUTES	COMMENTS
Clams in Shell	Medium or small clams are best for grilling	Tender	About 6	Optimal size to use are Topneck, Small Cherrystones, or Littlenecks.
Crab: Dungeness in Shell	1¼–4 lbs.	Tender firm	About 7*	*Most often crabs are precooked, so just heat.
Crab, Legs and Claws: King Crab Legs, Snow Crab Claws	1–4 oz.	Tender firm	About 3	Both King Crab Legs and Snow Crab Claws are available frozen and precooked.
Crab: Soft-Shell	3", 4", 5", 6"	Tender/crisp	3"–4"—about 4 5"–6"—about 6	Although grilling is not the most popular preparation, Soft-Shells are great grilled. Extremities crisp up and bodies and claws stay moist.
Crayfish, Whole	12–40 per lb.	Tender firm	About 4	Size dictates cooking time. Large Crayfish are more desirable for grilling.

SHELLFISH	SIZE VARIANCE	TEXTURE	COOKING TIME IN MINUTES	COMMENTS
Lobster Tails: Australian, New Zealand, Bahamian, Japanese, Honduran, Danties	2 oz.–2 lbs.	Tender firm	About 18 per lb.	To prepare for grill, remove undershell by cutting up sides with kitchen shears. Remove meat by separating, wedging fingers between meat and shell at top of tail and working back, leaving tail attached. Push meat back in tail. Cook ⅔ time on shell side, ⅓ on meat side.
Lobster, Whole, in Shell: Maine, Spiny	1–6 lbs.	Tender firm	About 10 per lb.	Can be par-cooked 2–3 min. on stove to kill lobster. Should be turned halfway through grilling.
Mussels, Skewered: Maine, New Zealand	Small, 1″; med., 1½″; large (greenlip), 2″	Tender	About 3	Can be bought already shucked or can be removed from shell after grilling.
Scallops, Bay: Calico, Florida	40–70 per lb.	Tender	About 4	Skewered or put on a screen.
Scallops, Sea	8–20 per lb.	Tender	About 8	Need delicate care on the grill. Turning often prevents overcooking and drying.
Shrimp: Prawns, Scampi	2–200 per lb.	Medium firm	About 4	Bigger is not better. Ideal size to go directly on grill is 15–20 count; skewered is 36–40 count.
Squid Mantles, Skewered	3″–12″	Medium tender, chewy	About 5	Quick cooking is essential.
Squid Steaks	4–12 oz.	Slightly chewy	About 3	Prepounded from large squid. Ideal for fast grilling.

TIPS FOR COOKING FISH AND SHELLFISH ON THE GRILL

• Fish is done when it begins to flake when tested with a fork. This means, specifically, when pressure is applied with a fork to the thickest part of the fish, the fish will easily split along its natural separations.

• If shellfish is frozen, defrost it in the refrigerator whenever possible—this will take longer than thawing at room temperature but will keep the shellfish fresh.

• You'll have a better chance of removing delicate fillets from the grill if you cut them so that they're no larger than 4 inches square.

• When grilling a fillet with the tail section, fold this section under; this will help even out the thickness of the fish and so make possible a more uniformly cooked fillet.

• If possible, buy a grill basket with a narrow grid so that shellfish will not fall through. If you don't have a grill basket, simply skewer the shellfish and cook them, then unskewer them onto the serving platter when cooked. Another alternative is to substitute a bed of seaweed (ask your fishmonger for some) or to lay a sheet of aluminum foil on the grill, then poke it full of holes so that the smoke flavor will permeate the shellfish.

• Today's trend is to undercook fish, rather than cook it until dry. Fish should be moist and opaque. It should have just lost its translucency. Always err on the side of undercooking shellfish.

• If you want to take extra precautions to keep a piece of fish moist, marinate it in a plastic bag full of several spoonfuls of oil, turning it before cooking. When grilling it, however, give it your full attention. Marinating fish in oil will not ensure that it will not overcook.

• Feel free to throw handfuls of any of your favorite fresh herbs on the grill fire, to impart a subtle flavor to the shellfish.

FROM GRILL TO PLATTER

To remove the fish (whether fillet, steak, or whole fish) from the grill, oil a spatula. If the fish sticks (in spite of it being oiled before getting grilled) carefully and slowly loosen it with a gentle back-and-forth motion, using the spatula. You may want to use two greased spatulas to remove a large fish. Serve your fish on slightly warmed platters and plates. Do not let them get too hot or the fish may continue cooking after being removed from the grill.

SPECIAL STRATEGIES, TIPS, IDEAS, AND RECIPES

FIVE-MINUTE FISH

Your boss keeps you late at the office, despite the fact that your newest boyfriend or girlfriend is coming to dinner for the first time. Never mind. Forget the dinner you planned. Stop at the fish store and buy some fillets of whatever kind is freshest, and then hurry home with confidence. Your dinner should take only minutes to make.

It really is almost that easy. There are, however, a few things to keep in mind:

• Once you're at the fish store, be sure to choose a quick-cooking cut. A thin fillet, such as sole or whitefish, will take just minutes on the grill and doesn't need to be turned. A fish steak also cooks in a short time. If you're really rushed, don't buy a whole fish; it takes too long. And don't buy fish for shish kabob, it takes several minutes just to thread the fish and vegetables on the skewers.

• Plan your meal on the way to the fish store. Plan side dishes and sauces or butters that are made of ingredients you have on hand. It helps if you've anticipated a possible emergency and stockpiled ingredients—such as olives (needed for olive spread) or dried tarragon (needed for our sole with tarragon)—for just such emergencies.

• Also, if you're a beginning cook and estimating how long a dish will take you, the time you figure should be doubled or tripled. What the experienced cook can put together in 5 minutes, may take the novice as much as 20 minutes.

• When you're pressed for time and need a quick marinade, run to the refrigerator and take out your leftover salad dressing. Pour this into a bowl, add the fish fillet and let it sit for 30 minutes. If the dressing tastes good on salad, it will taste good on grilled fish.

TIPS FOR MAKING SIMPLY SUBLIME QUICK BUTTER SAUCES

• You can invent your own delicious butter-based sauces by mixing almost anything that has a strong, hearty flavor—be it fish roe in a jar, anchovies, savory herbs (tarragon, rosemary, sage, thyme, etc.), capers, horseradish, mustard, garlic, or shallots—with enough butter at room temperature (for a spreading consistency). Then, when your fish is hot off the grill, transfer it to a serving dish, put a dollop or two of seasoned butter on the fish (it will melt), and serve immediately. Be sure to pass the remaining butter mixture.

• Nut butters go wonderfully with all the fish varieties in this book. What's a nut butter? It's finely chopped or ground nuts combined with softened butter which can be spread on fish. Try pecan butter, walnut butter, or cashew butter. Add a squeeze of lemon juice, pinch of salt, and a half teaspoon or so of chopped onion and you've got something special. Serve it as a log, for guests to slice, or just put a dollop on each piece of hot fish and wait for it to melt. Delicious!

• Herbs and herb butters go well with most types of fish in this book. You may want to mix a few herbs together, fresh or dried, and combine them with butter to taste. Parsley adds a green note and combines well with almost anything. Parsley is especially effective when used fresh, even when combined with dried herbs, because its overall effect is freshness.

• When added judiciously with dried herbs, chives act as a flavor complement, adding pungency. A small amount of very finely chopped onion or green onion will do the same.

• When mixing herb butters, be sure the butter is soft, room temperature, so the herbs combine evenly. As soon as you get home, take the butter out of the refrigerator, measure it, cut it into pieces, and place it in a bowl in a warm place (maybe right near the stove). When speed is important, nothing is more exasperating that trying to stir something into cold butter.

• If you really have no time, not even for the butter to soften at room temperature, melt it in a pan over low heat with the herbs. Then brush it over the just-grilled fish. It works as well as the more solid varieties.

CLARIFIED BUTTER

❧

Clarified or drawn butter is butter that has been separated into pure fat and milk solids.
Clarified butter does not burn readily and is very useful in preparing sauces.

¼ pound unsalted butter or margarine

Melt butter in small saucepan over low heat. Skim off the white foam that forms on the top of the butter. Pour the remaining butter into a covered glass container, cool, and refrigerate until needed.

LEMON BUTTER

❧

Lemon butter is delicious with any kind of fish in this book.

4 tablespoons (½ stick) butter or
margarine, room temperature
2 teaspoons minced fresh parsley
2 tablespoons fresh lemon juice
1 teaspoon grated lemon zest

Cream butter until soft. Add minced parsley, lemon juice, and zest. Continue beating until butter is fluffy. Can be stored.

Yield: 4 servings

TROPICAL FRUIT GARNISH

❧

1 papaya or mango, peeled, seeded, and
*   sliced*
1 large firm banana, sliced
1 kiwifruit, peeled and sliced
2 tablespoons fresh orange juice

Toss all ingredients in a large mixing bowl. Spoon the fruit mixture over grilled fish fillets or steaks.

Yield: 4 servings

BASIL MAYONNAISE

❧

This lovely mayonnaise will complement any seafood, especially leftover shrimp. The sauce is improved by using homemade mayonnaise for a base (see Index). However, commercial mayonnaise is fine when you have last-minute company.

If you find yourself with a piece of cold, leftover grilled fish, a sandwich spread with basil mayonnaise will turn a leftover into a delight.

1 cup regular, homemade, or light
*   mayonnaise*
¼ cup lightly packed fresh basil leaves
¼ teaspoon each: salt, white pepper

Process mayonnaise, basil leaves, salt, and pepper in a food processor fitted with a steel blade, until smooth. Taste and adjust seasonings. Place basil mayonnaise in a covered container and chill until ready to serve.

Yield: 1¼ cups

BEER SAUCE

This hearty, but easy, sauce goes well with any fish, particularly the heartier varieties. Try it on a cold day (sure, you can grill in the cold—all you need is a coat and a few minutes time).

> 1 cup regular, homemade, or light
>   mayonnaise
> ¼ cup catsup
> ¼ cup dark beer
> 2 teaspoons prepared mustard
> ½ teaspoon fresh lemon juice
> ¼ teaspoon, or to taste, white horseradish

Combine mayonnaise, catsup, beer, mustard, lemon juice, and horseradish in a small bowl. Cover and refrigerate until ready to serve.

Yield: 1½ cups

BASIC MARINADE

Though not a sauce in the strictest sense, we include this basic marinade here because it is so easily put together and is called for often in many of the recipes in Part II. It can be used to enhance virtually any of the fish varieties in this book.

> ½ cup imported good-quality mild olive oil
> 3 tablespoons fresh lemon juice
> 2 large cloves garlic, minced fine
> ¼ teaspoon salt
> ¼ teaspoon freshly ground pepper
> 1 bay leaf, crumbled
> ¼ small onion, cut into chunks (optional)

Mix all ingredients together in a food processor fitted with a steel blade and pulse several times to combine ingredients.

Yield: ½ cup

These delicious recipes make use of leftover grilled fish.

REGRILLED FISH PATTIES

🌿

When grilling these patties, remember that the fish is already cooked and must be watched carefully so it does not burn. Note that this recipe serves only four. We suggest you serve it along with french-fried or baked potatoes.

> *2 cups flaked leftover grilled fish*
> *1½ cups fine fresh bread crumbs*
> *2 tablespoons evaporated milk*
> *2 eggs*
> *2 egg whites*
> *4 scallions, chopped fine*
> *¼ cup dried currants*
> *6 tablespoons coarsely chopped pecans*
> *1 teaspoon ground allspice*
> *½ teaspoon salt*
> *Few grinds of pepper*
> *Oil for brushing patties*

1. Combine all ingredients except the oil in a large bowl.

2. Scoop out a scant ½ cup and form into a compact, 3-inch-diameter round patty. Repeat with the remaining mixture; you should have eight patties.

3. Brush the patties with oil and place on the prepared grill. Grill for about 3 minutes on one side, then brush with oil and carefully turn the patties using a spatula. Cook for an additional 3 minutes or until done. Transfer to a serving platter and serve immediately.

Yield: 4 servings (2 patties per person)

FISH SALAD IN
A TOASTED LOAF

This company dish, made of leftovers, consists of a round white or sourdough loaf that is hollowed out and filled with a delicious fish salad. The filled loaf is served cut into wedges. Hollowed-out breads filled with different preparations such as this one were popular in the 1950s and are now coming back into style. Note that this dish will serve only six. Serve it with cold vegetables tossed with vinaigrette or a green salad.

DRESSING
1 egg
2 tablespoons red wine vinegar
1 cup vegetable oil
¼ medium-sized onion
2 scallions, cut into 1-inch lengths
Large handful fresh parsley
2 tablespoons sweet pickle relish
¼ cup pimiento-stuffed green olives
1 tablespoon fresh lemon juice
1 teaspoon sugar
½ teaspoon salt (or to taste)

FISH
2 cups flaked leftover grilled fish
½ cup coarsely chopped pecans

TOASTED LOAF
1 1¼- to 1½-pound round bread
    (use white or sourdough if possible;
    otherwise substitute rye or
    pumpernickel)

1. *Make the dressing:* Place egg, wine vinegar, and ¼ cup of the oil in a food processor fitted with the steel blade and process for a few seconds to combine. Measure out the remaining ¾ cup oil and turn on the motor; add

the oil in a thin, steady stream with the motor running. When all the oil has been added, turn off the motor. (You can use a blender for this step.)

2. Add onion, scallion lengths, and parsley to the food processor and process until these ingredients are chopped coarse. Then add relish, green olives, lemon juice, sugar, and salt and pulse a few times to chop the olives coarse and combine seasonings.

3. *Make the salad:* Place flaked fish and pecans in a serving bowl. Stir in ½ cup of the dressing and toss lightly to combine. Taste, then add a few more tablespoons of dressing if desired. Reserve the remaining dressing for another use, such as tuna, salmon, or chicken salad. Let salad sit at room temperature until ready to stuff the bread.

4. *Hollow out the bread:* Preheat the oven to 350°F. With a small, serrated knife, cut a 4-inch circle in the top of the bread (use a 4-inch cardboard circle as a guide for the knife if desired). Carefully cut the bread under the circle so the circle can be lifted off the top of the bread.

5. Using your fingers, carefully pull out the center of the bread, hollowing out the shell. Leave no more than a ½-inch-thick bread crust.

6. Place the bread in the oven for 10–15 minutes or until the outside crust is crisp.

7. Immediately remove the bread and 4-inch circle from the oven and spoon the fish salad into the bread. Top with the 4-inch circle and serve immediately, cut into wedges.

Yield: 6 servings (1¼ cups dressing, 3 cups fish salad)

VEGGIES ON THE GRILL

Many vegetables can be grilled along with the fish for an easy, thematic meal. Eggplant, pepper strips, onion slices, even carrots and tomatoes can be brushed with oil and grilled. Remember to watch vegetables closely, because they cook quickly. Sprinkle with salt and pepper, if desired, and serve.

GARLIC ON THE GRILL

Garlic on the grill is incomparable. Place a large garlic clove at the outer edges of the coals. Cook, turning occasionally, 15–20 minutes until soft and spreadable. Then, squeeze and spread on french bread, or directly onto the grilled fish. The taste is mild and almost nutty—delectable.

FISH ON THE GRILL FOR ENTERTAINING

Many of the recipes in this book have been developed with entertaining specifically in mind. Most of these recipes give a list of accompaniments that work well with the particular type of fish being prepared. These serving suggestions range from salads and vegetable side dishes to fresh breads, fruit dishes, and desserts. Also listed are suggestions for fish substitutions just in case your local fishmonger has run out of your first choice. The fish substitutions are specific to each recipe and are in addition to the fish substitution suggestions at the beginning of each chapter.

We've intended these recipes for entertaining to inspire you to be a little more creative in preparing meals. They call for the best and most flavorful ingredients. For example, extra-virgin olive oil is specified. This attention to detail will make your meals especially elegant, whether they're served to family, friends, or both. We hope you'll have as much fun preparing and serving them as we did developing them for you.

Menu Planning

In the late 1950s and early 1960s it was easy—even for inexperienced brides— to cook the perfect dinner for guests. It usually consisted of six courses: cocktails and potato chip dips, shrimp cocktail, lettuce with bottled dressing, giant steaks or a large roast beef served with baked potato and sour cream, green bean/mushroom soup casserole, and a dessert that was usually cake and ice cream with chocolate sauce, followed by the candy someone had brought to the hostess.

The rationale for this meal was simple: everyone liked and expected it, and it was considered fancy, which meant expensive enough to serve to guests. It was considered healthy and well balanced too in those days before we were concerned about cholesterol and weight-watching.

Today, few of us—certainly not those who think about health—would serve such a fat-laden dinosaur. Our tastes have changed, too. As we've traveled in other countries or eaten in the ethnic restaurants that have opened up in profusion around the country, our palates have become more sophisticated and our tastes more exotic.

Therefore, a whole new set of menu-planning rules has to be considered when planning a dinner party. Some have to do with nutrition; others, stemming from the haute cuisine of the past, have to do with flavors, textures, and presentation. Still others have to do with the sophistication of today's guests. With this in mind, we've assembled a few loose rules you might want to consider the next time you're having company for dinner.

1. Serve what the nutritionists call a balanced meal, consulting the USDA nutritional guidelines if necessary. If possible, avoid weighing a menu too heavily on any one side of the basic food groups. Balanced meals include raw vegetables, tossed with unsaturated or monosaturated oils; some protein such as fish; a side dish of bread, potatoes, noodles, or rice; and perhaps a cooked vegetable such as asparagus, green beans, brussels sprouts, carrots, or cauliflower. You might decide to serve fresh fruit with simple cookies—at least some of the time—rather than rich desserts.

2. Keep these "gourmet" rules in mind when planning:
    • Include within one meal dishes at all different temperatures: hot, cold, and room temperature.
    • Foods within a meal should be as varied in texture as possible, from soft and pureed to slightly chewy to crunchy.
    • Try to include all of the tastes—salty, sweet, sour, bitter, bland, and even piquant—within one meal. If you're at a loss for a way to add the bitter taste, remember that coffee, grapefruit, eggplant, and beer are all considered bitter foods.

3. Keep the colors of your proposed dinner in mind, making everything as bright as possible. Bright green vegetables, colorful sauces and garnishes, and

multicolored condiments all make the final plate beautiful. Try not to serve white fish on white plates. Fish is more appetizing when set on a plate of an attractive, contrasting color.

4. One semiobsolete gourmet rule advises against serving the same food twice within one meal. While you may not want to serve two sauces within a meal (sauces can be fattening), and you may not want to repeat strong flavors (such as anchovies in the salad and anchovy sauce with the fish), there's no reason why you can't begin a meal with a simple fish broth, then move to a fish entree. Here your instincts should guide you.

5. Most important, find out beforehand what kinds of food your guests like and serve those or similar kinds of food to them. If you're inviting guests who say they hate fish but like beef, try serving swordfish, which has a texture similar to that of beef and a bland taste, or serve shrimp or lobster. Of course there are always a few folks who don't like fish no matter what, so it doesn't hurt to have a steak you can throw on the grill in emergencies. Your guests should always come first.

PART II
THE RECIPES

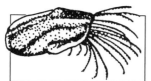

BARNACLES

Barnacles are becoming such a trendy shellfish item on both coasts that we felt we should at least include instructions for preparing them as an appetizer.

Barnacles are crustaceans that taste like a cross between shrimp and lobster. They grow in clusters, each resembling a clump of strange undersea flowers from which five or six stalks protrude. The two- to three-inch stalks—the part that is eaten—are each topped with a tiny mouth that resembles a shell. The stalks are covered with a thick skin, which you pull off as you would pull the paper off a chocolate cigarette.

GRILLED BARNACLES

To eat barnacles: With one hand, pick up a skin-covered stalk. Hold the shell-like mouth section in your left hand. Carefully move your hands in opposite directions against each other to loosen the connection between the skin and the mouth section. Then slip the skin off. You'll see a thin stalk of white meat connected to the shell-mouth section. Dip this in any delicate sauce or melted butter and put the whole thing in your mouth, using your teeth to pull the meat off the inedible portion of the stalk.

8 barnacles
Melted butter

Hold the clump of raw barnacles in one hand and break off all of the stalks at the base of the clump. Lay barnacles in a single layer on a heated, well-oiled grill and cook them for 4 minutes on each side. Then examine one barnacle by pulling off skin (directions above). It should have lost its translucent look. If it has not, return it to the grill for a few more minutes.

Yield: 4 appetizer servings

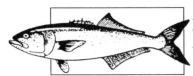

BLUEFISH

This fish has a delicate yet distinctive flavor. When bluefish is not available, substitute mackerel or whitefish.*

BLUEFISH WITH TOMATO BUTTER

TOMATO BUTTER
3 shallots, minced
1 tablespoon tomato paste
3 tablespoons water
3 tablespoons wine vinegar
16 tablespoons (2 sticks) butter, cut into
  small pieces
2 teaspoons crumbled dried oregano
1 teaspoon fresh lemon juice
Salt and white pepper to taste

FISH
4 7-ounce bluefish fillets or whole cleaned
  mackerel, split in half
Crumbled dried oregano to taste
Oil for greasing grill

1. *Make tomato butter:* Mix shallots, tomato paste, water, and wine vinegar in a saucepan. Reduce mixture by cooking over medium heat until approximately 2–3 tablespoons of liquid remain. Whisk in butter, 2 pieces at a time. Mix in oregano and lemon juice. Season tomato butter to taste with salt and white pepper. Refrigerate until ready to serve.

2. *Grill bluefish:* Sprinkle bluefish with oregano to taste. Place fish on oiled grill and cook for 4–5 minutes. Turn fish over and continue cooking 2 minutes or until fish begins to flake when tested with a fork. Place on individual serving plates and serve with Tomato Butter.

Yield: 4 servings

Note: Here and in some other fish specie descriptions, a few suggested substitutions are supplied. For a more complete breakdown of easily interchanged fish, see chart on pages 5–7.

This lake fish has a distinctive flavor. When it is not available, substitute snapper.

BUFFALOFISH STUFFED WITH PECANS AND SHERRY

STUFFING

2 tablespoons butter

4 ounces fresh mushrooms, chopped

¼ cup finely chopped onion

¼ teaspoon each: salt, pepper, dried thyme, and celery seed

⅛ teaspoon each: ground nutmeg, and ground mace

¾ cup chopped pecans

2¼ cups toasted bread crumbs

3 tablespoons dry sherry

FISH

1 3-pound whole buffalofish, scaled and boned

Oil for brushing fish and greasing fish basket

4 lemon slices

1. *Make stuffing:* Melt butter in large frying pan. Add mushrooms and onion and sauté over low heat, stirring often, for about 10–15 minutes or until the liquid has evaporated.

2. Add salt, pepper, thyme, celery seed, nutmeg, and mace. Continue cooking another moment.

3. Remove from heat. Stir in pecans, bread crumbs, and sherry. Mix well.

4. Lightly pack stuffing into cavity of fish.

5. Oil outside of fish on both sides. Then oil inside of fish basket. Lay 2 slices of lemon on bottom of fish basket. Lay fish over lemon slices. Top with 2 additional lemon slices. Attach top of basket.

6. *Grill buffalofish:* Grill stuffed fish about 10 minutes on each side or until fish flakes easily with a fork and outside is beginning to be crispy and brown. Transfer to serving platter. Serve immediately.

Yield: 4 servings

CATFISH
A sweet, medium-firm freshwater fish. Substitute orange roughy or walleye pike when catfish is tough to find.

CATFISH WITH CREOLE SAUCE

It's hard to beat catfish with Creole sauce for a real Southern treat. We suggest serving it with hush puppies.

CREOLE SAUCE
2 tablespoons butter
1 large clove garlic, minced
1 large onion, minced
2 stalks celery, chopped
1 medium green bell pepper, seeded and
  chopped
1 bay leaf
½ teaspoon paprika
3 cups peeled, diced fresh or canned
  tomatoes
½ cup chili sauce

FISH
4 7-ounce catfish fillets
Oil for brushing fish and greasing grill
½ teaspoon garlic powder
1 teaspoon paprika
Pepper to taste
½ teaspoon crumbled dried tarragon

1. *Make sauce:* Heat butter in medium saucepan and add garlic, onion, celery, and bell pepper. Sauté for 3–5 minutes, stirring often, until vegetables are tender.

2. Add remaining sauce ingredients. Simmer, uncovered, stirring occasionally, for 20 minutes.

3. Remove and discard bay leaf. Place cooled sauce in a covered container and store in refrigerator until ready to use. Reheat before serving.

4. *Grill catfish:* Brush catfish fillets with oil and sprinkle with seasonings. Arrange fish on prepared grill. Cook for 3 minutes, brush with oil, and turn. Continue cooking until fish begins to flake easily when tested with a fork, 2–4 minutes, depending on the size of the fish.

5. Arrange catfish on heated platter. Pass heated creole sauce at table with catfish.

Yield: 4 servings

CATFISH WITH FRIED ONIONS

We suggest serving this dish with grilled potato skins, marinated asparagus salad, and corn bread. This recipe may be prepared with pollack, as well as pike or roughy.

FISH
1 recipe basic marinade (see Index)
3 pounds catfish fillets, cut into 8 serving pieces
2 oranges, sliced thin (you'll need 16 slices altogether)

FRIED ONIONS
2 tablespoons butter or margarine
2 large red onions, sliced thin
¼ cup golden raisins
3 tablespoons dry white wine
¼ teaspoon salt
⅛ teaspoon freshly ground pepper
½ teaspoon caraway seed

1. *Marinate the fish:* Pour the marinade into a large plastic bag and place the bag in a bowl. Add the catfish, secure the bag with a twister seal, and turn the bag several times to make sure all fish surfaces touch the marinade. Let sit at room temperature for 1 hour.

2. *Meanwhile, make the fried onions:* Melt the butter in a skillet over medium heat. Cook the onions and raisins, stirring occasionally, until the onions are well cooked. Transfer the onions to a plate and reheat the skillet. Stir in the wine and heat. Pour over onions and combine. Sprinkle with salt, pepper, and caraway seeds. Set aside.

3. *Grill the catfish:* Arrange the orange slices in pairs on the prepared grill. Place each catfish fillet on pair of orange slices. Grill for 5 to 6 minutes, without turning, or until the fillets have lost their translucence and are slightly browned on the edges.

4. When the fillets are cooked, transfer them to a serving platter and garnish with the hot fried onions.

Yield: 8 servings

CATFISH STUFFED
WITH WALNUTS

❧

STUFFING

2 tablespoons butter

½ cup finely chopped onion

*½ teaspoon finely chopped fresh hot
  pepper*

¼ teaspoon salt

3 pinches dried rosemary

2 pinches dried thyme

*1 cup each: chopped walnuts and bread
  crumbs*

FISH

*1 3-pound farm-raised catfish, scaled,
  boned, head cut off*

*Oil for brushing fish and greasing fish
  basket*

4 lemon slices

1. *Make stuffing:* Melt butter in a medium-sized frying pan, add onion and pepper, and sauté 10 minutes or until onion is translucent.

2. Add salt, rosemary, and thyme and mix well over low heat for a moment. Remove from heat and combine with walnuts and bread crumbs, mixing well.

3. Fill catfish cavity with stuffing.

4. Oil catfish on both sides. Oil fish basket. Lay 2 slices of lemon in middle of fish basket. Then arrange catfish so it is lying on lemon slices. Top with 2 more lemon slices, then fasten top of grill basket over fish.

5. Grill over ashen coals. Grill 6–7 minutes on each side or until fish flakes easily when tested with a fork. Serve immediately.

Yield: 4 servings

STUFFED CATFISH
WITH COUSCOUS

This dish is based on couscous, grains of durum wheat semolina that are used to make the various couscous dishes of Morocco. Couscous comes in different-sized grains, any of which will work for this recipe, and is available at Middle Eastern stores or by mail (see Appendix). If desired, substitute cooked rice. Since this is a sweet couscous—one that includes nuts and currants—we've eliminated the hot sauce traditionally served with savory couscous dishes. If you wish to make this couscous savory, simply eliminate the nuts and currants and serve a side bowl of commercially available harissa *(Moroccan hot sauce), available at Middle Eastern stores or by mail (see Appendix).*

If you have a favorite chicken stuffing and wish to use that one instead of our couscous stuffing, just follow our directions for stuffing and grilling the fish. It is necessary to use a grill basket to cook a fish larger than 1 pound, or it will break when you try to turn it. This recipe can also be prepared with trout.

This recipe intentionally allows extra stuffing, which should be reheated and served in a separate serving bowl along with the grilled fish.

This dish has many complex flavors. We suggest you serve it with a green salad.

STUFFING

1½ cups water

3 cups medium-grain or other size couscous

4 tablespoons butter or margarine

½ teaspoon freshly grated nutmeg (more to taste)

8 scallions, green part only, minced fine or snipped fine with scissors

1 cup pine nuts

½ cup dried currants (more to taste)

1½ teaspoons salt

FISH

2 3-pound farm-raised dressed (headless, skinless, scaled and gutted) catfish

Salt and freshly ground pepper to taste

12–16 ¼-inch-thick slices lemon

Lemon wedges

Oil for greasing fish basket

1. *Make the stuffing:* Heat the water to a boil and immediately stir in the couscous grains. Stir a few times, then allow to cool, stirring occasionally.

2. Melt the butter in a large frying pan, then add the couscous grains, breaking up any clumps that have formed with your hands or with a fork. Stir in the nutmeg, scallions, pine nuts, currants, and salt and cook for 2–3 minutes, stirring constantly. Remove from the heat and allow to cool.

3. Sprinkle the inside of each fish liberally with salt and pepper. Stuff each fish with the couscous mixture, packing tightly. Don't bother using skewers to close; the grill basket will hold each fish shut.

4. *Grill the fish:* Place each fish in an oiled fish basket, placing 3–4 lemon slices on each side of the fish between the fish and the basket. Place the fish basket on the prepared grill and cook for about 15 minutes on each side or until the fish is cooked through on both sides and has lost its translucence.

5. While the fish cooks, reheat extra stuffing in a saucepan, then transfer to a serving dish just before removing the fish from the grill. Carefully transfer each fish to a large serving platter and serve immediately, 1 fish for each 3 to 4 people. Pass the bowl of heated stuffing and lemon wedges.

Yield: 8 servings

CATFISH WITH MEXICAN RED SAUCE

You may substitute ocean perch or small rockfish for the catfish in this recipe. We suggest you serve this dish with warm corn tortillas and a salad of lettuce with fresh fruit and pine nuts.

RED SAUCE
4 large tomatoes, peeled, seeded, and
    chopped
¾ cup chopped cilantro
½ small onion, minced
1 poblano chili, seeded and chopped
1 tablespoon drained capers
¼ teaspoon salt
¼ teaspoon freshly ground pepper

FISH
3 pounds catfish fillets, cut into 8 serving
    pieces
Good-quality olive oil for brushing fish
¼ cup fresh lime juice
½ cup minced cilantro
16 ¼-inch lime slices
2 ripe avocados, peeled and sliced

1. *Make the sauce:* Combine the tomatoes, cilantro, onion, chili, capers, salt, and pepper in a bowl. Cover and refrigerate until ready to serve.

2. *Grill the fish:* Brush the fish fillets with olive oil and sprinkle with lime juice and cilantro. Arrange the lime slices in pairs on the prepared grill. Place each catfish fillet on a pair of lime slices. Cook on the grill for about 3 minutes, without turning. Check and continue grilling for about 3 minutes, until it tests done.

3. Put the fish on a heated platter, ladle the tomato sauce next to the fish, and garnish with avocado slices.

Yield: 8 servings (3 cups sauce)

CLAMS
Although any of the numerous varieties of this bivalve mollusk will roast well on the grill, we suggest using only the smaller varieties for grilling because the larger ones are tough and best when put into chowders or subjected to slower cooking with moist heat. Hard-shell clams, or quahogs, are most often chopped and used in chowder, while the medium-sized clams, the cherrystones, or the small clams such as littlenecks are used for grilling, steaming, and frying. Clams are available on both the West Coast and the East Coast.

BABY CLAM APPETIZER

This recipe for baby clam appetizers can easily be doubled.

EASY SWEET SAUCE
1 12-ounce jar apricot jam
3 tablespoons white vinegar
3 tablespoons water
1 2-ounce jar minced pimiento, drained

SHELLFISH
1 10-ounce can baby clams in water,
* drained*
8 10-inch wooden presoaked barbecue
* skewers*
Oil for greasing grill

1. *Make sauce:* Combine apricot jam, white vinegar, water, and pimiento in a small saucepan. Heat to boiling point, stirring to combine ingredients. Reduce heat to simmer. Continue simmering for 1 minute. Remove sauce from heat and pour into serving dish. Cool.

2. *Prepare clams:* Force baby clams onto skewers, jamming them tightly onto the skewers. Brush with sauce. Cover and refrigerate extra sweet sauce for another use.

3. *Grill clams:* Grill skewered clams on prepared grill over ashen coals for 1½ minutes, being careful not to burn them. Turn skewers and grill an additional minute or until glazed (clams will cook quickly). Arrange decoratively on serving dish and serve hot or warm. Serve two skewers per person.

Yield: 4 appetizer servings (1¾ cups sauce)

CLAMS ITALIAN

This dish works nicely on your buffet, as an appetizer.

BREADING
2 tablespoons butter
2 cloves garlic, minced
1 small onion, minced
2 teaspoons crumbled dried oregano
1 teaspoon crumbled dried basil
2 cups fine bread crumbs
3 tablespoons grated fresh Parmesan
  cheese

SHELLFISH
2 dozen medium clams, shucked, bottom
  shells and any juice reserved

1. *Make breading:* Melt butter in large heavy skillet; sauté garlic and onion over medium heat, stirring occasionally, until onion is soft. Stir in oregano, basil, bread crumbs, and Parmesan. Blend in ¼ cup of clam juice if available.

2. *Prepare clams:* Sprinkle 1 tablespoon of breading over each clam in the shell.

3. *Grill clams:* Arrange clams, open side up, on prepared grill over hot coals. Cook clams for 8 to 10 minutes. Test one clam to see if ready to eat. Arrange clams on four individual plates or put on a tray for a buffet-style dinner. Serve with a small antipasto.

Yield: 4 appetizer servings

CLAM-STUFFED MUSHROOMS ON THE GRILL

24 medium-large fresh shiitake mushrooms
2 dozen medium-sized clams, shucked,
reserving liquid
1½ cups bread crumbs
1 teaspoon dried oregano
1 teaspoon dried basil
2 cloves garlic, minced
¼ teaspoon salt
¼ teaspoon freshly ground pepper
2 tablespoons butter, melted and cooled
¼ cup grated fresh Parmesan cheese
Oil for greasing grill

1. Remove stems from mushrooms, wipe caps with damp towel, and set aside.

2. *Prepare stuffing:* Toss clams, crumbs, oregano, basil, garlic, salt, and pepper in mixing bowl. Lightly mix in 1 tablespoon liquid from clams, if available, and 2 tablespoons melted butter.

3. Stuff mushrooms lightly with mixture, making sure there is one clam in each mushroom. Sprinkle with Parmesan cheese.

4. *Grill mushrooms:* Arrange mushrooms on prepared grill over ashen coals, about 3 to 4 inches from heat source. Grill mushrooms for 3 to 4 minutes or until just cooked. Serve hot.

Yield: 4 appetizer servings

GRILLED CLAMS
ON THE HALF SHELL

TOPPING
3 tablespoons butter, cut into small pieces
½ teaspoon dried tarragon
½ teaspoon dried fennel seed
¾ cup fine bread crumbs

SHELLFISH
2 dozen medium-sized clams such as
    topnecks, shucked, leaving clams and
    some liquid in bottom shells

1. *Prepare topping:* Puree butter, tarragon, and fennel in food processor fitted with steel blade. Blend in bread crumbs.

2. *Prepare clams:* Spoon a small amount of flavored butter on each clam.

3. *Grill clams:* Arrange clams on prepared grill over ashen coals, about 3 inches from heat source. Cover grill and cook for 2 to 3 minutes or until clams are done to your taste. Serve hot.

Yield: 6 appetizer servings or 4 entree servings

GRILLED CLAMS WITH CORN AND ONION

 ❧

Aluminum foil
2 dozen medium-sized clams, washed
4 ears corn, shucked and cut into thirds
1 large onion, sliced
3 tablespoons butter
2 tablespoons fresh lemon juice

1. *Prepare clam packages:* Cut 6 double sheets of aluminum foil large enough to hold four clams and 2 pieces of corn each.

2. Arrange clams, corn, and sliced onion in center of each package. Dot with butter and sprinkle with lemon juice. Seal packages tightly.

3. Arrange packages directly on hot coals. Grill for 3 to 4 minutes, turn packages, and grill 2 to 3 minutes. Test one package to see if it is done. Discard any unopened clams. Serve hot.

Yield: 6 servings

CLAMBAKE, GARLIC BUTTER, AND GRILLED POTATO SKINS

❧

POTATO SKINS
12 medium baking potatoes, about 3½
*   inches long*
Aluminum foil
Peanut oil
Salt to taste
1 cup sour cream
3 slices bacon, cooked, drained, and
*   crumbled*
½ cup chopped green onion

SHELLFISH
2 quarts cold water
¼ cup salt
2 dozen cherrystone clams
1½ dozen mussels, cleaned
¼ cup cornmeal
Enough fresh seaweed to make a bed for
*   shellfish*
Oil for greasing grill

GARLIC BUTTER
6 tablespoons butter, melted
2 cloves garlic, minced
3 tablespoons minced flat-leaf parsley

1. *Prepare potatoes:* Prick potatoes with tines of fork. Wrap each potato in aluminum foil. When coals are medium-hot and almost ashen, place potatoes directly on coals. Cook about 30 minutes, turning potatoes twice. Potatoes are done when they feel soft when pierced with a fork. (If you are in a hurry, pierce potatoes with tines of a fork and microwave at high for 4 minutes. Wrap with aluminum foil and cook on coals for about 15 minutes, turning once.)

2. *While potatoes cool, soak clams (and mussels if necessary):* To rid clams and mussels of sand, put 2 quarts of water and ¼ cup salt in a large pot. Add shellfish and sprinkle cornmeal over water. Let soak for 1 hour.

3. *Prepare garlic butter:* Pour butter into bowl. Mix in garlic and parsley. Set aside until ready to use.

4. *Prepare potato skins:* Cut baked potatoes in half horizontally. Remove cooled potato pulp, leaving between ¼ and ½ inch of pulp inside skins.

5. Brush outside of potato skins with peanut oil. Cut potatoes in half lengthwise. Sprinkle with salt to taste.

6. *Grill potato skins:* Place potato skins on prepared grill, 3-4 inches away from the coals, and cook for 2 to 4 minutes. Turn over and grill 2 to 4 minutes or until done to taste.

7. *Grill shellfish:* Drain clams and mussels. Make a bed or nest of seaweed on prepared grill. Place shellfish randomly on seaweed. Cover and grill for 10 minutes. Remove cover and discard any unopened shellfish. Serve hot with garlic butter.

8. Serve potato skins hot with sour cream, bacon bits, and chopped green onion.

Yield: 6 servings

CHEESE-CRUSTED CLAMS

This recipe can easily be doubled.

CHEESE MIXTURE
2 tablespoons butter
½ cup fine bread crumbs
¾ cup grated fresh Parmesan cheese
¼ teaspoon dried thyme
¼ teaspoon dried rosemary
2 egg whites, slightly beaten

SHELLFISH
2 dozen medium-sized clams, shucked
6 10-inch wooden presoaked barbecue
   skewers
Oil for greasing grill

1. *Prepare cheese mixture:* Melt butter and toss with bread crumbs, cheese, and herbs. Place in a shallow bowl. Pour egg whites into another bowl.

2. Dip each clam in egg whites. Roll in cheese-crumb mixture.

3. *Grill clams:* Thread four clams on one end of each skewer. Grill for 2 minutes on prepared grill over ashen coals. Turn and grill 1 to 2 minutes longer or until clams are done. Serve hot.

Yield: 6 servings

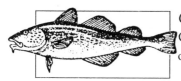

COD
Cod has a low fat content and a delicate flavor; scrod or flounder will do in its stead.

COD WITH SPANISH ALMOND-GARLIC SAUCE

ALMOND-GARLIC SAUCE
2 tablespoons oil
½ cup finely chopped onion
1–2 fresh hot peppers, seeds removed, chopped fine
5 cloves garlic, chopped fine
4 tomatoes, peeled, seeded, and chopped fine
22 whole blanched almonds
½ teaspoon salt
½ cup finely chopped fresh parsley

FISH
Oil for brushing fish and greasing grill
2 pounds fresh cod fillets

1. *Make sauce:* Heat 2 tablespoons oil in large saucepan. Sauté onion and peppers in oil over medium heat for 10 minutes. Add garlic and cook for an additional 1–2 minutes, taking care that it doesn't burn. Add tomatoes, heat to simmer, and let cook for 3–4 minutes.

2. Meanwhile, spread almonds on small cookie sheet or baking dish in a single layer. Place in a 350°F oven for 10 minutes or until lightly browned. Grind in blender until coarsely grated.

3. Add grated almonds to sauce along with salt. Stir well. Then remove from heat and stir in parsley.

4. *Grill cod:* Lightly oil cod fillets on both sides. Place on greased grill over ashen coals. Cook 4–5 minutes on both sides or until fish just turns white. Transfer cod to heated serving platter. Spoon sauce over cod. Serve immediately.

Yield: 4 servings

SKEWERED COD WITH GREEK SKORDALIA SAUCE

This smooth, creamy white Greek sauce takes only minutes to make and is delicious with any kind of fresh grilled fish. The garlic flavor is very delicate.

SKORDALIA SAUCE
15 slices white bread, crusts removed
¾ cup hot water
5 medium-sized garlic cloves, peeled
¾ cup olive oil
½ cup white wine vinegar
1 squeeze from a lemon half

FISH
5 pounds fresh cod, skinned and boned
Oil for brushing fish and greasing grill
1 cup freshly toasted pine nuts or sliced
  almonds (optional) for garnish

1. *Make sauce:* Put bread in food processor container and pour hot water over top to soften. Allow to sit for a moment.

2. Add garlic, olive oil, wine vinegar, and the squeeze of fresh lemon juice.

3. Turn on food processor and process for a few moments or until well blended. Sauce should be very smooth.

4. Cut cod into large squares, about 1¼–1½ inches. Thread onto 4 10-inch skewers and arrange skewers in a dish with raised sides. Brush fish with oil.

5. *Grill cod:* Grill kabobs on prepared grill over ashen coals turning every 3 minutes until done.

6. Transfer to serving dish and bring to table. Serve immediately, passing sauce and toasted nuts for garnish if desired.

Yield: 12 servings

MEDITERRANEAN
PITA POCKETS

You may substitute scrod or pollack for the cod. We suggest you serve a Greek salad or deep-fried zucchini rounds.

EGGPLANT

1 medium-large eggplant
Salt
Good-quality olive oil
½ cup dried oregano, crumbled
2 large red bell peppers, cored, seeded, and
    sliced into rings

FISH

1½ pounds cod fillets
Olive oil for brushing fish and greasing
    grill
4 tablespoons fresh lemon juice
4 pita bread rounds, halved and wrapped
    in foil
1 cup sliced black olives

1. *Grill the eggplant:* Cut eggplant crosswise into ½-inch slices. Sprinkle with salt and let stand on paper toweling for 20 minutes. Wash off the salt and pat dry. Brush with olive oil and sprinkle each slice with ¾ teaspoon of the oregano. Brush the pepper slices with oil. Grill the eggplant slices and pepper strips until done to taste. Reserve in a bowl.

2. *Grill the fish:* Sprinkle the remaining oregano over the hot coals. Brush the fish fillets with olive oil and sprinkle with the lemon juice. Place the fillets on the prepared grill. Cover and grill for 3–6 minutes. Remove the cover, turn fish, and grill until done to taste.

3. Heat the foil-wrapped pita bread on the grill, turning once.

4. *To assemble:* Allow your guests to stuff their own pita pockets. Arrange the pita bread in a round basket. Cut the fish into chunks and toss with the vegetables and olives, in a bowl.

Yield: 8 servings

COD STEAKS WITH WATERCRESS SAUCE AND WATERCRESS SANDWICHES

This recipe can also be prepared using haddock or orange roughy. We suggest you serve it with grilled cinnamon apple slices and Cotswold cheese.

SANDWICHES

12 slices white bread, crusts removed

6 tablespoons butter or margarine, softened

2 bunches watercress, stems removed, minced

½ cup good-quality mayonnaise

WATERCRESS SAUCE

1 bunch watercress, stems removed

4 tablespoons butter or margarine

4 large shallots, minced

2 tablespoons flour

1 cup whipping cream

½ cup sour cream

Salt and freshly ground white pepper to taste

FISH

3 pounds cod, cut into 8 steaks

Melted butter or margarine for brushing cod

Salt and freshly ground white pepper to taste

1 teaspoon ground ginger

Oil for greasing grill

1. *Make the sandwiches:* Cut the bread slices into 1½- to 2-inch rounds with a cookie cutter. Spread one side of the bread rounds with softened butter. Sprinkle lightly with watercress and make into sandwiches.

2. Spread mayonnaise around the outer edges of each sandwich. Scatter the remaining watercress in a flat dish and roll each sandwich edge in watercress. Arrange the sandwiches on a plate, cover with a damp paper towel, and refrigerate for 1 hour. When ready to serve, place the sandwiches on a serving dish, rims up.

3. *Prepare the sauce:* Blanch the watercress for 2 minutes, rinse in cold water, and drain. Pat dry with paper toweling. Puree the watercress in a blender or a food processor fitted with the steel blade, and reserve.

4. Melt the butter in a medium saucepan, add the shallots, and sauté until tender, approximately 2 minutes. Whisk in the flour until absorbed, about 1½–2 minutes. Blend in the pureed watercress and the whipping cream; heat slowly, being careful not to boil. Remove from the heat, cool slightly, and blend in the sour cream. Add salt and pepper to taste.

5. *Grill the fish:* Brush the cod steaks with melted butter and season with salt, pepper, and ginger. Place the steaks on the prepared grill and cook for 3–6 minutes on each side or until done. Transfer to individual plates.

6. Serve the fish hot off the grill with the warm sauce and the watercress sandwiches.

Yield: 8 servings (3 cups sauce)

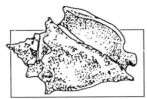

CONCH

The conch is really a snail—a univalve mollusk. The conch spends most of its life inside a beautiful porcelainlike shell, moving about on a powerful muscular foot, which is, incidentally, the edible portion of the animal. Conch is available fresh, frozen, and canned. If it has not already been tenderized by pounding, it should be pounded with a wooden mallet; otherwise it will be too tough to eat.

CONCH ON THE GRILL

BREADING
1½ cups fine bread crumbs
1 teaspoon paprika
½ teaspoon garlic powder
½ teaspoon onion flakes
¼ teaspoon salt
1 egg white, slightly beaten

SHELLFISH
1 pound frozen conch, defrosted in
*   refrigerator or at room temperature*
Oil for greasing grill or grill rack

1. *Prepare breading:* Toss bread crumbs, paprika, garlic powder, onion flakes, and salt in a shallow dish. Pour egg white into a shallow glass dish.

2. *Prepare conch:* Put conch on waxed paper on a kitchen counter, cut into portion-sized pieces and pound with a tenderizer or wooden mallet. Roll in egg white and lightly press on bread crumbs.

3. *Grill conch:* Arrange conch on prepared grill or rack over hot coals and grill 1½ minutes on each side. Some of the crumbs may char or even fall off, but it will not affect the flavor. Serve warm on individual plates. The conch can also be sliced thin and tossed with a pasta salad.

Yield: 4 servings

CRAB
Yes, crab can be grilled!

SOFT-SHELL CRAB WITH GARLIC BUTTER

8 soft-shell crabs
¼ cup clarified butter (see Index)
2 cloves garlic, minced
Salt, pepper, and paprika to taste

1. To clean soft-shell crabs, put the crabs, one at a time, on cutting surface. Cut off face portion of crab. Lifting the shell easily on either side of back, scrape off the gills. Lift shell and remove sand receptacle from under the mouth area. Discard all removed portions from the crab. Wash crab and pat dry with paper toweling. (If you make friends with your fishmonger, he may clean them for you.)

2. Lay each crab on a square of aluminum foil. Begin to fold foil, envelope style, but do not seal.

3. Heat butter in small saucepan over medium heat. Sauté garlic in it until tender, stirring often.

4. Drizzle garlic butter over crabs. Sprinkle crabs with salt, pepper, and paprika to taste. Fold and seal envelopes securely.

5. Arrange crab packages over hot grill in a single layer. Cook for 4–5 minutes. Open one envelope and check to see if crab has steamed (crabs will turn a reddish color when done). If not, rewrap and continue grilling until crabs have cooked. Serve soft-shell crabs on individual plates, allowing guests to open packages themselves.

Yield: 4 servings

SOFT-SHELL CRABS
SKEWERED WITH VEGETABLES

If you don't want to deal with shell on a soft-shell crab, but love blue crab, try eating it between the months of May and October. The shell is soft at this time because crabs have molted.

VEGETABLES
1 medium-sized zucchini
¾ pound large white mushrooms

HOT CAJUN SPICE
2 teaspoons cayenne
1 teaspoon ground sweet pepper
2 teaspoons dried minced onion
½ teaspoon garlic powder
¼ teaspoon dried thyme
¼ teaspoon salt
⅛ teaspoon white pepper

SHELLFISH
8 soft-shell crabs
3 tablespoons butter, melted
4 wooden presoaked barbecue skewers
Oil for greasing grill

1. *Prepare vegetables:* Cut zucchini into 1½-inch pieces. Trim mushrooms. Set vegetables aside.

2. *Clean soft-shell crabs:* Put crabs, one at a time, on cutting surface. Cut off face portion of crab. Lifting the shell easily on either side of back, scrape off the gills. Lift shell and remove sand receptacle from under the mouth area. Discard all portions removed from crab. Wash crab and pat dry with paper toweling. Or ask your fishmonger to clean them for you.

3. *Prepare cajun spice:* Stir all ingredients together until combined. They will yield about 2½ tablespoons. Reserve 1½ tablespoons for another use.

4. Mix 1 tablespoon hot cajun spice with melted butter. Brush crabs and vegetables with seasoned butter. Thread vegetables and crabs onto skewers, threading the crabs through the top edge.

5. *Grill crabs:* Arrange skewers on prepared grill over ashen coals and grill for 3 minutes. Brush with seasoned butter, turn over, and continue grilling until crabs are a reddish color, about 3 to 4 minutes longer. Serve hot over fluffy rice or noodles.

Yield: 4 servings

STONE CRAB CLAWS WITH PLUM DIPPING SAUCE

Somewhere in their evolution, stone crabs learned a trick that human scientists are trying their darnedest to imitate. Stone crabs, like lobsters, regenerate. If you pull off their claws and return them to the ocean, they will grow another set. Since stone crabs are often sold precooked, their grilling time will be short. You can substitute split king crab legs. You might serve this dish with a spring green salad with goat cheese and bacon bits or chilled artichoke with dill mayonnaise and hot rolls.

PLUM SAUCE

1 12-ounce jar Damson plum preserves
3 tablespoons red wine vinegar
1 teaspoon Dijon mustard
2 tablespoons light brown sugar
1 teaspoon finely grated orange zest

BREADING

1½ cups fine bread crumbs
6 tablespoons minced hazelnuts
2 tablespoons finely grated orange zest
1 tablespoon dried tarragon, crumbled
1 teaspoon ground chervil
2 tablespoons melted butter or margarine,
  cooled

SHELLFISH

Oil for greasing grill
24 stone crab claws, cracked, loose shell
  removed, leaving top of claw exposed
Melted butter for brushing crab claws

1. *Make the sauce:* Mix together the preserves, vinegar, mustard, sugar, and zest in a small, heavy saucepan. Bring the mixture to a boil and reduce the heat to a simmer. Continue cooking for 4 minutes, stirring often. Cool

slightly. Puree the sauce in food processor fitted with the steel blade or in a blender. Place the sauce in a serving dish and refrigerate until ready to serve. Remove the sauce from refrigerator 30 minutes before serving.

2. *Make the breading:* Combine the bread crumbs, hazelnuts, zest, herbs, and butter in a small bowl. Set aside.

3. *Prepare the shellfish:* Brush the claws with butter and roll in the breading, making sure the crumbs stick to the claws.

4. *Grill the shellfish:* Put the crab claws on the prepared grill and cook for 1 minute. Turn the claws and continue grilling for 1 minute or until the crab meat is warm. Transfer the crab claws to a platter and serve 3 claws per person with plum dipping sauce.

Yield: 8 servings (1 cup sauce)

SOFT-SHELL CRABS WITH BASIL BUTTER

Blue crabs that have just "busted" out of their shells become soft-shell crabs; it is part of the natural molting process. Allow two or three soft-shell crabs per person. Sea scallops may be substituted for crabs.

Lime-marinated bay scallops, a salad of red leaf, Boston, and romaine lettuce with chive vinaigrette, and fried string potatoes would go well with this dish.

BASIL BUTTER
¼ cup (½ stick) butter or margarine, melted
¼ cup minced fresh basil leaves
4 tablespoons minced fresh parsley
¼ teaspoon cayenne pepper

SHELLFISH
Oil for greasing grill
24 soft-shell crabs
¼ cup sliced almonds
Basil leaves for garnish

1. *Make the basil butter:* Blend together the butter, basil, parsley, and cayenne. Set aside.

2. *Clean the crabs:* Put the crabs, one at a time, on a cutting surface. Cut off the face portion of the crab. Lifting the shell easily on either side of the back, scrape off the gills. Lift the shell and remove the sand receptacle from under the mouth area. Discard all removed sections of the crab. Wash the crab and pat dry with paper toweling. (Your fishmonger might clean them for you.)

3. *Grill the crabs:* Brush the crabs with some of the basil butter. Place them directly on the prepared grill or thread them onto skewers. Grill for about 3 minutes on each side, until they turn a reddish color. Be sure that the crabs are cooked through, but do not overcook them. Serve immediately, sprinkled with the almonds, garnished with basil leaves.

Yield: 12 servings

SOFT-SHELL CRABS WITH PISTACHIO BUTTER

PISTACHIO BUTTER
¼ cup shelled pistachios
4 tablespoons butter at room temperature
2 tablespoons minced fresh parsley
1 teaspoon fresh lime juice

SHELLFISH
12 soft-shell crabs
Melted butter for brushing crabs
Oil for greasing grill

1. *Prepare pistachio butter:* Blend pistachios and butter in food processor fitted with steel blade. Add parsley and lime juice and combine. Mound pistachio butter in a small bowl, cover, and refrigerate. Remove from refrigerator 45 minutes before serving time so that the pistachio butter will be at room temperature.

2. *Clean soft-shell crabs:* Put crabs, one at a time, on cutting surface. Cut off face portion of crab. Lifting the shell easily on either side of back, scrape off the gills. Lift shell and remove sand receptacle from under the mouth area. Discard all the portions removed from crab. Wash crab and pat dry with paper toweling. Or ask your fishmonger to clean them for you.

3. Brush crabs with melted butter. Arrange crabs on prepared grill over hot coals. Grill for 3 minutes. Brush with butter, turn, and continue grilling for 3 minutes or until crabs are a reddish color. Place two crabs on each plate, top with a dollop of pistachio butter while hot, and serve immediately. Pass extra pistachio butter at the table for guests to help themselves.

Yield: 6 servings

MESQUITE-GRILLED SPLIT KING CRAB LEGS WITH PICKLED GINGER AND WASABI

Wasabi powder (Japanese green horseradish powder) and pickled ginger are available at most Oriental food stores.

WASABI
2 teaspoons cold water
2 tablespoons wasabi powder
1 cup (or to taste) pickled ginger

SHELLFISH
4 pounds frozen split king crab legs,
    presliced in half, defrosted in
    refrigerator
3 to 4 4-inch pieces mesquite or 2 cups
    mesquite chips, soaked in water 30
    minutes and drained
Oil for greasing grill

1. *Prepare wasabi:* Stir 2 teaspoons water with 2 tablespoons wasabi powder in shallow dish until a thick paste is formed. If necessary, add more water, ½ teaspoon at a time. Allow wasabi to stand for 15 minutes and stir.

2. Remove pickled ginger from packet, divide, and mound onto four individual dinner plates. Dollop wasabi next to ginger on plates and set aside.

3. *Grill crab legs:* Arrange mesquite over hot coals and replace prepared grill. Put crab legs cut side down on prepared grill. Cover grill and smoke for 2 to 4 minutes or until crabmeat is flavored to taste. It will have a light brownish smoked appearance.

4. Arrange crab legs on dinner plates and provide a bowl for crab shells.

Yield: 4 servings

HICKORY·SMOKED KING CRAB LEGS WITH NO·COOK ORANGE SAUCE

❧

Both king crab legs and snow crab claws are available frozen and precooked. It's best to defrost them in the refrigerator.

NO-COOK ORANGE SAUCE
½ cup orange marmalade
3 tablespoons fresh orange juice
3 tablespoons fresh lemon juice
2 teaspoons prepared white horseradish
¾ teaspoon grated fresh gingerroot
¼ teaspoon salt
2 tablespoons brandy

SHELLFISH
4 pounds frozen king crab legs, presliced
  in half, defrosted in refrigerator
Melted butter for brushing crab legs
2 cups hickory wood chips, soaked in
  water for 30 minutes and drained
Oil for greasing grill

1. *Prepare sauce:* Blend all sauce ingredients in a food processor fitted with steel blade or a blender. Place in covered container and refrigerate until ready to serve.

2. *Grill crab legs:* Brush crab legs with melted butter. Sprinkle hickory chips over hot coals and carefully replace prepared grill. Arrange crab legs cut side down on prepared grill. Cover grill and smoke for 2 to 3 minutes or until crabmeat is flavored to taste. It will have a brownish smoked appearance.

3. Serve crab legs with orange dipping sauce.

Yield: 4 servings

SPICY SNOW CRAB CLAWS
WITH HORSERADISH SAUCE

HORSERADISH SAUCE
2 cups crème fraîche (see Index)
1 tablespoon prepared red horseradish
1 small red onion, chopped
2 teaspoons fresh lime juice
1 teaspoon fennel seeds

BREADING
1½ cups fine bread crumbs
1 teaspoon paprika
½ teaspoon garlic powder
1½ teaspoons onion flakes
½ teaspoon salt
½ teaspoon crushed red pepper
2 egg whites, slightly beaten

SHELLFISH
2 dozen frozen snow crab claws,
    defrosted
Oil for greasing grill

1. *Prepare horseradish sauce:* Mix together sauce ingredients and spoon sauce into a serving bowl. Chill until ready to serve.

2. *Prepare breading:* Combine bread crumbs, paprika, garlic powder, onion flakes, salt, and crushed red pepper in a shallow bowl or pie plate. Pour egg whites into a shallow dish.

3. Roll exposed crab section in egg whites and then in crumb mixture. Put paper toweling in bottom of cookie sheet and place crab claws on the paper.

4. *Grill crab claws:* Arrange claws across grid of prepared grill, about 3 to 4 inches from heat source, and grill for 2 minutes. Turn crab claws over and grill for 1 to 2 minutes or until done.

5. Serve on individual plates with horseradish dipping sauce.

Yield: 4 servings

DUNGENESS CRAB WITH SHALLOT BUTTER AND GRILLED SHALLOTS

Dungeness crab is from the Pacific Northwest; it is cooked and then frozen. Each crab averages about 1½ to 2 pounds.

SHALLOT BUTTER

3 medium shallots

4 tablespoons (½ stick) butter

2 tablespoons evaporated milk

½ teaspoon crumbled dried thyme

1 teaspoon crumbled dried green peppercorns

2 medium shallots (for grilling)

SHELLFISH

4 1½-pound frozen Dungeness crabs, defrosted in refrigerator or at room temperature

Oil for greasing grill

1. *Prepare shallot butter:* Puree 3 peeled shallots in food processor fitted with steel blade. Blend in butter. Add milk, thyme, and green peppercorns; mix all ingredients together. Spoon into a small bowl, cover, and refrigerate. Bring to room temperature before serving.

2. Arrange remaining shallots, with skins on, at outer edge of ashen coals. Cook for 8 minutes, turn, and continue cooking for 3 to 4 minutes or until soft. The outer wrapping may char. Place shallots on serving dish.

3. *Grill crabs:* Put crabs, shell side up, on prepared grill and grill for 3 to 4 minutes. Turn crabs over and grill 1 to 2 minutes longer. The crabs will turn red. Place crabs on serving dish.

4. Serve crabs hot with shallot butter and roasted shallots. Squeeze warm shallots out of skin and eat with vegetables or on roasted potatoes or tomatoes. Serve crabs with picks.

Yield: 4 servings

MARYLAND-STYLE CRAB CAKES ON A BED OF PARSLEY

MUSTARD SAUCE

½ cup mayonnaise

¾ cup sour cream

1 teaspoon dry mustard

2 teaspoons prepared rough-grained
   mustard

CRAB CAKES

1 pound crabmeat, picked over, cartilage
   discarded, and any liquid squeezed out

¼ cup fine bread crumbs

1 egg, beaten

1 tablespoon mayonnaise

½ teaspoon (or to taste) Worcestershire
   sauce

½ teaspoon dry mustard

½ teaspoon salt

¼ teaspoon white pepper

3 tablespoons minced fresh parsley

All-purpose flour

2 eggs, slightly beaten

Bread crumbs

Oil for greasing grill

2–3 cups parsley sprigs

1. *Prepare mustard sauce:* Stir together sauce ingredients; place in a covered container, and refrigerate until needed.

2. *Prepare crab cakes:* Combine ¼ cup fine bread crumbs, egg, mayonnaise, Worcestershire, mustard, salt, pepper, and 3 tablespoons parsley in a deep bowl. Form into six firm patties.

3. Roll patties in flour, then dip into the beaten eggs. Roll in bread crumbs.

4. *Grill crab cakes:* Spread parsley as a nest on prepared grill. Arrange patties over parsley. Or you can grill the crab cakes in a fish basket. Cook for 3 to 4 minutes over medium-hot coals. Turn patties with spatula and grill 3 minutes longer or until done. Serve hot with mustard sauce.

Yield: 4–6 servings

MOCK CRAB SALAD
SANDWICHES

If you're troubled by the word mock, don't worry; you're still eating fish. Imitation crab is made by a Japanese process called surimi in which fresh fish is pounded to a paste, flavored, re-formed into a crablike shape, then cooked. The mesquite smoke imparts a wonderful flavor to the mock crab.

FISH
1 pound mock crab legs
Melted butter for brushing crab legs
3 to 4 4-inch pieces mesquite or 2 cups
   mesquite chips, soaked in water 30
   minutes and drained
Oil for greasing grill

SALAD
6 ounces mild goat cheese, cut into ½-inch
   chunks
½ cup chopped walnuts
½ cup chopped fresh chives
3 tablespoons mayonnaise
Best-quality white bread

1. *Grill crab legs:* Brush crab legs with melted butter and set aside. Arrange mesquite on hot coals and replace grill carefully. Set crab legs on prepared grill, cover, and cook for 2 minutes. Remove cover, turn legs over, and continue cooking for 2 minutes.

2. Remove crab legs, cool, and chop them into ¾- to ½-inch chunks; place in deep mixing bowl. Toss crab with goat cheese, walnuts, chives, and mayonnaise. Prepare sandwiches on best-quality fresh bread.

Yield: 6–8 sandwiches

MARINATED MOCK CRAB LEGS WITH PASTA

Mock crab products are often based on pollack—a saltwater whitefish found in Alaskan waters. The pollack is pounded to a paste, and in many cases the finished product contains 17 percent real crab along with crab shell extracts and flavorings. The paste is molded into crab leg shapes and cooked before being put out in the fish display cases.

MARINADE
1 cup virgin olive oil
¼ cup red wine vinegar
½ teaspoon paprika
½ cup chopped green onion

FISH
1¼ pounds mock crab legs
3 to 4 4-inch pieces mesquite or 2 cups mesquite chips, soaked in water 30 minutes and drained
Oil for greasing grill

PASTA SALAD
¾ pound spiral noodles, cooked according to package directions
1 cup sliced celery
1 small red onion, chopped
2 tomatoes, peeled, seeded, and chopped
2 teaspoons crumbled dried basil
½ teaspoon salt
¼ teaspoon freshly ground pepper
½ cup sour cream
½ cup mayonnaise

1. *Prepare marinade:* Combine marinade ingredients in a shallow bowl or glass pie plate. Marinate crab legs for 30 minutes, turning once.

2. *Grill crab legs:* Arrange mesquite on hot coals and carefully replace grill. Set crab legs on prepared grill, cover, and cook for 2 minutes. Remove cover and turn legs over; they will tend to separate, so turn carefully with a spatula. Continue cooking for 1 to 2 minutes.

3. Remove legs and chop into ¾- to ½-inch chunks; place in deep mixing bowl. Toss crab with drained, cooled pasta, celery, onions, and tomatoes. Season with basil, salt, and pepper. Stir in sour cream and mayonnaise. Arrange on individual plates or use as a buffet item.

Yield: 6 servings

CRAYFISH

These freshwater shellfish resemble lobsters but are much smaller—not to mention trickier to eat!

GRILLED CRAYFISH FINNISH STYLE

In summer, during crayfish season, the Finnish people consume an unbelievable amount of crayfish, which they boil in highly flavored water instead of putting them on the grill. The crayfish are then allowed to steep in this water until they're ready to eat. We prefer them grilled and flavor them by serving a highly seasoned dill butter with them. The Finns, who eat crayfish tails cold, say that custom dictates that a drink of aquavit, beer, or white wine be taken with each tail. Certainly, if you follow this dictum, it should make for a lively, uninhibited party. You may want to serve a dessert of fresh berries in season and sweetened whipped cream.

DILL BUTTER
4 tablespoons (½ stick) butter
¼ cup minced fresh dill
3 tablespoons aquavit
1 teaspoon dill seeds

SHELLFISH
6 pounds crayfish, prepared for grilling by
*   fishmonger*
Oil for greasing basket
2 cups fresh dill

1. *Prepare dill butter:* Melt butter in small heavy saucepan over low heat. Stir in dill, aquavit, and dill seeds. Pour dill butter into serving dish.

2. *Grill crayfish:* Rinse crayfish. Arrange in prepared hinged grill basket or on grill. Cover crayfish with ¾ cup fresh dill sprigs and secure basket.

Unless you have two or more grill baskets, it will be necessary to repeat procedure until all the crayfish have been grilled. Put basket on grill over hot coals 3 to 4 inches from heat source. Grill 2 to 3 minutes, turn basket, and grill 2 minutes longer. Crayfish will turn a bright red.

3. Scatter remaining dill on a large platter. Mound crayfish in the center over dill. Serve hot or cool with dill butter as a dipping sauce. Guests open their own crayfish. Provide a bowl for shells. To eat crayfish, see Index.

Yield: 6 servings

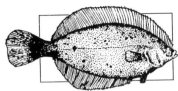

FLOUNDER
The flounder is a mild flat fish found in both the Atlantic and Pacific Oceans.

GRILLED WHOLE FLOUNDER ORIENTAL STYLE

We suggest you serve Oriental noodles with chopped scallions and minced garlic and stir-fried Oriental vegetables.

Sole, sea bass, or whitefish may be used instead of flounder in this recipe.

SEASONINGS
1 tablespoon freshly grated gingerroot
3 cloves garlic, minced
1 bunch scallions, cut into 1½-inch
    lengths
3 tablespoons julienned tangerine peel
1 small bunch cilantro, trimmed and
    chopped
2 tablespoons peanut oil
2 tablespoons soy sauce
½ teaspoon Oriental sesame oil
2 tablespoons dry white wine
6 tablespoons fresh tangerine juice

FISH
2 2-pound flounders, scaled and cleaned,
    head and tail intact
Oil for greasing grill

1. *Prepare the seasonings:* In a small bowl, toss the gingerroot, garlic, scallions, tangerine peel, and cilantro. Divide the mixture and lightly place one-quarter of the seasonings in each fish cavity.

2. Heat the peanut oil in a wok or small heavy skillet. Stir-fry the remaining ginger mixture for 2 minutes or until blended; set aside.

3. Combine the soy sauce, sesame oil, wine, and tangerine juice. Add to ginger mixture. Brush the flounder generously with the mixture on both sides.

4. *Grill the fish:* Arrange the fish on a sheet of aluminum foil and cook for 5–8 minutes. Turn the fish carefully with a spatula, being sure not to break the fish. Continue grilling until fish is done to taste.

5. Place the fish on a heated platter. Bring the fish whole to the table and serve hot.

Yield: 8 servings

FLOUNDER IN
SPINACH PACKETS

These delicate green spinach wrappings not only add flavor but also protect the flounder from the direct heat of the grill. You'll find that the fish stays moist in its colorful wrapping.

You might serve it with grilled tomatoes and grilled potatoes. You may substitute shark or marlin in this recipe.

MARINADE

⅓ cup good-quality olive oil

3 tablespoons red wine vinegar

1 small clove garlic, minced

¼ teaspoon dry mustard

FISH

30 ounces flounder fillets (about
    2½ ounces per packet), cut into 2-inch
    strips

SPINACH MOUSSE

2 cloves garlic, minced

1 10-ounce package frozen chopped
    spinach, thawed and drained well

1 egg

¼ teaspoon salt

⅛ teaspoon freshly ground pepper

4 teaspoons milk or evaporated milk

SPINACH PACKETS

24–36 fresh spinach leaves (about
    1 pound including stems), trimmed and
    blanched

Oil for greasing grill

1. *Make the marinade:* Combine the marinade ingredients and pour into a large plastic bag. Add the flounder fillets. Secure with a twister seal and turn the bag several times to make sure all fish surfaces touch the marinade. Place the bag in a bowl and let sit at room temperature for 1 hour.

2. *Meanwhile, make the mousse:* Mince the garlic in a food processor fitted with the steel blade; add spinach, egg, salt, and pepper. Drizzle in the milk and blend.

3. *Make the packets:* Lay a spinach leaf on a paper towel. Place a flounder strip in the center of the leaf (reserve the leftover marinade). Spread 1–2 tablespoons of mousse over the fish. Roll the top of the leaf to the center and bring up the bottom of the leaf, creating a package. Arrange a second spinach leaf on a paper towel and place the spinach packet in the center of the leaf. Again make a packet by folding and bringing the top of the leaf to the center of the fish and the bottom of the leaf over and around the fish. Secure the fish package with a toothpick. Use a third leaf, if necessary, to cover the fish. The ends of the fish packet can be open or closed as desired. Continue making packets until ingredients are used up; you should have about 12 packets in all.

4. Brush each spinach packet with the remaining marinade.

5. *Grill the packets:* Place the spinach packets on the prepared grill (coals should be medium-hot) or on a well-oiled grill screen. Grill for 4 minutes over medium-hot coals. Brush again with marinade, turn over, and continue grilling for 2–4 minutes or until done.

6. If the outer leaf chars to excess, remove it before serving.

Yield: 6 servings

SALMON QUENELLES IN FLOUNDER

Risotto and a warm spinach salad would go well with this dish. Sole substitutes for flounder with this recipe.

SALMON QUENELLES
1 pound salmon fillet, all bones removed,
  cut into strips
2 egg whites
1 teaspoon dried tarragon
¼ teaspoon ground mace
½ cup evaporated milk

FISH
8 flounder fillets, each cut into
  2 horizontal strips
Melted butter or margarine for brushing
  fillets and greasing grill rack
Oil for greasing grill
½ cup dried tarragon leaves
Fresh tarragon sprigs or thin slices truffle
  for garnish

1. *Make the quenelles:* Puree the salmon in a food processor fitted with the steel blade or in a grinder. Slowly add the egg whites, tarragon, and mace. With the food processor running, add the milk in a slow, steady stream until incorporated. The salmon mixture will be delicate and light. Cover and refrigerate until ready to assemble.

2. Place a flounder strip on the work surface and cover with waxed paper. Pound the flounder thin and discard the paper. Mound about 2 tablespoons of the quenelle filling on the fillet, roll the fillet lightly, and place it on a tray, seam side down. Continue until all the fillets have been rolled. Brush with butter.

3. *Grill the fish:* Arrange the rolled fillets on the prepared grill or on a grill rack that has been brushed with butter. Sprinkle the tarragon over the hot coals. Cook the fish for 2–3 minutes, rotate so that they will grill evenly, and continue grilling until the filling is cooked.

4. Serve 2 rolled fillets to each guest. Garnish with tarragon sprigs or thin slices of truffle.

Yield: 8 servings

GRILLED FLOUNDER MELT

This recipe is the perfect choice for a lunch at the seashore or in your own backyard. Grilled Tuna Sandwiches (see Index) is another tempting sandwich recipe. Dover sole also works well in this recipe. With it, you might serve potato salad and tomato slices topped with a sprinkling of balsamic vinegar and chopped fresh basil.

BREAD
2 French bread baguettes
1 tablespoon sesame seed
4 tablespoons (½ stick) butter or
    margarine, melted

FISH
Oil for brushing peppers and scallions and
    greasing grill
2 large green bell peppers, tops removed,
    seeded, sliced into rings
2 pounds flounder fillets, cut into
    8 serving pieces
8 thin slices (or to taste) Colby or baby
    Swiss cheese
8 scallions, trimmed
8 crisp, trimmed lettuce leaves
¾ cup radish sprouts

1. *Prepare the bread:* Slice the baguettes horizontally and cut each on the diagonal into four sandwich-sized pieces. Stir the sesame seeds into the melted butter. Brush onto the cut sides of bread and set aside.

2. *Grill the fish:* Oil the pepper slices and place on the prepared grill. Arrange a slice of cheese on each fillet, trimming so that the cheese does not overlap the fillet. Place the fillets on slices of pepper and grill for about 2–6 minutes, without turning, or until fish is cooked to taste. At the same time, grill the oiled scallions until done, laying the scallions across the grill. Also at the same time, briefly grill (about 30–40 seconds) the cut sides of the bread.

3. *Assemble the sandwiches:* Put a lettuce leaf on the bottom piece of each baguette and top with flounder, pepper, and cheese. Sprinkle with the sprouts and top with a grilled scallion. Cover with the tops of the baguettes and serve hot.

Yield: 8 servings

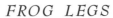

FROG LEGS

Frogs are neither fish nor shellfish; they are amphibians with long hind legs adapted for jumping. But they're so often put into this category gastronomically that we decided to include them in this book. Frog legs taste like a combination of lobster and chicken. They are commercially grown and marketed all over the United States and are available frozen in many supermarkets. Although they come in small, medium, and large sizes, we suggest buying only the smallest and most tender you can find.

FROG LEGS WITH TROPICAL FRUIT

FRUIT SAUCE
1 cup mashed mango pulp
½ cup sweetened flaked coconut
¼ cup crushed pineapple with juice
2 teaspoons fresh lime juice

SEAFOOD
12 pairs frozen frog legs, defrosted in refrigerator or at room temperature
¾ cup chili sauce
3 green onions, minced
Oil for greasing grill

1. *Prepare fruit sauce:* Combine sauce ingredients in a bowl and stir together until blended. Cover and refrigerate until needed.

2. *Prepare frog legs:* Wash legs and pat dry; arrange in a shallow glass pan. Stir together chili sauce and onions. Brush frog legs with chili sauce and let stand for 20 minutes.

3. *Grill frog legs:* Place frog legs on prepared grill over ashen coals about 3 to 4 inches from heat source. Grill 3 to 4 minutes. Brush with extra sauce. Turn and continue grilling for 2 minutes or until legs are cooked. Serve hot with hot rice and fruit sauce.

Yield: 6 servings

FROG LEGS ORIENTAL

This recipe yields two pairs of frog legs per person, but sometimes three pairs are considered a serving, so grill more if you wish. Serve hot rice or noodles.

Hoisin sauce is available at Oriental food markets and some large supermarkets (see Appendix).

HOISIN SAUCE MIXTURE
1 cup hoisin sauce
1 teaspoon soy sauce
1 teaspoon sugar
½ teaspoon Oriental sesame oil

SEAFOOD
*12 pairs frozen frog legs, defrosted in
    refrigerator or at room temperature*
Oil for greasing grill

1. *Prepare hoisin sauce mixture:* Combine sauce ingredients in small heavy saucepan. Cook over low heat until hot. Cool, cover, and refrigerate until needed. Reheat before serving.

2. *Grill frog legs:* Brush with hoisin sauce mixture and grill on prepared grill over ashen coals for 3 minutes. Flip frog legs and again brush with hoisin sauce mixture and continue grilling for 2 to 3 minutes or until done. Serve hot with extra hoisin sauce mixture at the table.

Yield: 6 servings (with 1 scant cup sauce)

FROG LEGS WITH PESTO SAUCE

Pesto is best prepared in late summer when fresh basil is plentiful. This sauce freezes very well.

PESTO SAUCE
½ cup pine nuts
2 cloves garlic, peeled
2 cups fresh basil leaves
¼ teaspoon salt
½ cup grated fresh Parmesan cheese
1 cup good-quality olive oil

SEAFOOD
24 pairs frozen frog legs, defrosted in
*   refrigerator or at room temperature*
Oil for greasing grill

1. *Prepare pesto sauce:* Puree pine nuts and garlic in food processor fitted with steel blade. Add basil and puree. Mix in salt and cheese. With the machine still running, add oil in a slow, steady stream until it is incorporated. Place sauce in a covered container and refrigerate until needed.

2. *Grill frog legs:* Brush frog legs with pesto sauce and place on prepared grill. Cook for 3 minutes. Brush again with pesto sauce and turn over. Continue grilling for 3 minutes or until done. Serve frog legs hot with a pasta dish.

Yield: 12 servings (with 1½ cups sauce)

FROG LEGS WITH BARBECUE SAUCE AND GRILLED TOMATILLOS

Tomatillos are readily available in most of the larger supermarkets, as well as in Mexican and Cuban food stores.

BARBECUE SAUCE

1 tablespoon butter
3 green onions, chopped
2 cloves garlic, minced
½ cup chili sauce
¼ cup catsup
1 tablespoon Gebhardt chili powder, or a
  good quality chili powder
½ teaspoon Worcestershire sauce
1 teaspoon prepared mustard
3 drops (or to taste) hot pepper sauce

SEAFOOD AND TOMATILLOS

8 tomatillos
Oil for greasing grill and tomatillos
12 pairs frozen frog legs, defrosted in
  refrigerator or at room temperature

1. *Prepare barbecue sauce:* Heat butter in medium-sized saucepan and sauté onions and garlic in it only until tender. Mix in remaining sauce ingredients. Simmer for 10 minutes, stirring occasionally. Cool.

2. Brush tomatillos with oil, leaving outer skin in place. Set aside.

3. Arrange frog legs in a glass dish and cover with barbecue sauce. Marinate for 1 hour, turning once.

4. *Grill frog legs:* Place frog legs on prepared grill and cook for 3 minutes. Brush with sauce, turn over, and continue cooking for 2 minutes or until done.

5. *Grill tomatillos:* Cut tomatillos in half, brush with oil again, and grill cut side up for 2 minutes. Turn over and grill 2 minutes or until done. Serve frog legs with tomatillos.

Yield: 6 servings (with ¾ cup sauce)

FROG LEGS WITH SHIITAKE MUSHROOMS AND HERBS

❧

Shiitake mushrooms are available at many gourmet markets and by mail order (see Appendix). Store mushrooms in refrigerator, covered loosely with a damp cloth and not in a plastic bag.

SHIITAKE MUSHROOMS
½ pound fresh shiitake mushrooms
Melted butter for brushing mushrooms
½ cup dried rosemary
½ cup dried thyme

MARINADE
⅓ cup good-quality olive oil
3 tablespoons fresh lemon juice
3 tablespoons minced fresh parsley
½ teaspoon garlic powder

FROG LEGS
12 pairs frozen frog legs, defrosted in
*   refrigerator or at room temperature*
Oil for greasing grill

1. *Prepare mushrooms:* Remove and discard stems. Wipe caps with damp towel. Brush mushroom caps with melted butter. Sprinkle with 3 tablespoons each of rosemary and thyme and set aside.

2. *Prepare marinade:* Combine marinade ingredients in a shallow glass bowl. Marinate frog legs for 1 hour, turning once, and drain, reserving marinade.

3. *Grill mushrooms and frog legs:* Sprinkle remaining herbs over hot coals. Working quickly, put mushroom caps (cap side down) and frog legs on prepared grill. Cover and cook for 3 minutes. Remove mushrooms, brush frog legs with marinade, turn over, and continue grilling for 2 to 3 minutes or until done. Serve mushrooms with frog legs.

Yield: 6 servings

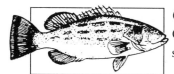

GROUPER

Grouper, a firm fish, can be substituted with all snappers.

GROUPER WITH SWEET AND SOUR SAUCE

SWEET AND SOUR SAUCE

1 tablespoon cornstarch
½ cup firmly packed dark brown sugar
⅓ cup red wine vinegar
6 tablespoons pineapple juice, reserved
    from canned pineapple
2 teaspoons soy sauce
1 20-ounce can pineapple chunks,
    drained, juice reserved
1 green bell pepper, seeded and cut into 1-
    inch cubes

FISH

4 7-ounce grouper fillets
Peanut oil for brushing fish and greasing
    grill
Garlic powder
Sesame seeds for garnish

1. *Make sauce:* Combine cornstarch and brown sugar in a small saucepan. Mix in remaining ingredients except pineapple and pepper. Bring sauce to a boil over medium heat. Reduce heat to a simmer and continue cooking for 1½ minutes, stirring constantly. Mix in pineapple chunks and pepper cubes. Remove sauce from heat. Reheat sauce when ready to serve.

2. *Grill grouper:* Brush grouper fillets with peanut oil and sprinkle with garlic powder. Arrange fillets on prepared grill and cook for 4 minutes. Turn fish over and continue cooking about 2 minutes or until fish begins to flake when tested.

3. Place grouper on a serving platter and drizzle with warm sweet and sour sauce. Sprinkle with sesame seeds; serve with rice.

Yield: 4 servings

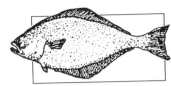

HALIBUT
A sweet-flavored fish with a moderately high fat content.

COLD HALIBUT HORS D'OEUVRES WITH MUSTARD SAUCE

This is a rich appetizer. All other dishes served—whether a main course or additional appetizers—should be lean in taste and texture. A plain fillet, first marinated in our basic marinade (see Index), then grilled, along with French bread and a green salad, would be ideal.

This yummy appetizer could be made with monkfish, scrod, or any fish that is delicate in flavor but strong enough to hold together when speared with a cocktail toothpick.

FISH
2 pounds halibut fillets, about ¾ inch
    thick
Oil for brushing fish and greasing grill

MUSTARD SAUCE
2 cups plain yogurt
2 tablespoons Dijon mustard
1 tablespoon white vinegar
1½–3 teaspoons sugar (to taste)
¼ teaspoon salt (more to taste)

1. *Grill the fish:* Brush the halibut with oil. Place the fillets on the prepared grill and cook for 3–6 minutes. Turn the fillets carefully and cook until the fish has lost its translucence.

2. Transfer the fillets to a platter (do not use metal), cover, and refrigerate until well chilled. Then cut each fillet into bite-sized chunks. Arrange the chunks carefully on a large platter.

3. *Make the sauce:* Combine yogurt, mustard, vinegar, sugar, and salt. Taste and adjust seasoning, adding more sugar or salt if desired.

4. Serve chunks of fish topped with dabs of sauce.

Yield: 8 appetizer servings

HALIBUT STEAKS WITH TOMATO-BASIL SAUCE

This is a delightful fall recipe, when fresh basil is abundant. Sauce can be made a day or two in advance, making this a potentially no-time-needed recipe.

TOMATO-BASIL SAUCE
2 tablespoons olive oil
1 clove garlic, minced
1 medium onion, minced
2½ cups peeled, diced fresh tomatoes
¼ teaspoon each: salt and freshly ground
  pepper
3 tablespoons finely chopped fresh basil

FISH
4 7-ounce halibut steaks
Melted butter
Freshly ground white pepper
1 teaspoon crumbled dried basil
Oil for greasing grill

1. *Make sauce:* Heat oil in saucepan and add garlic and onion. Sauté for 3 minutes, stirring often, until vegetables are tender. Add remaining sauce ingredients. Simmer, uncovered, stirring occasionally, for 10 minutes. Place cooled sauce in covered container and store in refrigerator until ready to use.

2. *Grill halibut steaks:* Brush halibut steaks with butter and sprinkle steaks with white pepper and basil. Place halibut steaks on prepared grill and cook for 4–5 minutes. Brush fish again, turn, and continue cooking 2–3 minutes until halibut begins to flake when tested. Arrange on individual plates. Reheat sauce and pass at the table.

Yield: 4 servings

HALIBUT CURRY
WITH CHUTNEY

This dish is extra delicious with the chutney. Make a double batch of the chutney and give it as your next gift to the host and hostess.

CHUTNEY
2 cups dried apricots
1½ tablespoons chopped candied ginger
1 cup dark raisins
½ lime, sliced thin
1 large onion, sliced thin
1½ cups firmly packed dark brown sugar
½ cup wine vinegar
3 cloves garlic, minced
1 teaspoon dry mustard
½ cup canned tomato sauce
½ teaspoon each: ground cinnamon,
 ground allspice, and ground cloves

FISH
Curry powder
3 tablespoons cup melted butter
4 7-ounce halibut steaks
Oil for greasing grill

1. *Make chutney:* Wash and chop apricots. Combine all chutney ingredients in a medium-sized heavy saucepan. Simmer for 25 minutes, stirring often, until mixture blends together and has a thick consistency. Pour the cooled chutney into a covered container and refrigerate until ready to serve.

2. *Grill halibut steaks:* Mix curry powder to taste with melted butter. Brush halibut with curry-butter mixture. Cook steaks on prepared grill for 4–5 minutes. Turn halibut with a greased spatula and continue cooking until fish begins to flake, 2–3 minutes. Remove fish to individual plates. Pass chutney at the table as a sauce for the halibut.

Yield: 4 servings

HALIBUT FILLETS WITH MISO SAUCE

When prepared in this delicate Japanese sauce, sweet-flavored halibut is especially delicious. You could also use red snapper, mahimahi, yellowtail, or scrod. Serve with rice and pickled ginger slices.

Shiro miso, Japanese light soy sauce, and pickled ginger slices are each available in Oriental food stores or by mail; see Appendix.

SAUCE
½ cup plus 2 tablespoons water
½ cup plus 2 tablespoons mirin
2 tablespoons sugar
¾ cup shiro miso
1 tablespoon Japanese light soy sauce
Salt (optional)

FISH
3 pounds halibut fillets, cut into 8 serving
　　pieces
16 ¼-inch-thick lemon slices
Oil for brushing fish

1. *Make the sauce:* Combine the water, mirin, and sugar and heat to a boil. Reduce the heat to a simmer and cook for 15 minutes. Stir in the miso and soy sauce. Taste for seasoning, adding salt if desired. Let sit in a saucepan at room temperature until ready to serve.

2. *Grill the fish:* Brush fish with oil. Place the lemon slices in pairs on the prepared grill. Arrange each fillet on 2 lemon slices. Grill for 6–8 minutes without turning, until the fish has lost its translucence. Carefully remove the fillets from the grill using two spatulas and discard the lemon slices.

3. While the fish is grilling, reheat the sauce and pour it into a serving bowl. Bring the sauce to the table and spoon liberally over each fillet.

Yield: 8 servings (2 cups sauce)

HALIBUT STEAKS WITH CILANTRO AND LIME BUTTER, GRILLED SHALLOTS, AND MUSHROOMS

If you're watching calories, try preparing the lime butter with low-calorie margarine. Or, if you feel the dish will suffer greatly from the substitution, mix the two or buy one of the butter-margarine combinations commercially available. You may substitute black sea bass, snapper, or yellowtail for halibut.

We suggest you serve this dish with buckwheat noodles or rice and a salad of endive, watercress, and a sprinkle of pine nuts.

LIME BUTTER
1 lime
4 tablespoons butter or margarine, at
   room temperature

FISH
3 pounds halibut, cut into 8 steaks
3 cups fresh shiitake mushrooms, trimmed
Melted butter or margarine for brushing
   fish and vegetables
½ cup minced cilantro
Oil for greasing grill
16 large shallots, unpeeled
1 lime, sliced paper-thin, for garnish

1. *Make the lime butter:* Grate the zest of the lime, place in a bowl, with the juice of the lime. Mix in the butter until combined, using the back of a wooden spoon or a food processor fitted with the steel blade.

2. Brush the halibut steaks and the tops of the mushrooms with melted butter. Sprinkle the fish with cilantro, patting to help the cilantro adhere to the halibut.

3. *Grill the vegetables:* Put the mushrooms and shallots on the grill. The shallots will take about 8–10 minutes to cook, and the mushrooms will cook quickly, so watch them carefully.

4. *Grill the fish:* Grill the halibut steaks on the prepared grill for about 6–8 minutes. Turn fish over and continue grilling until done to taste; be sure not to overcook fish.

5. Place the halibut steaks on a large serving platter and scatter the mushrooms and shallots around the fish. Put a dab of lime butter over each steak and place the lime slices decoratively around the platter.

Yield: 8 servings

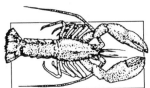

LOBSTER

The lobster is a crustacean of the northern hemisphere. The American lobster is also called the *Maine lobster* and is distinguished by its two large claws called the *crusher* claw and the smaller *quick* claw. Hard-shell lobsters are preferred because the contain more meat, and female lobsters are also favored because of the roe. Usually, one should bring them home alive from the market.

ROCK LOBSTER TAILS WITH PERNOD BUTTER

If the solid Pernod butter is served at room temperature, it will melt into the hot lobster immediately.

PERNOD BUTTER
4 tablespoons (½ stick) butter, room
    temperature
2 tablespoons Pernod liqueur, or to taste
2 teaspoons dried crumbled tarragon

LOBSTER
4 7–8-ounce rock lobster tails, defrosted
Melted butter
Oil for greasing grill

1. *Make Pernod butter:* Combine 4 tablespoons butter with Pernod and tarragon. Beat until fluffy. Cover and refrigerate until ready to serve.

2. *Grill lobster tails:* With kitchen shears, cut top membrane and discard. Partially loosen meat from shell with your hand, leaving tail section connected. Brush lobster tails with melted butter.

3. Arrange tails on prepared grill, cut side down, and cook for 2–3 minutes. Turn tails over and continue cooking until done, 7–9 minutes. (Grilling lobster shell side down for most of the cooking time helps the lobster meat retain its juices.) The lobster meat is cooked when it turns opaque. The shell may char. Serve lobster tails immediately with Pernod butter (don't melt the butter; the heat of the lobster will melt it for you.

Yield: 4 servings

WHOLE LOBSTERS WITH VANILLA SAUCE A LA CHEF THIERRY LEFEUVRE

❧

Thierry LeFeuvre is the talented young chef-owner of Froggy's Cafe, 306 Green Bay Road, Highwood, Illinois.

VANILLA SAUCE
2 teaspoons butter
3 shallots, minced
4 tablespoons dry white wine
1 vanilla bean, slit
3 cups heavy cream
¾ pound bay scallops
⅛ teaspoon salt
⅛ teaspoon white pepper

SHELLFISH
6 Maine lobsters, 1¼–1½ pounds each,
    prepared for grilling
Melted butter

1. *Make vanilla sauce:* Melt 2 teaspoons butter in a medium saucepan over low heat. Sauté shallots for 3 minutes or until tender, stirring often. Stir in white wine and vanilla bean. Mix well and cook over medium-high heat until mixture is almost dry. Stir in cream and bring mixture to a boil. Reduce heat and simmer about 3 minutes. Add scallops, salt, and white pepper and continue cooking until scallops are just cooked. Remove scallops. Strain sauce and return scallops. Set aside. Keep warm.

2. *Grill lobsters:* Using a pastry brush, brush cut sides of prepared lobsters with melted butter. Arrange lobsters shell side up on prepared grill, 3 to 4 inches from ashen coals, and cook for 6 to 8 minutes. Brush with butter, turn lobsters over, and continue grilling for 2 minutes or until done. Lobster is cooked when the meat is opaque and it starts to separate from shell. *Do not overcook lobsters.* Serve lobsters on top of warm sauce.

Yield: 6 servings (with about 3 cups sauce)

WHOLE MAINE LOBSTERS HOT FROM THE GRILL WITH LEMON BUTTER OR CHILLED WITH HERB MAYONNAISE

❧

Prepare only one of the two sauces below—lemon butter if you plan to serve the lobsters hot from the grill or herb mayonnaise if you wish to serve the lobsters cold.

LEMON BUTTER
2 recipes lemon butter (see Index)
Dash hot pepper sauce

HERB MAYONNAISE
2 egg yolks at room temperature
2 tablespoons red wine vinegar
1 tablespoon Dijon mustard
1 tablespoon chopped fresh parsley
1 tablespoon chopped fresh tarragon
¼ teaspoon salt
¾ cup olive oil

SHELLFISH
6 Maine lobsters, about 1¼–1½ pounds
   each
Melted butter
Oil for greasing grill
Lemon slices for garnish

1. *Prepare lemon butter:* Stir hot pepper sauce into lemon butter. Spoon into a serving dish and refrigerate. Bring to room temperature 45 minutes before serving.

2. *Prepare herb mayonnaise:* Put egg yolks in food processor or blender container along with red wine vinegar, mustard, parsley, tarragon, and salt. Process for about 5 or 6 seconds or as necessary to combine.

3. With motor running, begin adding the oil in a slow, steady stream. Keep motor running until all oil is added, then turn off machine. Let mayonnaise sit at room temperature for 5 minutes before serving. Cover any leftover mayonnaise; it will keep from 1 to 2 days in refrigerator.

4. *Grill lobsters:* Using a pastry brush, brush cut sides of prepared lobsters with melted butter. Arrange lobsters shell side up on prepared grill, 3 to 4 inches from ashen coals, and cook for 6 to 8 minutes. (Grilling shell side up prevents loss of juice.) Brush with butter, turn lobsters over, and continue grilling for 2 minutes or until done. Lobster is cooked when the meat is opaque and it starts to separate from shell. Do not overcook lobsters.

5. Serve lobsters hot with lemon butter or chilled with herb mayonnaise. Garnish with lemon slices. Give each diner a disposable bib, a lobster cracker, a pick, and a damp finger towel.

Yield: 6 servings (with 1 cup lemon butter or 1⅔ cups herb mayonnaise)

SPINY LOBSTER WITH EASY CREAMY ROQUEFORT SAUCE

Spiny lobsters are usually shipped frozen and should be defrosted in the refrigerator or at room temperature before using. The color of the lobster can vary from a dark red to a mottled color with or without spots. The meat tends to be somewhat softer in texture and slightly less sweet than the meat of the cold-water tails.

ROQUEFORT SAUCE
2½ cups evaporated skim milk
4 ounces Roquefort or other veined cheese,
    crumbled
3 tablespoons minced fresh chives

SHELLFISH
8 1¼-pound frozen spiny lobsters,
    defrosted
Oil for greasing grill
Melted butter for brushing lobsters

1. *Make Roquefort sauce:* Warm milk in medium saucepan over low heat. Mix in cheese and chives and simmer for 1 minute. Remove from heat.

2. Cut and remove membrane from center to tail. Cut away underpart of lobster without disconnecting from shell completely.

3. Arrange lobsters cut side up on prepared grill over medium-hot ashen coals about 3 to 4 inches from coals. Brush with melted butter. Grill about 6 minutes. Bottom of lobster shell may char. Brush lobster meat with butter, turn over, and grill for 1 to 2 minutes or until meat is opaque and pulling away slightly from sides of shell.

4. Place lobster on individual plates and serve with warm Roquefort sauce. Place disposable bibs, nutcrackers, and picks at table around place settings. Serve damp finger cloths after dinner.

Yield: 8 servings (2⅔ cups sauce)

LOBSTER TAILS WITH NEWBURG BUTTER

❧

Sometime in the 1890s, Delmonico's, a famous restaurant in New York, decided to bestow the ultimate honor upon one of its customers and name a dish after him. The customer—Benjamin Wenberg—had been such a frequent customer at the restaurant that Mr. Delmonico decided to call a special lobster dish Lobster Wenberg. Unfortunately, Delmonico and Wenberg had a bitter quarrel from which the friendship did not recover. Delmonico soon renamed the dish Lobster Newburg, which is the name used today.

NEWBURG BUTTER
6 tablespoons butter, cut into chunks
3 tablespoons heavy cream
4 tablespoons sherry
¼ teaspoon grated nutmeg

SHELLFISH
*4 frozen lobster tails, 12–14 ounces each,
   defrosted*
Melted butter for brushing lobster tails
Oil for greasing grill

1. *Make Newburg butter:* Puree ¼ pound butter in a food processor fitted with steel blade. Incorporate cream and mix in sherry and nutmeg. Mound butter in serving dish, cover, and refrigerate. Bring to room temperature before serving.

2. *Grill lobster tails:* Cut and remove outer membrane from lobster tails. Brush with melted butter. Arrange tails cut side up on prepared grill over ashen coals, about 3 to 4 inches from heat. Grill for 8 to 10 minutes. Lobster meat will turn from translucent to opaque during cooking. Turn lobster tails over and continue cooking for 2 to 3 minutes or until lobster is cooked. Shells may char on bottom.

3. Place a tail on each plate and spread soft Newburg butter over hot lobster meat. Pass extra butter at table for guests to help themselves.

Yield: 4 servings (1 cup sauce)

FLAMING LOBSTER TAILS WITH LEMON-LIME MARINADE

The effect of flaming at the table is very dramatic, but this recipe can be prepared without flaming if you wish.

MARINADE
4 tablespoons olive oil
2 tablespoons fresh lemon juice
2 tablespoons fresh lime juice
1 tablespoon grated lime zest
2 bay leaves
2 cloves garlic, minced
¼ teaspoon white pepper

SHELLFISH
6 frozen lobster tails, 10–12 ounces each,
   defrosted at room temperature
Oil for greasing grill
3 ounces brandy

1. *Make marinade:* Combine marinade ingredients in a shallow glass bowl or pie plate.

2. Cut away and remove the membrane from top of lobster tails. Partially loosen meat from shell but leave connected. Arrange lobster tails cut side down in marinade and marinate for 1 hour. Drain, reserving marinade.

3. *Grill lobster tails:* Arrange lobster tails cut side up on prepared grill over ashen coals, about 4 inches from heat. Cook 8 minutes. Brush with reserved marinade and turn over. Continue grilling for 2 minutes or until tails are cooked. Lobster meat will be opaque.

4. Remove tails from grill to a flameproof serving dish. Bring to table cut side up. Heat brandy and pour over tails. Carefully ignite brandy. Wait until flame burns out, about 1 minute, and serve.

Yield: 6 servings

STUFFED LOBSTER TAILS

Lobster tails are harvested from both warm and cold waters. The warm areas are the Caribbean, Mexican, and South African waters; the cold-water tails are from New Zealand and Australia. Cold-water tails seem to have a firmer texture and somewhat sweeter taste.

In America, lobster and deep-sea tails are usually sold frozen in sizes ranging from three ounces to over two pounds each. The best way to defrost them is slowly, uncovered, in the refrigerator or at room temperature. Always defrost them before grilling.

STUFFING
2 tablespoons butter
4 tablespoons chopped fresh chives
2 tablespoons chopped fresh parsley
¼ teaspoon salt
⅛ teaspoon freshly ground pepper
1½ cups bread crumbs

SHELLFISH
6 frozen lobster tails, about 10 ounces
  each, defrosted at room temperature
Melted butter
Oil for greasing grill

1. *Prepare stuffing:* Melt 2 tablespoons butter in medium frying pan. Add chives and sauté over low heat, stirring, for 2 minutes. Add parsley, salt, and pepper. Remove from heat. Stir in bread crumbs, mixing well.

2. With kitchen shears, cut top membrane off lobster tails and discard. Partially loosen meat from shell, leaving tail section connected. Brush lobster tails with melted butter.

3. Lightly pack stuffing into cavity between the meat and the shell.

4. *Grill lobster tails:* Arrange tails shell side down on prepared grill, 3 to 4 inches from heat source, and cook for 8 to 10 minutes. Brush with butter, turn over, and continue cooking for 2 to 3 minutes or until lobster is cooked. Meat will be opaque and firm. Serve with melted butter.

Yield: 6 servings

MACKEREL

This Atlantic fish has a distinctive flavor and a high fat content; it is similar to bluefish. Butterflied mackerel will cook quickly on a hot grill; consider it when you need to cook in a hurry.

MACKEREL APPETIZER MARINATED IN THE JAPANESE MANNER

For this delicious Japanese appetizer, called yuan zuke *in Japan, grilling gives the mackerel skin a crisp black texture that complements the marinated fish pieces. Mackerel may be substituted with ono or yellowtail. Mirin is Japanese sweet rice wine used for cooking, available in Oriental food strores or by mail; see Appendix. Serve this dish with mild pasta tossed with cooked vegetables, butter/margarine blend, and salt.*

MARINADE
½ cup Japanese light soy sauce
½ cup mirin
1 cup canned or fresh chicken broth
3 tablespoons sugar
1 lemon, cut into thin slices

FISH
2 pounds mackerel fillets with skin
Oil for greasing grill
Lemon wedges

1. *Make the marinade:* Combine the soy sauce and mirin and heat to a boil. Add the chicken broth and sugar, return to a boil, and remove from the heat. Let sit at room temperature until cool. Then pour the soy-mirin mixture into a large plastic bag, add lemon slices, and set the bag in a large bowl.

2. *Marinate the fish:* Cut the mackerel fillets into 2-inch pieces, each containing some skin. Place the mackerel pieces in the marinade in the plastic bag and secure the bag with a twister seal. Turn the bag several times, making sure the marinade touches all fish surfaces. Place the bag and bowl in the refrigerator for 8–12 hours, turning the bag occasionally while the mackerel marinates.

3. Remove the mackerel from the plastic bag and discard the lemon slices. Transfer the marinade to a saucepan and set aside.

4. *Grill the fish:* Place the mackerel slices skin side down on prepared grill. Grill until the skin becomes crisp and black. Then turn the mackerel with tongs or a spatula and grill flesh side down for another few minutes or until the fish is lightly browned and cooked through.

5. Carefully transfer the mackerel pieces to a serving platter. Heat the marinade to a boil and spoon a little over each piece of mackerel. Garnish the platter with lemon wedges and serve immediately.

Yield: 8 appetizer servings

MACKEREL WITH GARLIC AND TOMATOES

Roasting garlic on the grill transforms the flavor from pungent to mellow. Soft, roasted cloves can actually be squeezed out and spread onto toasted French bread.

4 large fresh tomatoes, peeled and chopped
½ teaspoon crumbled dried oregano
Salt and pepper to taste
1 head garlic with large cloves
2 mackerel, about 1½ pounds each,
    cleaned and split in half
Crumbled dried rosemary
Oil for greasing grill

1. Toss tomatoes with oregano, salt, and pepper. Set aside.

2. Loosen unpeeled cloves of garlic and place on grill at edge of hot coals about 10–15 minutes before starting to grill fish.

3. Sprinkle mackerel with rosemary. Arrange fish on prepared grill or in an oiled double-hinged grill basket. Secure basket. Sprinkle 2 tablespoons rosemary over hot coals. Grill mackerel for 3 minutes, turn fish over, and continue cooking about 3 minutes, or until fish begins to flake when tested. Turn garlic occasionally as you are grilling the mackerel. Roast garlic for 20 minutes altogether, or until the insides of the cloves are soft. Place mackerel on heated platter. Arrange tomato mixture around grilled fish. Separate garlic cloves and sprinkle over fish. Garlic, when grilled, has a mild, somewhat nutty taste. Serve fish and allow guests to squeeze out the garlic from individual cloves and spread over mackerel.

Yield: 4 servings

GRILLED DO·IT·YOURSELF SUSHI BAR

❧

The word sushi *means "vinegared rice" and refers to a small, bite-sized preparation of rice and fish in combination with other ingredients. But since the fish in sushi is usually—not always, but usually—raw, many people who don't like raw fish are missing out on the fun of this healthful, delicious dish.*

The delicious flavors of sushi can be experienced by raw fish haters with ease. Simply follow our directions for a grilled sushi bar. For those who are scandalized at the thought, relax. We're not breaking completely with tradition. Many of the fish used to make traditional sushi dishes are cooked, including shrimp, crab, and imitation crab.

Here are instructions for setting up your own grilled sushi bar. The type of sushi we're making here is called temaki-sushi, *which means "hand-rolled sushi." Some of the ingredients in our bar may sound odd to you, but once you try them you'll see how delicious they are. These include nori (sheets of pressed seaweed); wasabi paste (horseradish), which comes in tubes; and pickled ginger. All of these ingredients are available by mail (see the Appendix for a list of sources), as are Japanese rice and Japanese rice vinegar.*

Grilled yellowtail, shrimp, or tuna can be substituted for mackerel in this dish. Serve it with rice and fresh orange slices or orange sherbert for dessert.

SUSHI RICE
1⅛ cups uncooked Japanese rice
1⅛ cups water
⅓ cup Japanese rice vinegar
2 tablespoons sugar
¼ teaspoon salt

SUSHI
Oil for greasing grill
1⅓ pounds mackerel fillets
4 teaspoons wasabi paste or powder
1 package nori (10 8-inch square sheets)
1 pound imitation crab fingers
2 medium-sized avocados
1 large cucumber
2–3 ounces red salmon roe
3 ounces pickled ginger
1 bowl Japanese soy sauce

1. The night before your sushi party, rinse the Japanese rice in a colander, drain, place in a bowl, cover, and refrigerate overnight.

2. *Grill the fish:* Arrange the mackerel fillets on the prepared grill. Cook for 4–8 minutes, then turn fillets and continue cooking for 4–8 minutes or until done. Remove from the grill and allow to cool. Place the cooled mackerel on a serving platter and cut into very thin strips.

3. Place the rice in a medium-sized saucepan or an electric rice cooker. Stir in the water. Bring to a boil over medium-high heat, and cook for 8–10 minutes. Reduce the heat to a simmer, cover, and cook for 18–20 minutes. Turn off the heat and allow the pan to sit with the cover on for 15 minutes before removing the lid. If using an electric rice cooker, follow the manufacturer's directions.

4. Combine the rice vinegar, sugar, and salt in a small pan over medium heat. Cook until the sugar dissolves, stirring occasionally.

5. Working lightly, with a wooden spoon, work the mixture into the rice. Place in a serving bowl.

6. Spoon some wasabi paste into a small bowl or place wasabi powder in a bowl and stir a few drops of water into it—just enough to make a paste.

7. Cut the sheets of nori in half so that each measures 8 inches by 4 inches. Lay them in a stack on a serving plate.

8. Arrange the crab fingers on a flat serving plate. Then peel the avocados and cut them into thin, 1-inch-long slices and place on a separate serving platter. Peel the cucumber, cut in half lengthwise, remove the seeds, and cut the cucumber into thin matchsticks, ¼ inch wide and 1 inch long. Arrange the cucumber sticks on a separate serving platter.

9. Spoon the salmon roe into a small bowl and arrange the pickled ginger in another small bowl. Pour Japanese soy sauce into a small serving bowl.

TO ASSEMBLE THE SUSHI BAR

Lay the dishes of ingredients on the table in the following order, so guests may begin at one end and proceed toward the other, adding ingredients to their temaki-sushi as they go: nori, sushi rice, wasabi, mackerel, imitation crab, avocado, cucumber, salmon roe, pickled ginger, soy sauce.

TO MAKE TEMAKI-SUSHI

1. Pick up a half sheet of nori and hold it in your left hand (assuming you are right-handed). Spoon 2 to 3 tablespoons of rice into the center of the nori and flatten it slightly. Dip a finger into the wasabi paste and run a very thin line of it down the center of the rice; use wasabi paste sparingly, as it is very hot.

2. Arrange a strip of mackerel or a small piece of imitation crab over the wasabi and rice. Top with a few avocado pieces, a few cucumber matchsticks, and a sprinkling of salmon roe.

3. Finally, roll the filled nori slowly and carefully into a cone shape—it should resemble an ice cream cone with a pointed bottom. Twist the bottom of the cone carefully to make certain that it will not leak at the bottom and will stay closed.

4. Place two or three pieces of pickled ginger on your plate. Then dip your temaki-sushi cone into the bowl of soy sauce. Begin to eat, taking small bites from the wide end of the cone. Eat slices of pickled ginger in between bites.

Yield: 20 temaki-sushi, 6–8 servings

SADA HAKANATA'S SABA NO MISO YAKI (GRILLED MACKEREL IN MISO SAUCE)

This traditional Japanese recipe is based on an ingredient called miso, *which is a fermented soybean paste with a delicate, distinctive flavor. Miso can be ordered by mail through the Star Market (see Appendix). The two basic types of miso are* aka miso, *which is reddish-colored, and the more delicate* shiro miso, *which is white and best for fish marinades. Since the different brands of shiro miso on the market vary considerably in sweetness, you may want to add sugar to our recipe below.*

Once your package of miso is opened, simply place any unused portion in a plastic bag and secure with a twister seal. Then set the plastic bag in a jar or container with a lid and store it in the refrigerator. Even after having been opened, it will keep for up to a year.

Although this dish sounds odd, we strongly urge you to try it. It is very simple to prepare; the miso is mixed with brown sugar and mirin, *a Japanese cooking wine also available at Japanese markets or by mail order (see Appendix). And it is absolutely delicious. The Japanese often leave the fish in the miso for up to three days or even longer, but for American tastes 24 hours should be sufficient. Although mackerel is particularly delicious when marinated in miso, almost any soft- to medium-firm-fleshed fish, such as red snapper, cod, bluefish, yellowtail, or even whitefish fillets, can be substituted.*

This particular recipe is a gift of Sada Hakanata, one of the owners of the Star Market in Chicago.

We suggest you also serve rice, green salad, and pickled ginger slices (available in Oriental food stores or by mail; see Appendix).

FISH
Salt
3 pounds mackerel fillets with skin, cut
    into 3-inch pieces
Oil for greasing grill

MARINADE
4 cups (about 2 pounds) shiro miso
1⅓ cups mirin
1 cup brown sugar (more to taste if bean
    paste is not faintly sweet)
Lemon wedges

1. Salt the mackerel fillets lightly on all sides and allow to stand for 10 minutes.

2. *Meanwhile, make the marinade:* Combine the shiro miso, mirin, and brown sugar in a bowl and taste. It should have a slightly sweet flavor. If it does not, add an additional teaspoon or more of brown sugar.

3. Add the mackerel fillets to the bowl and rub the marinade into the fish on all sides. Transfer the fish and miso to a large plastic bag, roll it up tightly, and wrap the fish-filled bag tightly with plastic wrap. Refrigerate for 24 hours.

4. *Grill the fish:* At serving time, remove the mackerel from the marinade and use paper towels to wipe some—not all—of the miso off the fillets. Place the fillets skin side down on the prepared grill. Cook for 4–8 minutes or until the skin becomes crisp and black. Immediately turn the mackerel carefully with a spatula or tongs and grill until done to taste. Transfer the mackerel pieces to a serving platter and serve immediately with lemon wedges.

Yield: 8 servings

GRILLED MACKEREL WITH GREEN GRAPES

❧

Yellowtail also works well in this recipe. Serve it with grilled mushrooms, a mixed green salad, and fresh raspberries and cream for dessert.

GRAPE SAUCE
1 16½-ounce can green grapes in light
  syrup
½ cup water
2 tablespoons sugar
1½ teaspoons cornstarch
1 tablespoon fresh lemon juice
1 tablespoon grated lemon zest

FISH
2 large lemons, each cut into 8 slices
8 10- to 12-ounce mackerel, split, heads
  removed
Oil for brushing fish and greasing grill
Salt and freshly ground pepper to taste

1. *Make the sauce:* Mix the grapes, ¼ cup of the grape syrup, and the water in a medium saucepan. Stir in the sugar and cook over medium heat until the grapes are warm but not broken. In a small dish, blend the cornstarch and 1 tablespoon of water. Blend the cornstarch mixture into the sauce and bring to a boil, stirring until the sauce thickens and is clear. Stir in the lemon juice and zest.

2. *Grill the fish:* Place 2 lemon slices in each fish cavity; brush the mackerel with oil and sprinkle with salt and pepper. Place on the prepared grill or aluminum foil and cook for about 4–8 minutes. Turn mackerel and grill until done to taste. Transfer the fish to a serving platter and drizzle the hot sauce over the fish.

Yield: 8 servings (1½ cups sauce)

Mahimahi is a medium-textured fish with a high fat content. Substitute snapper, yellowtail, and sea trout.

MAHIMAHI WITH ALMONDS

The cilantro, singed in the basket, will still be tasty when brought to the table.

¾ *cup cilantro (coriander) sprigs*
Peanut oil for greasing fish basket
3 oranges, sliced thin
4 7-ounce mahimahi fillets
2 cloves garlic, minced
½ *cup sliced almonds*

1. Arrange half of the cilantro sprigs over prepared double-hinged fish basket. Put orange slices over cilantro and top with mahimahi. Sprinkle fish with garlic and remaining cilantro. Secure basket. Grill mahimahi with orange and cilantro in place for 4–5 minutes. Turn grill basket over and continue cooking 2–3 minutes or until fish begins to flake when tested with a fork. Put fish on individual plates and sprinkle with sliced almonds.

2. Serve with corn tortillas warmed in the oven. If you wish, spread mahimahi on the warm tortilla, sprinkle with almonds, roll, and enjoy.

Yield: 4 servings

MAHIMAHI SEAFOOD RANCHERO

Halibut and black sea bass also work well with this recipe. You might serve it with Spanish rice, a mixed green salad with hearts of palm, and grilled Anaheim pepper strips.

3–4 4-inch pieces mesquite wood
Oil for greasing grill

RANCHERO SALSA
2 tablespoons good-quality olive oil
½ cup minced red onion
3 Anaheim chilies, seeded and chopped
2 cups diced fresh tomato
1 tablespoon fresh lime juice
½ cup minced cilantro
¼ teaspoon salt
2 dashes Tabasco sauce

MARINADE
⅓ cup good-quality olive oil
1½ cups fresh lime juice
½ teaspoon red pepper flakes
2 large bay leaves

FISH
3 pounds mahimahi, cut into 8 fillets
8 corn tortillas
2 cups shredded cheddar cheese
1 cup chopped scallions

1. Soak the mesquite in cold water to cover for 1 hour.
2. *Make the salsa:* Heat the oil in a saucepan, add the onion and chilies, and sauté until tender. Add the tomatoes, lime juice, cilantro, salt, and Tabasco. Continue cooking for 1 minute, stirring to combine.

3. *Make the marinade:* Combine the marinade ingredients, pour into a large plastic bag, and set the bag in a bowl. Add fillets and secure with a twister seal. Turn the bag several times to make sure all fish surfaces touch the marinade. Let sit at room temperature for 1 hour.

4. *Grill the fish:* Drain the mesquite and place it over the hot coals. Replace the grill and place the mahimahi on the prepared grill. Cook for 4–5 minutes, turn, and continue grilling for about 4 minutes until the fish is cooked to taste. Wrap the tortillas in aluminum foil and warm them on the grill.

5. Lay a warm tortilla on each plate. Ladle salsa over the tortilla and sprinkle with cheese. Arrange grilled mahimahi on top and sprinkle with chopped scallions. Serve hot.

Yield: 8 servings (3 cups sauce)

MAHIMAHI KABOBS WITH FRUIT

Kabobs should be turned every 3 minutes to ensure even cooking; remember, any firm-fleshed fish can make a delicious kabob.

2 cups fresh or canned pineapple chunks, drained
3 bananas, peeled and cut into 2-inch chunks
1½ pounds mahimahi fillets, cut into 1½-inch pieces
2 limes, sliced
4 tablespoons (½ stick) butter
4 tablespoons light brown sugar
Oil for greasing grill
Freshly grated coconut

1. Thread fruit, mahimahi pieces, and lime slices alternately on 4 10-inch skewers.
2. Melt butter with brown sugar in a saucepan.
3. Brush kabobs with sugar-butter mixture and arrange kabobs on prepared grill. Cook for 3 minutes, turn, and rotate kabobs every 3 minutes until mahimahi begins to flake when tested with a fork.
4. Arrange on individual plates and sprinkle with coconut. Allow guests to remove fish and fruit from skewers.

Yield: 4 servings

MARLIN
Marlin is a meaty fish with a mild flavor. It tastes great marinated.

MARLIN WITH BAY LEAVES AND BASIL BUTTER

❧

You may substitute shark or mahimahi in this recipe. We suggest you serve it with squid ink pasta or other flavored pasta and grilled shrimp salad.

FISH
1 recipe basic marinade (see Index)
⅓ cup large bay leaves
3 pounds marlin, cut into 8 steaks
Oil for greasing grill

BASIL BUTTER
¾ cup (6 ounces) butter or margarine, cut into ½-inch pieces
½ cup trimmed chopped fresh basil

1. *Marinate the fish:* Combine the marinade and bay leaves in a large plastic bag, place the bag in a bowl, add the fish, and secure with a twister seal. Turn the bag several times to make certain all fish surfaces touch the marinade. Let sit at room temperature for 1 hour, turning the bag occasionally.

2. *Make the basil butter:* In a food processor fitted with the steel blade or in a blender, cream the butter with the basil. Place the butter in a bowl and set aside.

3. *Grill the fish:* Remove the marlin from the marinade and place the fish on the prepared grill, making sure some of the bay leaves adhere to the fish. Cook the fish for about 4–8 minutes, turn marlin carefully and cook for 4–5 minutes or until the fish has lost its translucence. Remove the marlin skin, discard bay leaves, and serve fish hot with the soft basil butter.

Yield: 8 servings

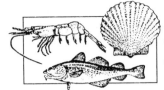

MIXED SEAFOOD
Combining shellfish with other fish will add a variety
of textures and flavors to any meal.

SEAFOOD BROCHETTES
WITH CHIVE BUTTER

BROCHETTES

3 slices bacon

1 pound medium to large raw shrimp,
*   peeled and deveined*

1 pound sea scallops

1 pound firm-fleshed fish such as scrod,
*   cut into 1-inch chunks*

Cherry tomatoes

Mushroom caps

Oil for greasing grill

CHIVE BUTTER

4 tablespoons (½ stick) butter

4 teaspoons snipped fresh chives (if
*   necessary, substitute frozen or freeze-*
*   dried chives)*

1. Cook bacon until just done. Drain, pat with paper towels to remove
as much fat as possible, and cut into 1½-inch pieces.

2. Thread shrimp, scallops, and scrod chunks onto 4 10-inch skewers,
alternating with bacon pieces, cherry tomatoes, and mushroom caps.

3. *Make chive butter:* Melt 4 tablespoons butter with chives. Transfer to
small bowl and set aside while skewered fish cooks.

4. *Grill brochettes:* Arrange skewers on well-oiled grill rack over ashen
coals. Cook 3–4 minutes on each side or until lightly browned. Serve
immediately with bowl of chive butter.

Yield: 4 servings

PAELLA KABOBS WITH SAFFRON RICE

❧

This dish can be cooked outdoors completely over an open fire, as they do on the beaches of southern Spain. We have chosen to prepare the rice indoors, grill the seafood outdoors, for its special flavor, and combine the two items into a delicious treat.

Saffron is expensive but worth the cost for the taste and lovely color. A small amount will impart a golden color and a subtle taste. You may substitute 2-inch chunks of tuna for the seafood in this recipe. We suggest you serve it with gazpacho, Andalusian salad (greens with olives and cheese), and pineapple flan for dessert.

16 8-inch wooden presoaked barbecue
  skewers

SAFFRON RICE
¼ cup good-quality olive oil
1 large onion, minced
1 pound spicy sausage, skin removed, cut
  into ½-inch pieces
3½ cups uncooked rice
6 cups fresh or canned chicken broth
¼ teaspoon saffron threads, dissolved with
  the back of spoon in 2 tablespoons
  water
1 2-ounce jar pimiento, including liquid
2 10-ounce packages frozen peas

SHELLFISH
Oil for greasing grill
Enough seaweed to cover half of the grill
  (available at most fish markets)
1½ pounds small farm-raised mussels,
  cleaned and debearded
1½ pounds cherrystone clams, cleaned
1½ pounds large shrimp, shelled and
  deveined
1 pound sea scallops
1 cup pitted black olives
2 lemons, sliced
Good-quality olive oil for brushing
  shellfish
2 cloves minced garlic or ½ teaspoon
  garlic powder

1. *Make the saffron rice:* Heat the olive oil in a large iron skillet or a paella pan; add the onion and sausage and cook over low heat until the onion is soft, stirring occasionally. Add the rice and stir until the rice is well coated with the oil. Add the broth and saffron, avoiding the hot steam that may occur when the broth is added. Cover with a tight-fitting lid and continue

cooking over low heat. After 10 minutes, stir in the pimiento and peas and cover quickly. Continue cooking about 10 more minutes, until all the liquid has been absorbed and the rice is tender.

2. *Meanwhile, prepare the seafood:* Spread the seaweed over the grill. Put the mussels and clams over the seaweed. Cover the grill and cook about 4 minutes or until the shellfish open. Discard any unopened shellfish.

3. Thread skewers with shrimp, scallops, olives, and lemon slices. Brush with olive oil and sprinkle with garlic.

4. Grill the kabobs, rotating every 2–3 minutes until the shellfish is cooked to your taste; do not overcook shrimp as it tends to get tough.

5. Arrange the shellfish and kabobs decoratively over the saffron rice and serve immediately.

Yield: 10 servings

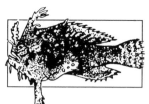

MONKFISH
Monkfish is also known as "poor man's lobster" because of its lobsterlike texture.

ORIENTAL KABOBS WITH MONKFISH

Five spice powder is available at Oriental food stores and in the Oriental food sections of some supermarkets.

MARINADE
½ cup rice vinegar
2 cloves garlic, minced
1 teaspoon chopped peeled fresh gingerroot
2 tablespoons soy sauce
¾ teaspoon five spice powder

SEAFOOD
1 pound monkfish, cut into 1½-inch chunks
2 oranges, cut into quarters
½ cup snow peas, outer string removed, trimmed
1 6½-ounce can water chestnuts, drained
4 10- to 12-inch wooden presoaked barbecue skewers
Oil for greasing grill

1. *Prepare marinade:* Combine marinade ingredients in shallow glass bowl or pie plate.

2. Arrange fish in marinade and marinate for 1 hour, turning after 30 minutes. Drain monkfish, reserving marinade.

3. Thread orange quarters, snow peas, water chestnuts, and monkfish on skewers. Brush with marinade.

4. *Grill monkfish:* Arrange skewers on greased grill over ashen coals, about 3 to 4 inches from heat source. Cook 4 to 5 minutes on each side or until lightly browned. Turn skewers as necessary and brush with marinade. Serve immediately with hot brown rice or Oriental noodles.

Yield: 4 servings

MONKFISH WITH CONCARNEU SAUCE

❧

We had some leftover grilled monkfish and ate it the following day, served cold and sliced with warm sauce. It tasted even more like lobster, firm and somewhat sweet in taste. Concarneu sauce hails from Brittany's rocky coast.

CONCARNEU SAUCE

2 tablespoons butter

1 tablespoon olive oil

1 small onion, minced

3 medium-sized shallots, minced

1 clove garlic, minced

1 tablespoon all-purpose flour

4 medium-large tomatoes, peeled, seeded, and chopped

1 tablespoon tomato paste

3 tablespoons minced fresh parsley

2 teaspoons minced fresh tarragon

¾ cup dry white wine

¼ teaspoon salt

⅛ teaspoon freshly ground pepper

MARINADE

¼ cup salad oil

2 tablespoons lemon juice

1 clove garlic, minced

¼ teaspoon salt

⅛ teaspoon freshly ground pepper

SEAFOOD

3 pounds monkfish (sometimes this fish is uneven in thickness; we butterflied the thicker part for more even grilling)

Oil for greasing grill

1. *Make Concarneu sauce:* Heat butter and olive oil in a medium saucepan. Sauté onion, shallots, and 1 clove minced garlic over medium heat for 3 to 4 minutes or until tender, stirring often, taking care that it doesn't brown. Whisk in flour and stir until it is absorbed. Add tomatoes, tomato paste, parsley, tarragon, and white wine. Simmer sauce for 10 minutes. Season with salt and pepper; set aside.

2. *Marinate monkfish:* Combine marinade ingredients in a shallow glass bowl or pie plate. Place fish in marinade and marinate for 1 hour, turning after 30 minutes.

3. *Grill monkfish:* Place drained fish on prepared grill and cook for 8 minutes. Brush with remaining marinade and turn. Continue cooking 8 minutes or until fish is cooked. Remember that cooking time depends on the heat of the coals, the distance from the coals, and the thickness of the fish you are preparing. Fish is cooked when it begins to flake when tested with a fork.

4. Place fish on platter, cut into serving pieces, and top with heated sauce.

Yield: 6 servings (with about 2 cups sauce)

MONKFISH WITH CRACKED GREEN OLIVES

&

This delicious and unusual combination of sour green olives and fresh fish is popular in Morocco. The olives are brought to a boil three times to rid them of bitterness. Monkfish is at its best here, when its bland flavor and thick, meaty texture is enhanced by the strong garlic marinade and the sour olive topping. Green Greek olives are available at Greek and Middle Eastern markets.

Swordfish can also be used in this recipe. With it, serve cracked wheat salad (tabbouleh) and grilled marinated eggplant and green pepper slices.

1½ cups drained green Greek olives

MARINADE
¾ cup fresh lemon juice
¼ cup imported mild, good-quality olive oil
Large handful parsley, stems removed
6 cloves garlic, peeled and quartered
1½ teaspoons paprika
¾ teaspoon salt
½ teaspoon freshly ground pepper

FISH
3 pounds monkfish, cut into 8 fillets
16 ¼-inch-thick slices lemon for grilling fillets

SAUCE
2 tablespoons butter or margarine
3 tablespoons imported mild, good-quality olive oil
2 medium onions, chopped fine (about 1 cup)
3 cloves garlic, minced fine
1½ large lemons, sliced paper-thin, seeds removed
1 teaspoon ground ginger
1 teaspoon salt
½ teaspoon freshly ground pepper
¼ teaspoon ground cumin
¼–½ cup water (as needed)
⅓–½ cup chopped fresh parsley

1. Put the olives in a single layer within a folded towel and lightly hit the top of the towel with a wooden mallet, hammer, or stone. Then pick out the pits and discard. Or, if desired, pit each olive individually, using a small, sharp knife.

2. Place the olives in a saucepan, cover with water, and heat to a boil. Drain the olives and return to the saucepan. Cover with water and heat again to a boil. Drain and repeat the process a third time, then drain olives again and reserve.

3. *Make the marinade:* Place the lemon juice, olive oil, parsley, garlic, paprika, salt, and pepper in a blender or a food processor fitted with the steel blade and pulse until the parsley and garlic are finely chopped and the mixture is well combined.

4. Pour the marinade into a large plastic bag and set the bag in a bowl. If the monkfish fillets are very uneven in thickness, butterfly the thick portions so that the fish will cook evenly. Prick the monkfish with fork tines several times, then place the fillets in the bag and secure the bag with a twister seal. Turn the bag several times to make sure all fish surfaces touch the marinade. Let sit at room temperature for 1 hour, turning occasionally.

5. *Meanwhile, make the sauce:* Heat the butter and oil in a large, heavy-bottomed frying pan until the butter is melted. Add the onions and garlic and sauté over medium heat for 15 or 20 minutes, until the onions are cooked through.

6. Add the paper-thin lemon slices, ginger, salt, pepper, and cumin along with ¼ cup of the water and heat to a simmer. Simmer for 15 minutes, stirring occasionally to make sure the mixture does not stick.

7. Add the parsley, drained olives, and additional water if needed. Heat again to a simmer, cook for a minute, then turn off the heat. The sauce should be thick.

8. *Grill the fish:* Remove the monkfish from the marinade. Arrange the ¼-inch-thick lemon slices in pairs on the prepared grill and place each fillet on two lemon slices. Grill for 15 minutes, without turning, or until the fish is completely cooked through. Transfer the fillets to a serving platter, discarding lemon slices.

9. Meanwhile, heat the olive sauce until hot, adding another ¼ cup water if needed. Remove the lemon slices from the sauce and discard. Transfer the sauce to a serving bowl and bring to the table. Serve each fillet topped with green olive sauce.

Yield: 8 servings

MONKFISH WITH GREEN CHILE SAUCE

❧

GREEN CHILE SAUCE

2 medium onions, quartered

3 4-ounce cans mild green chilies,
chopped and drained

1–2 canned jalapeño peppers, packed in
vinegar, water, and salt (do not use
oil-packed) or 1–2 fresh jalapeños,
seeded

¾ teaspoon salt

½ cup evaporated milk, heated (do not let
boil)

SEAFOOD

2 pounds monkfish fillets

Oil for brushing fish and greasing grill

1. *Prepare sauce:* Place quartered onions in food processor fitted with steel blade and pulse several times until coarsely chopped. Add drained green chilies and jalapeño peppers and pulse again until a coarse puree results. (If you do not have a food processor or blender, simply chop the onions, green chilies, and jalapeño peppers fine by hand.)

2. Heat butter over medium heat in medium saucepan. When butter sizzles, add chile mixture and salt. Cook 5 minutes, stirring often with a wooden spoon, watching mixture carefully to be sure that it does not burn. When excess moisture has evaporated, remove from heat and stir in warmed milk. Transfer sauce to serving bowl.

3. *Grill monkfish:* Brush monkfish with oil and arrange fillets on prepared grill. Cook 6 to 8 minutes on each side or until fish has lost its translucent appearance. Transfer to serving platter.

4. Serve immediately with green chile sauce. Pass heated French bread at the table.

Yield: 4 servings (with 1¾ cups sauce)

MUSSELS

For grilling purposes, we found that it was not necessary to "feed" these bivalve mollusks cornmeal or flour to force them to unload the grit lodged in their shells and intestines. So many of the mussels marketed today are farm grown that they are naturally much cleaner than those marketed previously. All you'll need to do is wash the shell and pull away any protruding "hairs" (called the *beard*) sticking out of the shell before putting them right on the grill in their shells.

MUSSELS ON THE COALS

Aluminum foil
2 dozen small mussels, cleaned
1 7-ounce can baby corn ears, drained
4 green onions, chopped
8 broccoli pieces
2 tablespoons butter
4 tablespoons white wine

1. *Prepare mussel packages:* Cut 4 double sheets of aluminum foil large enough to hold mussels and vegetables.

2. Arrange mussels, corn, and green onions in center of each foil sheet. Add broccoli, dot with butter, and sprinkle with wine.

3. *Grill mussels:* Secure packages tightly. Place directly on hot coals. Cook for 3 to 4 minutes, turn packages, and grill 2 to 3 minutes longer. Test one package to see if it is done. Discard any unopened mussels. Serve hot.

Yield: 4 appetizer servings

MUSSELS STUFFED WITH SHRIMP PASTE

SHRIMP PASTE
4 medium-sized shallots, minced
2 cloves garlic, minced
½ pound small shrimp, cooked, shelled,
   and pureed
1 egg, slightly beaten
¼ teaspoon salt
⅛ teaspoon white pepper

SHELLFISH
2 dozen mussels, cleaned

1. *Prepare shrimp paste:* Combine shrimp paste ingredients in a small bowl. Set aside.

2. *Steam mussels:* Put ½ inch water in a medium pot. Bring to a boil. Put in mussels, cover, and steam about 2 to 3 minutes. Discard any mussels that do not open. Cool. Discard top shells. Lightly top each mussel with 1 teaspoon of shrimp paste.

3. *Grill mussels:* Arrange mussels on grill over ashen coals. Cover and grill for 3 to 4 minutes or until done. Serve hot.

Yield: 4 appetizer servings

GRILLED MUSSELS ON THE HALF SHELL

SHELLFISH
2 dozen black mussels, cleaned

GARLIC-BACON BREADING
2 tablespoons butter
2 cloves garlic, minced
*4 strips bacon, cooked, drained, and
   crumbled*
1¼ cups fine bread crumbs
¼ teaspoon salt
⅛ teaspoon freshly ground pepper

1. *Steam mussels:* Put ½ inch water in large kettle, add mussels, cover pot, bring to a boil, and steam 2–3 minutes. Drain mussels, remove top half of shells, and cool. Discard any unopened mussels.

2. *Prepare garlic-bacon breading:* Heat butter in a heavy frying pan; sauté garlic in it until soft, about 1 minute. Stir in bacon bits, bread crumbs, salt, and pepper. Toss to combine; remove from heat and set aside.

3. *Prepare shellfish:* Lightly top each mussel with 2 teaspoons of garlic breading.

4. *Grill mussels:* Place mussels open side up on grill over hot coals. Cover and grill for 3 to 4 minutes. Test one mussel and continue grilling until cooked to taste. Serve hot.

Yield: 4 appetizer servings

MUSSELS WITH
BLACK BEAN SAUCE

❧

For a slightly different flavor, try adding 3 cups mesquite chips or hickory chips, soaked in water for 30 minutes and drained, over the hot coals. Black beans are available at Oriental food stores.

BLACK BEAN SAUCE
2 tablespoons dry white wine
½ teaspoon sugar
2 tablespoons soy sauce
6 tablespoons chicken stock
1½ teaspoons cornstarch blended with 2
*   tablespoons water*
2 tablespoons peanut oil
2 tablespoons salted black beans, washed,
*   drained, and mashed with back of*
*   spoon*
3 cloves garlic, minced
½ teaspoon minced peeled fresh gingerroot
½ teaspoon crushed red pepper
2 green onions, minced
2 red bell peppers, seeded and cut into ¾-
*   inch strips*

SHELLFISH
2 dozen medium-sized farm-grown
*   mussels, cleaned*
Oil for greasing grill

1. *Prepare black bean sauce:* Combine wine, sugar, soy sauce, and stock. Whisk in cornstarch mixture. Set aside.

2. Heat oil in wok or heavy skillet. Add black beans, garlic, ginger, crushed red pepper, and green onions. Cook for 1 minute on high heat,

stirring continuously. Add red bell pepper and wine mixture and stir until sauce thickens slightly, about 2 minutes. Set aside.

3. *Grill mussels:* Arrange mussels on prepared grill. Cover and cook for 5 minutes. Discard any unopened mussels.

4. Place mussels in a deep heavy bowl. Drizzle hot black bean sauce over mussels. Serve immediately.

Yield: 4 appetizer servings

HICKORY-SMOKED MUSSELS
WITH FRUIT COMPOTE

These smoked mussels can also be shelled after grilling and tossed in a green salad or pasta salad. To remove the skin of the peaches soak the peaches in boiling water 2 minutes, then rinse with cold water. The skins can then be removed easily.

SUMMER FRUIT COMPOTE

¼ cup water
½ cup sugar
½ teaspoon ground cinnamon
½ teaspoon ground ginger
6 peaches, peeled and sliced
1 pint raspberries, washed and drained
2 cups seedless red grapes, washed and
    drained
4 cooking apples or other fruit of your
    choice, peeled, cored, and sliced

SHELLFISH

3 cups hickory chips, soaked in water 30
    minutes and drained
3 dozen mussels, cleaned

1. *Prepare fruit compote:* Bring water and sugar to boil in medium pan. Reduce heat to simmer, add spices and fruit, and stir to combine. Continue simmering for 5 minutes, stirring occasionally. Cool, pour fruit into bowl, and refrigerate until ready to serve.

2. *Smoke mussels:* Sprinkle drained hickory chips over hot coals and carefully replace grill. Arrange mussels in center of grill. Cover and smoke for 6 minutes or until done. Discard any unopened mussels. Mussels can be served warm or hot with the fruit compote.

Yield: 6 appetizer servings

MUSSELS WITH MARINARA SAUCE

MARINARA SAUCE

2 tablespoons good-quality olive oil

2 cloves garlic, minced

½ cup chopped green onion

1 28-ounce can tomatoes chopped, with
  liquid

¼ teaspoon dried thyme

1 bay leaf

¼ cup dry white wine

3 tablespoons minced Italian parsley

Salt and pepper to taste

SHELLFISH

3 to 4 4-inch pieces mesquite or 2 cups
  mesquite chips, soaked in water 1 hour
  and drained

2½ dozen medium-sized mussels, cleaned

1. *Prepare marinara sauce:* Heat oil in a small heavy saucepan. Sauté garlic and onion in it until lightly browned. Stir in tomatoes with their liquid. Add thyme, bay leaf, wine, parsley, salt, and pepper. Cook over medium heat for 15 minutes, stirring occasionally.

2. *Grill mussels:* Arrange mesquite wood over hot coals and carefully replace grill. Arrange mussels over grill in the center. Cover and smoke for 3 to 5 minutes or until done. Discard any unopened mussels. Divide mussels among wide soup plates. Ladle hot sauce over mussels.

Yield: 4 servings

SKEWERED GREEN LIP MUSSELS, SHRIMP, AND KIWIFRUIT WITH KIWIFRUIT BEURRE BLANC SAUCE

❧

Green lip mussels are large, tender, meaty mussels from New Zealand, yielding about eight to a pound. They are available fresh in the shell at the fishmarket or frozen and packaged at Oriental food markets.

KIWIFRUIT BEURRE BLANC
SAUCE
2 kiwifruit, peeled
4 medium shallots, minced
1 cup dry white wine
½ pound (2 sticks) butter, cut into ½-inch pieces

SHELLFISH
½ cup water
½ cup dry white wine
2 large bay leaves
1 small carrot, sliced thin
1 pound green lip mussels, cleaned
¾ pound large shrimp, shelled and deveined
8 cherry tomatoes
2 kiwifruit, cut into quarters (unpeeled)
4 green onions, cut into 2-inch pieces
4 10-inch wooden presoaked barbecue skewers
Melted butter for brushing kabobs
Oil for greasing grill

1. *Prepare sauce:* Puree 1 peeled kiwifruit and reserve. Slice the other peeled kiwifruit and set aside for garnish. Combine shallots, 1 cup wine, and kiwifruit puree in heavy nonaluminum saucepan; cook until mixture is reduced to 2 to 3 tablespoons. Remove saucepan from heat, add 1 piece of butter, and whisk until incorporated. Whisk in remaining butter, 2 pieces at a time, being careful not to allow the sauce to separate. If sauce separates, whisk quickly and try to emulsify. Keep sauce warm over simmering water or serve immediately.

2. *Steam mussels:* Combine water, ½ cup wine, bay leaves, and carrot in a medium saucepan. Bring mixture to a boil over medium-high heat. Add mussels, cover, and steam for 2 to 3 minutes, shaking pan during cooking. Discard any unopened mussels. Remove mussels from shells and set aside to cool.

3. Thread mussels, shrimp, tomatoes, quartered kiwifruit, and onions on skewers, beginning with and ending with shrimp. Mussels are threaded horizontally onto skewers. Brush with melted butter.

4. *Grill kabobs:* Arrange skewers on greased grill over ashen coals, about 3 to 4 inches from heat source. Cook 3 to 4 minutes on each side or until lightly browned. Tend to undercook shrimp and barely grill mussels. Serve immediately on bed of rice on individual plates. Garnish with kiwifruit slices. Drizzle with sauce.

Yield: 4 servings

MUSSEL·CLAM KABOBS

DRESSING
½ cup tarragon vinegar
¼ cup good-quality olive oil
1 tablespoon chopped fresh parsley
1 clove garlic, minced
½ teaspoon paprika

SHELLFISH
1 dozen medium clams, shucked
1 dozen mussels, cleaned and shucked
8 broccoli flowerets
12 cherry tomatoes
1 large red onion, quartered and leaves
  separated
4 10-inch wooden presoaked barbecue
  skewers
Oil for greasing grill

1. *Prepare dressing:* Pour vinegar into a bowl and whisk in olive oil, parsley, garlic, and paprika. Set aside.

2. Divide shellfish and vegetables and thread on skewers. Brush generously with dressing.

3. *Grill kabobs:* Arrange kabobs on prepared grill over ashen coals and grill for 2 to 3 minutes. Brush with dressing and continue grilling for 2 to 3 minutes or until done. Serve hot.

Yield: 4 servings

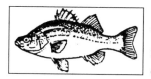 *OCEAN PERCH*
This small freshwater fish has a mild taste and a medium texture. Orange roughy, flounder, and turbot can be substituted for ocean perch.

OCEAN PERCH WITH PINE NUT BUTTER SAUCE

Pine nuts have such a delicate taste that we've combined them with an equally delicate fish—ocean perch fillets. Rockfish, sea trout, or orange roughy also work well in this recipe. Serve it with rice and a green salad.

PINE NUT BUTTER SAUCE
½ cup pine nuts
½ cup (1 stick) butter or margarine
4 teaspoons finely chopped chives

FISH
12 ¼-inch-thick slices lemon for grilling
3 pounds ocean perch fillets

1. *Toast the pine nuts:* Preheat the oven to 350°F. Arrange the pine nuts in a single layer on a baking sheet and toast them in the oven for about 10 minutes, watching carefully. After the first 5 minutes, check every minute or so to make sure they don't burn. As soon as they are lightly browned, remove from the oven.

2. Place the butter in a small saucepan and heat until melted. Add the toasted pine nuts and chives, stir thoroughly, and transfer to a serving bowl.

3. *Grill the fish:* Arrange the lemon slices on the prepared grill. Place the fillets on the lemon slices and grill for 2–6 minutes without turning, or until they have lost their translucence and are thoroughly cooked.

4. Use two spatulas to remove the fillets carefully from the grill and transfer them to a serving platter. Discard the lemon slices. Serve immediately, topped with pine nut butter sauce.

Yield: 8 servings

 *ONO*

Ono, a delicate-flavored fish in the mackerel family, is caught commercially in the Pacific. It can be substituted with swordfish.

ONO GRILLED ON A BED OF TARRAGON LEAVES

You might serve garlic-basil fettucini and a salad of Bibb lettuce and yellow cherry tomatoes with this herbaceous dish, in which pompano would serve as a substitute for ono.

1 recipe basic marinade (see Index)
3 pounds ono fillets, cut into 8 serving
  pieces
Oil for greasing grill
3 cups fresh tarragon
½ teaspoon fennel seed

1. *Marinate the fish:* Pour the marinade into a large plastic bag, place the bag in a bowl, and add the ono fillets. Secure with a twister seal and turn the bag several times to make sure all fish surfaces touch the marinade. Let sit at room temperature for 1 hour.

2. *Grill the fish:* Arrange a bed of tarragon on the prepared grill. Some of the leaves will fall through the grill onto the hot coals, adding their own special essence to the fish. Place the ono on the tarragon and sprinkle with the fennel. Cook the fish for 4–8 minutes, turn, and continue grilling until the ono is cooked to taste. Serve hot.

Yield: 8 servings

ONO STEAKS WITH GRILLED PINEAPPLE

Delicious served with grilled corn on the cob.

PINEAPPLE SAUCE
Reserved pineapple juice
Extra pineapple juice
1½ tablespoons cornstarch, mixed with
* 2 tablespoons pineapple juice*
¼ teaspoon each: ground cumin and
* ground ginger*

MARINADE
¼ cup pineapple juice
2 tablespoons fresh orange juice
4 tablespoons soy sauce
3 tablespoons chili sauce

FISH
4 7-ounce ono or shark steaks
1 5¼-ounce can pineapple slices, juice
* reserved, or 1 fresh pineapple, pared*
* and cut into 1½-inch slices*
Oil for greasing grill
1 teaspoon minced garlic
White pepper

1. *Make sauce:* Measure reserved pineapple juice and add enough extra juice to measure 1½ cups. In a small saucepan, combine juice and remaining sauce ingredients. Cook over medium heat, stirring often, until sauce thickens slightly. Remove pan from heat. Reheat sauce when ready to serve.

2. *Marinate ono steaks:* Combine marinade ingredients in a shallow glass bowl or pie plate. Marinate fish in mixture for 1 hour, turning once. Drain, reserving extra marinade.

3. *Grill ono steaks:* Arrange steaks on prepared grill, sprinkle with garlic and pepper to taste, and cook for 4 minutes. Grill pineapple slices 3–5 minutes on each side and reserve. Brush ono steaks with reserved marinade and turn fish. Continue grilling for 2–3 minutes, depending on the thickness of fish, until fish begins to flake when tested with a fork.

4. Place fish on heated platter and drizzle with sauce. Place grilled pineapple around fish.

Yield: 4 servings

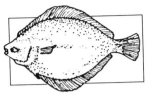

ORANGE ROUGHY

Orange roughy is a very mild, delicate fish; sole or turbot would also work well in orange roughy recipes.

ORANGE ROUGHY FILLETS ON A BED OF SAUTEED GREEN ONIONS

We suggest you serve this dish with tangy cole slaw.

2 tablespoons butter
2 cloves garlic, minced
1 bunch green onions, trimmed and cut
    into 2-inch pieces
½ teaspoon crumbled dried chervil
4 7-ounce orange roughy fillets
Melted butter
Oil for greasing fish basket
1 tablespoon capers, drained, for garnish

1. While coals are heating, prepare green onions. Melt butter in skillet. Sauté garlic in it until soft. Add green onions and chervil and sauté until tender, stirring occasionally. Arrange onions in a nest design on a serving platter.

2. Brush roughy fillets with butter. Arrange in a prepared fish basket and grill for 2–4 minutes. Turn fish and continue grilling for about 3 minutes, depending on the thickness of the fish, until fish begins to flake when tested with a fork. Place fish over green onions and sprinkle with capers.

Yield: 4 servings

ORANGE ROUGHY WITH BLACK BUTTER SAUCE

We suggest you serve grilled mushrooms sprinkled with chives and a celery root salad. Ocean perch may be substituted for orange roughy.

FISH
*3–4 limes, sliced thin (you'll need 16
    slices altogether)
3 pounds orange roughy fillets, cut into 8
    serving pieces
Good-quality olive oil for brushing fish*

BLACK BUTTER SAUCE
*½ cup (1 stick) butter
2 tablespoons red wine vinegar
4 tablespoons drained capers*

1. *Grill the fish:* Arrange the lime slices in pairs on the prepared grill. Place one roughy fillet on each pair of limes. Brush the fish with the olive oil. Grill for about 4–6 minutes, without turning, until the fillets have lost their translucence and are slightly browned on the edges.

2. *Make the sauce:* Melt the butter in the frying pan over medium heat on the stove or over a hot grill and brown the butter but do not burn.

3. Drizzle the butter over the fish on a serving platter. Quickly add the vinegar to the pan and reduce the mixture by half over medium heat; this will take about a minute. Drizzle the sauce over the fish and sprinkle with the capers. Serve immediately.

Yield: 8 servings

ORANGE ROUGHY WITH CHAMPAGNE SAUCE

❦

Serve a Waldorf salad, clusters of grapes, and hot French bread with this festive dish. You may substitute flounder or ocean perch for orange roughy in this recipe.

CHAMPAGNE SAUCE
2 tablespoons butter or margarine
1 tablespoon flour
1 cup dry champagne
1¼ cups whipped cream
½ teaspoon dried basil, crumbled
½ teaspoon minced fresh parsley
Salt and freshly ground white pepper to
  taste

FRIED LEEKS
2 cups peanut oil
2 cups finely julienned leeks
Salt to taste

FISH
3 oranges, sliced thin (you'll need 16
  slices for grilling; use any remaining
  slices for garnish)
3 pounds orange roughy fillets, cut into 8
  serving pieces
3 tablespoons dried basil, crumbled

1. *Make the sauce:* Melt the butter in a medium saucepan and whisk in the flour. Stir in the champagne. Continue cooking over medium heat until the liquid is reduced by half. Stir in the cream, basil, parsley, and salt and pepper. Cook over medium-low heat until the sauce thickens slightly. Taste and adjust seasonings.

2. *Fry the leeks:* Heat the oil to 375°F in a large, heavy skillet. Pat the leeks dry with paper toweling and slide into the oil. The leeks will brown quickly. Remove with a slotted spoon almost immediately and drain on paper toweling. Reserve for garnish.

3. *Grill the fish:* Arrange 16 of the orange slices in pairs on the prepared grill. Place one fillet on each pair of orange slices and sprinkle with basil. Grill for 4–6 minutes, without turning, or until the fillets have lost their translucence and are slightly browned on the edges.

4. When the fillets are cooked, transfer them to a serving platter and garnish the platter with fried leeks and any remaining orange slices. Serve with the warm champagne sauce.

Yield: 8 servings (1¾ cups sauce)

ROUGHY BURRITOS

※

The chilies predominate in this dish. Also serve refried beans, corn chips, and cold fruit.
Flounder works as a substitute for the orange roughy.

BURRITO SALSA
4 large tomatoes
2 fresh or canned jalapeño peppers, seeded
   and chopped fine
2 cloves garlic, minced
5 scallions, minced
½ cup chopped cilantro
¼ teaspoon salt
⅛ teaspoon freshly ground pepper

FISH
1¾ pounds orange roughy fillets
Oil for brushing fish and greasing grill
1 teaspoon pure chili powder
1 teaspoon ground cumin
2 green bell peppers, cored, seeded, and
   sliced into thin rings
½ cup chopped pitted black olives
8 10-inch flour tortillas
2 8-ounce cans green chilies, drained
3 fresh or canned jalapeño peppers, seeded
   and chopped fine
1 cup shredded Monterey Jack cheese

1. *Make the salsa:* Blanch the tomatoes in boiling water for 45 seconds or until the skins are loose. Remove and discard skins. Chop the tomatoes and put in a bowl with the jalapeños. Add the garlic, scallions, cilantro, salt, and pepper. Taste and adjust seasonings. Let the salsa stand for 1 hour before serving.

2. *Grill the fish:* Brush the fish with oil and sprinkle with chili powder and cumin. Grill for about 4–6 minutes, without turning, on slices of green pepper on the prepared grill, until the fillets have lost their translucence or until done to taste. Break the fish into chunks and place in a bowl with the pepper rings. Sprinkle with olives.

3. Wrap the tortillas in aluminum foil. Heat the tortillas on the grill until warm and wrap in a cloth napkin. Put the green chilies, jalapeños, and shredded cheese into three bowls. Toss the salsa ingredients in the bowl. Arrange the grilled roughy, green chilies, jalapeños, cheese, and salsa on the table.

4. Assemble a burrito by laying the tortilla flat in front of you on a plate. Place about ⅓ cup of the grilled roughy in the center of the tortilla and sprinkle with green chilies, jalapeños, and cheese to taste. Ladle on a small amount of salsa and roll up the tortilla, folding in one end so that the burrito can be eaten starting at the open end.

Yield: 8 burritos (about 2½ cups salsa)

ORANGE ROUGHY WITH PECAN SAUCE

❧

We suggest you serve a tart green salad, rice, and fruit for dessert with this dish. Catfish, scrod, or halibut may be substituted for the orange roughy.

PECAN SAUCE
½ cup (1 stick) butter or margarine
⅓ cup chopped fresh parsley
1 tablespoon fresh lemon juice
2 tablespoons finely chopped green part
   of scallion
¼ teaspoon freshly grated nutmeg
⅛ teaspoon Tabasco sauce (more to taste)
1¼ cups pecan halves

FISH
3 pounds orange roughy fillets, cut into
   8 serving pieces
Oil for brushing fish
16 ¼-inch-thick slices lemon for grilling
   fillets

1. *Make the sauce:* Melt the butter in a small frying pan or saucepan. Add the parsley, ground pecans, lemon juice, scallion, nutmeg, and Tabasco. Simmer over low heat for 1 minute. Then add the pecan halves, tossing them well with the butter mixture. Turn off the heat until ready to serve.

2. *Grill the fish:* Brush fish with oil. Arrange the lemon slices in pairs on the prepared grill, then place each fillet on two lemon slices. Grill for 4–6 minutes, without turning, or until the fish is cooked through and has lost its translucence. Transfer the fillets carefully to a serving platter and discard the lemon slices.

3. Reheat the sauce, transfer it to a serving bowl, and serve each fillet topped with pecan sauce.

Yield: 8 servings (¾ cup sauce)

OYSTERS

According to old wives' tales, one should only eat oysters in months that contain an *r*. Due to modern methods in transportation, refrigeration, and aquaculture (oyster farming) you can now enjoy them all year long. Oysters can be eaten raw or cooked. When cooked, do so lightly (only on the outside) as oysters should be juicy and plump.

OYSTERS EN BROCHETTE

Oysters are elegant—but kabobs are versatile. Shrimp, salmon chunks, swordfish, and many other firm-fleshed seafood would be delightful in this recipe.

> *8 slices lean bacon, cut in half widthwise,*
> *   partially cooked, and drained*
> *16 medium-large fresh mushroom caps*
> *3 dozen oysters, shucked*
> *1 large red onion, cut into 6 chunks,*
> *   sections loosened*
> *12 large firm fresh cherry tomatoes*
> *Salt and pepper to taste*
> *Oil for greasing grill*

1. Wrap a bacon strip securely around each mushroom. Thread 4 10-inch skewers alternately with oysters, vegetables, and bacon-wrapped mushroom caps. Add extra oysters as you thread. Sprinkle with salt and pepper to taste.

2. Arrange skewers on oiled grill in single layer and grill for 3 minutes on each side or until cooked. Place skewers on individual plates and allow guests to remove food themselves.

Yield: 4 servings

OYSTER ROAST

Oysters can be cooked very successfully in the shell on the grill—a welcome change from struggling to open them by hand. But, whatever kind of oysters you use, be sure to lay a bed of leaves, parsley, lemon slices, or seaweed on the grill first, to act as protection, then place oysters on this in a single layer.

Gremolata is an Italian seasoning mix made most often of chopped garlic, parsley, and finely chopped lemon rind, although other ingredients are sometimes used. The gremolata is then passed around the table to garnish soups and stews. Some cooks sprinkle gremolata directly on the grilled oysters, but we've made the gremolata into a butter, which adds both richness and moisture to the grilled oysters. Six oysters, as we call for here, are an appetizer serving. To make a main dish, serve at least 12 each.

GREMOLATA BUTTER
8 tablespoons (1 stick) unsalted butter,
*   very soft but not melted*
⅓ cup chopped fresh parley
1 teaspoon finely minced garlic
1 teaspoon finely minced shallots
1 teaspoon finely grated lemon

SHELLFISH
24 oysters in the shell

1. *Prepare gremolata butter:* Mix butter, parsley, garlic, shallots, and lemon rind together well. Transfer to four small bowls (French stoneware butter containers work well) and place on the serving table. (If you make gremolata butter early in the day, cover it carefully before storing in the refrigerator so it doesn't perfume everything else; remember to remove it from the refrigerator 2 hours in advance of serving so it softens sufficiently.)

2. *Grill oysters:* Scrub oysters with a vegetable brush under running tap water and place in shells on grill in a single layer. Grill oysters just a few moments, until you hear little popping noises, which signals that their shells have opened. Serve immediately, using tongs to transfer oysters to serving platter. Spoon soft gremolata butter onto each oyster.

Yield: 12 appetizer servings

OYSTERS WITH CAPER BUTTER

CAPER BUTTER

8 tablespoons (1 stick) butter, at room
   temperature
2 tablespoons capers, drained
Small bunch fresh parsley, stems removed
1 teaspoon tarragon

SHELLFISH
24 oysters in the shell

1. *Prepare butter:* Place butter, capers, parsley, and tarragon in a food processor container or blender and process with steel blade until well combined. Transfer to serving bowl, cover, and refrigerate. Let butter come to room temperature before serving.

2. *Prepare and grill oysters:* Scrub oysters with a vegetable brush under running tap water and place in shells on grill in single layer. Grill oysters just 3 to 6 minutes or until you hear little popping noises which indicate the oysters have opened. Serve immediately, using tongs to transfer oysters to serving platter and taking care that liquid does not spill. Serve topped with caper butter.

Yield: 12 appetizers

OYSTERS WITH COGNAC BUTTER

❧

COGNAC BUTTER
8 tablespoons (1 stick) butter, at room
  temperature
6 tablespoons chopped pecans
2 teaspoons orange rind
1 tablespoon cognac or to taste

SHELLFISH
24 oysters in the shell

1. *Prepare butter:* Place butter, pecans, orange rind, and cognac in food processor container or blender and process with steel blade until combined. Taste and adjust seasonings, adding more cognac or orange rind as desired. Transfer to serving dish, cover, and refrigerate. Bring to room temperature before serving.

2. *Prepare and grill oysters:* Scrub oysters with a vegetable brush under running tap water and place in shells on grill in single layer. Grill oysters just a few moments, anywhere from about 3 to 6 minutes, depending on size of oysters and grill and/or outdoor temperature. Cover grill. You will hear little popping sounds as each oyster opens. Using tongs, transfer oysters to serving platter carefully, so liquid does not spill. Spoon softened cognac butter onto each oyster.

Yield: 12 appetizers

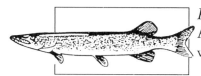

PIKE
A medium-firm freshwater fish that can be substituted with flounder or rainbow trout.

PIKE FILLETS IN GRAPE LEAVES

This beautiful dish would make a sensational centerpiece—but it never seems to last long enough to get a good look.

1 9-ounce jar grape leaves, washed and
    drained
4 7-ounce pike fillets
Olive oil for brushing fish and greasing
    fish basket
Minced fresh parsley and chives
1 lemon, sliced, for garnish
Greek olives for garnish

1. Layer grape leaves, dull side up, on the bottom of a prepared double-hinged fish basket. Arrange pike fillets over leaves. Brush with olive oil. Sprinkle with parsley and chives. Cover with a layer of grape leaves and secure basket.

2. Grill 7–10 minutes and turn basket over. Continue grilling about 3 minutes or until fish begins to flake when tested with a fork. Remove fish and grape leaves to individual serving dishes. Serve with lemon slices and sprinkle with Greek olives.

Yield: 4 servings

POMPANO
A medium-textured fish with a high fat content.
Pompano are relatively small, each averaging about
2 pounds, and are found in waters from Massachusetts
to South America. When pompano is not available, ono or swordfish will do.

POMPANO IN FOIL PACKETS

2 tablespoons butter
3 large shallots, peeled and minced
½ pound mushrooms, minced
4 5- to 6-ounce pompano fillets
¼ teaspoon each: salt and white pepper
4 large mushrooms, sliced

1. Melt butter in medium-sized skillet; sauté shallots and mushrooms in butter until vegetables are tender and dry. Reserve.

2. Cut 4 sheets of aluminum foil, each twice the size of a fish fillet. Arrange a piece of fish on each sheet of foil. Season with salt and pepper. Distribute the mushroom mixture over the fish. Arrange a sliced mushroom decoratively over each piece of fish. Fold foil envelope style.

3. Arrange fish packages over hot grill in single layer. Grill for 10–15 minutes and check one envelope to see if the fish has cooked. If not, rewrap and continue grilling until cooked. Serve pompano packages on individual plates, allowing guests to open packages themselves.

Yield: 4 servings

REDFISH
A mild-flavored fish with a low fat content. When redfish is not available substitute black bass, halibut, or bluefish (fillets).

BLACKENED REDFISH

If you wish, cook this dish indoors an hour before your guests arrive, then finish it on the grill. We suggest you serve it with corn bread.

> 4 7-ounce redfish or bluefish fillets
> Melted butter
> 1 tablespoon paprika
> ½ teaspoon each: salt, freshly ground
>   black pepper, and freshly ground white
>   pepper
> 1 teaspoon dried minced onion
> ½ teaspoon crumbled dried thyme
> ¼ teaspoon garlic powder

1. Rinse fish and pat dry with paper toweling. Place a large cast iron skillet over high heat on stove and allow it to preheat 3–4 minutes. (Open kitchen windows as the high heat will cause a great deal of smoke. Use proper ventilation.) Brush fish fillets with melted butter. Combine remaining ingredients and sprinkle both sides of fish with spice mixture.

2. Carefully place the redfish, one piece at a time, in the dry hot skillet. Brush fish with more melted butter. Sear fish 30 seconds on each side, turning with a spatula.

3. Using a pot holder, carry skillet outdoors and place on prepared grill. Continue cooking, turning fish every minute, for about 3–4 minutes, depending on thickness of fish, until it cooks and is darkened. Add more butter as necessary. To serve, remove redfish to individual plates.

Yield: 4 servings

REDFISH WITH CREOLE-CHORON SAUCE

BEARNAISE SAUCE

4 teaspoons tarragon vinegar or red wine
   vinegar
4 teaspoons dry white wine
1 small shallot, peeled and minced
Dash pepper
1 egg yolk, room temperature
⅓ cup butter, cut in ½-inch pieces
⅓ teaspoon crumbled dried tarragon leaves
Dash salt
⅓ teaspoon fresh lemon juice

CHORON SAUCE

¼ cup creole sauce (see Index)
½ cup béarnaise sauce

FISH

4 7-ounce redfish, sea trout, or grouper
   fillets
Melted butter
Pepper to taste
Oil for greasing grill
Tomato slices for garnish
Fresh tarragon leaves for garnish

1. *Make béarnaise sauce:* In a heavy nonaluminum saucepan, combine vinegar, wine, shallot, and pepper. Cook over medium heat until mixture is reduced. Remove pan from heat and whisk in the egg yolk. Place mixture in top of a double boiler over simmering water. Whisk butter into sauce, one piece at a time, until all the butter has been incorporated. Mix in tarragon, salt, and lemon juice. Keep sauce warm over a pan of hot, but not boiling, water.

2. *Make choron sauce:* Heat creole sauce in small saucepan over medium-low heat until sauce is reduced by half. Whisk in béarnaise sauce and continue cooking until sauce is combined and heated, about 1 minute. Set aside and reheat before serving.

3. *Grill redfish:* Brush redfish fillets with butter and season with pepper to taste. Arrange fish on prepared grill and cook for 5 minutes. Brush fish with melted butter and turn fish over. Continue cooking until fish begins to flake easily when tested with a fork, about 5 minutes.

4. Transfer fish to warm serving platter. Ladle sauce over fish and surround platter with tomato slices sprinkled with chopped tarragon leaves. Serve immediately.

Yield: 4 servings

RED SNAPPER
This is a medium-firm fish with a mild flavor. All snappers are interchangeable in recipes; halibut will work as well.

RED SNAPPER WITH OLIVE SPREAD

OLIVE SPREAD
4 tablespoons (½ stick) butter
2 tablespoons chopped fresh parsley
4 teaspoons fresh lemon juice
¼ cup coarsely chopped green olives with
* pimiento*

FISH
Oil for brushing fish and greasing grill
2 pounds fresh red snapper fillets, cut
* into 4-inch-long pieces*

1. *Make olive spread:* Place butter in a small saucepan and melt over low heat. Stir in parsley, lemon juice, and olives. Mix well and transfer to serving bowl.

2. *Grill snapper:* Brush snapper fillet pieces with oil on both sides, then place on prepared grill. Cook for 3–4 minutes on each side or until fish just begins to flake with fork. Remove from heat immediately.

3. Divide fish pieces evenly among 4 heated dinner plates. Spoon small amount of olive spread over each serving. Serve immediately.

Yield: 4 servings

INDIVIDUAL RED SNAPPERS

*4 small red snappers, about 8–10 ounces
    each, cleaned, head and tail intact*
Italian salad dressing
Freshly ground pepper
Crumbled dried oregano
Freshly grated Parmesan cheese
Oil for greasing grill
Pretty Romaine lettuce leaves for garnish
Watercress for garnish
Black olives for garnish

1. Brush snappers with salad dressing and sprinkle with pepper, oregano, and Parmesan cheese.

2. Arrange fish on prepared grill. Cook fish about 4 minutes. Brush with salad dressing and turn, using a spatula. Continue grilling about 2–3 minutes, until fish begins to flake when tested with a fork.

3. Place Romaine lettuce leaves on a serving platter. Arrange snappers over lettuce and garnish with watercress and black olives.

Yield: 4 servings

RED SNAPPER FILLETS WITH BEURRE ROUGE SAUCE

❧

BEURRE ROUGE SAUCE

3 large shallots, minced

1 cup dry red wine

2 tablespoons wine vinegar

*8 tablespoons (1 stick) butter, room
    temperature, cut into ½-inch pieces*

FISH

8 7-ounce red snapper or grouper fillets

Oil for greasing grill

1. *Make sauce:* Combine shallots, wine, and vinegar in a heavy nonaluminum saucepan and reduce mixture until almost evaporated, leaving only 3 tablespoons of liquid. Strain. Remove saucepan from the heat, add 2 pieces of the butter, and whisk until combined. Continue whisking in butter, 2 pieces at a time, being careful not to allow the sauce to separate. If the sauce separates, quickly whisk and try to emulsify. Serve sauce immediately or keep warm in top of a double boiler over simmering water.

2. *Grill red snapper:* Arrange fish on prepared grill and cook 2–3 minutes, depending on thickness of fish, until fish begins to flake easily when tested with a fork. It is not necessary to turn fillets over. If desired, you can grill snapper fillets in a prepared double-hinged grill basket, turning once. Place red snapper fillets on individual serving dishes and drizzle with sauce.

Yield: 8 servings

RED SNAPPER IN THE STYLE OF VERACRUZ

This recipe is classically served with a tomato sauce and garnished with olives. We are sure that you will enjoy this adaptation. Serve with potatoes.

VERACRUZ SAUCE
2 tablespoons vegetable oil
3 cloves garlic, minced
2 medium onions, sliced
4 large fresh tomatoes, peeled and
quartered
½ cup sliced green olives
Salt and pepper to taste

FISH
1 2½- to 3-pound whole red snapper fillet
Oil for brushing fish and greasing grill
Fresh lime juice

1. *Make sauce:* Heat 2 tablespoons oil in a saucepan; sauté garlic and onions in it until tender, stirring occasionally. Mix in tomatoes and olives and continue cooking over medium heat for 6–8 minutes. Season to taste with salt and pepper. Remove saucepan from heat and reserve. Reheat when ready to serve.

2. *Grill red snapper:* Brush red snapper with vegetable oil and sprinkle with lime juice, including cavity. Place snapper on prepared grill and cook for 6–10 minutes or use a greased double layer of aluminum foil poked with holes. Brush fish with oil and turn with spatula. Continue cooking 2–3 minutes, depending on the thickness of fish, until the fish begins to flake when tested with fork. Place fish on heated platter and pour heated Veracruz sauce over top.

Yield: 4 servings

RED SNAPPER WITH RED SALSA

RED SALSA

2 tablespoons vegetable oil

1 clove garlic, minced

1 medium onion, chopped

2 large tomatoes, peeled and chopped

1 small fresh hot pepper, or to taste
  (1 pepper gives a sting; 2 peppers give
  a bite)

¼ teaspoon each: salt and freshly ground
  black pepper

3 tablespoons chopped fresh cilantro
  (coriander)

FISH

2 tablespoons peanut oil

Juice of 1 lime or lemon

4 7-ounce red snapper fillets

Oil for greasing grill

½ cup whole pitted green olives for
  garnish

1. *Make salsa:* Heat vegetable oil in saucepan and sauté garlic and onion in it until tender. Add remaining salsa ingredients except cilantro. Simmer sauce for 10 minutes, stirring occasionally. Adjust seasonings. Stir in cilantro and continue cooking 1 minute. Serve salsa hot or cold.

2. *Grill red snapper:* Mix peanut oil and lime juice and baste snapper with mixture. Cook fish on prepared grill for 6 minutes, baste, and turn snapper. Continue grilling 2–3 minutes, depending on thickness of fish, until fish begins to flake when tested with a fork. Place fish on heated platter, garnish with olives, and serve with spooned salsa over fish and on the side for dipping.

Yield: 4 servings

RED SNAPPER
WITH TWO BUTTERS

GARLIC-CASHEW BUTTER
8 tablespoons (1 stick) butter
1 small clove garlic, minced very fine
2 tablespoons chopped fresh parsley
½ cup finely chopped salted cashews

ROMANO OR PARMESAN
CHEESE BUTTER
8 tablespoons (1 stick) butter
½ cup each: freshly grated Romano or
Parmesan cheese (do not use pregrated
cheese) and finely chopped fresh parsley

FISH
Oil for brushing fish and greasing grill
2 pounds red snapper fillets, cut into
4-inch-long pieces
4 large sprigs parsley or watercress with
stems for garnish

1. *Make garlic-cashew butter:* Melt 8 tablespoons butter in a small saucepan. Stir in garlic, 2 tablespoons parsley, and chopped cashews. Transfer to serving bowl.

2. *Make romano butter:* Melt 8 tablespoons butter in a small saucepan over low heat. Stir in grated cheese and ½ cup parsley. Transfer to serving bowl.

3. *Grill red snapper:* Oil red snapper on both sides and place on prepared grill. Cook for just 3 minutes on each side or until fish has turned white.

4. Divide fish among 4 heated dinner plates, laying fish sections in center. Spoon a little garlic-cashew butter on one side of fish; then spoon a little romano butter on other side. Garnish each serving with a parsley sprig. Serve immediately.

Yield: 4 servings

SZECHWAN-STYLE
RED SNAPPER FILLETS

❧

We suggest you serve this dish with warm oriental noodles.

SZECHWAN SAUCE
1 tablespoon peanut oil
½ teaspoon minced fresh gingerroot
2 cloves garlic, minced
3 green onions, minced
1–2 fresh chili peppers, chopped
   (1 pepper gives a sting; 2 peppers give
   a bite)
2 tablespoons sugar
5 teaspoons dark soy sauce
3 tablespoons catsup
2 teaspoons dry white wine
1 teaspoon white vinegar
1 tablespoon water
½ teaspoon sesame oil

FISH
4 7-ounce red snapper fillets
Peanut oil for brushing fish and greasing
   grill
2 green onions, minced, for garnish

1. *Make sauce:* Heat 1 tablespoon peanut oil over medium heat in a small saucepan. Lightly brown ginger, garlic, onions, and chili pepper in it. Stir-fry as they cook. Stir in remaining sauce ingredients and cook until sauce is heated. Reserve.

2. *Grill red snapper:* Brush red snapper fillets with peanut oil and arrange on prepared grill. Cook for 5–6 minutes. Brush fillets with peanut oil and turn over with a spatula. Continue cooking 2–3 minutes, depending on thickness of the fish, until fish begins to flake when tested with a fork. Place fish on platter and pour heated Szechwan sauce over top. Sprinkle with green onions.

Yield: 4 servings

RED SNAPPER FILLETS
WITH GORGONZOLA

We suggest you serve with this fish recipe a tart green salad and steamed small new potatoes tossed with a minimal amount of butter or margarine. You may substitute black sea bass for the red snapper.

2 tablespoons plus 2 teaspoons cashews
½ cup Gorgonzola cheese or any good-
     quality blue cheese at room temperature
½ cup farmer cheese, at room temperature
3 pounds red snapper fillets, cut into 8
     serving pieces
16 ¼-inch-thick lemon slices for grilling
     fish

1. *Toast the cashews:* Place the nuts in a single layer in a frying pan and set over medium heat. Watch carefully, stirring often. As soon as the nuts begin to brown, stir constantly for about 1 minute, until lightly browned on all sides. Remove from heat and allow to cool, then chop the nuts.

2. Combine the Gorgonzola, farmer cheese, and chopped cashews in a small bowl. Spread and pat the mixture over the tops of the fillets to cover.

3. *Grill the fish:* Place the lemon slices on the prepared grill. Arrange the fillets, Gorgonzola side up, on the lemon slices. Grill for 4–8 minutes, without turning, or until the fillets are cooked through and have lost their translucence.

4. Use two spatulas to carefully remove the fillets from the grill and transfer them to a serving platter. Discard the lemon slices and serve the fish immediately.

Yield: 8 servings (1 cup spread)

CHINESE CABBAGE PACKETS

For a less charred effect you can wrap the fish packets in aluminum foil; seal tightly before grilling. Serve with fried rice or Oriental noodles. Grouper, black sea bass, or striped sea bass may be substituted for the red snapper.

FILLING

1 tablespoon corn oil

3 scallions, minced

½ teaspoon ground ginger

½ teaspoon garlic powder

2 cups bean sprouts, rinsed with hot
   water and drained

½ cup chopped water chestnuts

½ teaspoon soy sauce

½ teaspoon Oriental sesame oil

¼ teaspoon salt

⅛ teaspoon freshly ground pepper

FISH

24 large leaves (about 1 large head)
   Chinese cabbage

2¼ pounds red snapper fillets, cut into
   12 equal pieces

12 small snow peas, strings removed,
   trimmed

Oil for brushing packets and greasing grill
   or fish basket

   1. *Make the filling:* Heat the oil in a wok or heavy skillet; add the scallions, ginger, garlic powder, bean sprouts, and water chestnuts. Stir-fry for 2–3 minutes. Stir in the soy sauce, sesame oil, salt, and pepper. Remove from the heat.

   2. *Make the packets:* Remove the tough end of the cabbage leaves and discard. Blanch cabbage leaves until almost cooked; drain and pat dry. Lay on paper toweling.

3. Put a piece of red snapper in the center of each leaf. Place 2 tablespoons of the filling over the fish. Place 1 snow pea on top. Bring the top of the leaf down to cover the fish, then bring the bottom of the leaf up over the fish, envelope style. Place the packet on a second leaf in the opposite direction so that the exposed sides will be covered. Again bring the top of the cabbage down to the center and the bottom half up over the center. Turn the packet over, seal side down, on a tray. Brush lightly with oil. Repeat with the remaining ingredients; you should end up with 12 packets.

4. *Grill the packets:* Place the packets on the prepared grill (coals should be medium-hot) or in a prepared fish basket and grill for 4 minutes. Turn and continue grilling for 2–3 minutes or until done. If the outer leaf is too charred for your taste, you can remove it before serving, leaving the inner leaf in place. Serve hot.

Yield: 6 servings (2 packets per person)

RED SNAPPER WITH
SPANISH WINE BUTTER AND
BLACK OLIVE AIOLI

Serve saffron rice, grilled pepper strips, and flan for dessert with this dish. Black sea bass, mullet, or pollack may be substituted for the red snapper in this recipe.

BLACK OLIVE AIOLI
2 tablespoons fine white bread crumbs
½ teaspoon fresh lemon juice
2 large cloves garlic, crushed
1 cup drained pitted black olives
¼ teaspoon salt
1 egg yolk
½ cup good-quality olive oil

SPANISH WINE BUTTER
¾ cup Spanish red wine
1 onion, minced
¾ cup (6 ounces) butter or margarine,
  at room temperature, cut into 1-inch
  pieces
1 tablespoon fresh lemon juice
¼ teaspoon salt

FISH
2 large red onions, sliced thin
Good-quality olive oil for brushing onions
  and fillets and greasing grill
8 8- to 12-ounce red snappers, cleaned,
  heads removed, or red snapper fillets

1. *Make the black olive aioli:* Puree the bread crumbs, lemon juice, and garlic in a food processor fitted with the steel blade or a blender. Add the

olives, salt, and egg yolk and process again. With the machine running, pour in the olive oil in a *slow*, steady stream until a sauce is formed. Cover and chill until ready to serve.

2. *Make the wine butter:* Simmer the wine with the onion in a medium saucepan until the liquid is reduced to 3–4 tablespoons. Strain. With a wooden spoon, beat in the butter, a small chunk at a time. Season with lemon juice and salt. Cover and serve soft, at room temperature.

3. *Grill the fish:* Brush the red onion slices with the oil. Arrange the onion slices on the prepared grill and cook for about 3 minutes on each side. Then place the oiled snappers on the grill and cook for about 5–8 minutes. Turn and continue cooking until the fillets are cooked through and have lost their translucence. Or you can grill snapper fillets on the onion slices, without turning.

4. Serve with the wine butter and black olive aioli as a side relish.

Yield: 8 servings (1 cup aioli and 1½ cups wine butter)

RED SNAPPER
WITH MARZIPAN

This crowd-stopping dish is known as hut b'noua in the Moroccan fishing city of Safi, where it originated. The unlikely combination of orange-flavored almond paste and fresh fish is superb; your guests will be astonished when they taste it and will beg for the recipe. The original dish is made with a large whole red snapper that is gutted and scaled, filled with orange-flavored almond paste, and topped with more paste. The fish is then oven-baked on a bed of chopped onions. Our version is made with snapper fillets that are spread with an almond paste topping and grilled. We do not suggest that you try to grill this dish the traditional way, using a whole fish, because half-cooked large fish fall apart on the grill when they are turned. We like this dish better using fillets, in any case, because it is so refined in flavor and concept that no one should have to deal with the indignity of fish bones. Scrod fillets may be substituted. In the original recipe, the almond paste is flavored with cinnamon and orange flower water, but we have substituted grated orange zest and orange juice. When you make the almond paste, keep it fairly dry. If it is limp, too much of it will run off the fillet during grilling. We suggest you serve this dish with a tart green salad and hot French bread.

FISH
½ cup imported mild, good-quality olive
  oil
3 tablespoons fresh lemon juice
3 pounds red snapper fillets, cut into
  8 serving pieces
Salt and freshly ground pepper to taste
16 ¼-inch thick orange or onion slices, for
  grilling fish

ALMOND PASTE
1½ cups blanched almonds
1 scant cup sugar
Zest from ½ large orange, removed with
  vegetable peeler and diced coarse
3 tablespoons fresh orange juice
2 tablespoons salad oil

1. *Marinate the fish:* Mix the olive oil and lemon juice and pour into a large plastic bag. Set the bag in a bowl and add the fish fillets. Secure the bag with a twister seal and turn the bag a few times to make certain all fish surfaces touch the marinade. Let sit at room temperature for 1 hour.

2. *Meanwhile, make the almond paste:* Preheat the oven to 350°F. Place the almonds in a single layer on a baking sheet and place in the oven for 8–10 minutes, watching carefully. Check every couple of minutes after the first 3–4 minutes and remove the almonds when lightly toasted.

3. Transfer the toasted almonds to a blender or food processor fitted with the steel blade. Add the sugar, orange zest, orange juice, and salad oil. Process the mixture by pulsing and checking the consistency until a coarse paste results.

4. Arrange the fillets, skin side down, on a platter. Salt and pepper each fillet liberally, then use paper towels to pat the top of each fillet dry. Top each with a scant ¼ cup almond paste, spreading it as evenly as possible.

5. *Grill the fish:* Lay the orange or onion slices in pairs on the prepared grill. Arrange the fillets on top of the orange or onion slices. Grill without turning until the fillets are cooked through, watching carefully.

6. Using two spatulas, carefully transfer the fillets from the grill to a serving platter. Discard the orange or onion slices. Serve immediately.

Yield: 8 servings (2 cups almond paste)

GRILLED RED SNAPPER ALFREDO

❧

We suggest you serve this dish with an endive or a mixed green salad and warm Italian bread.

PASTA
1 pound fettuccine, cooked according to
*   package directions*
Parmesan cheese chunk

FISH
2 pounds red snapper fillets
Oil for brushing fish and greasing grill

ALFREDO SAUCE
2 cups evaporated skim milk
⅓ pound Parmesan cheese, grated
¼ teaspoon freshly grated nutmeg

    1. *While the fettuccine is cooking, grill the fish:* Brush fish with oil. Arrange the fish on the prepared grill and cook for 4–8 minutes. Turn the fish and continue grilling until done to taste.

    2. Transfer the fish to a plate and break it into small irregular pieces using two forks.

    3. *Make the sauce:* In a large saucepan, bring the evaporated milk to a simmer over moderate heat. Stir in the grated Parmesan and, as soon as it has melted and the sauce is thick and creamy, pour over cooked pasta and fish chunks. Season with nutmeg. Pass Parmesan cheese chunk with a grater at the table.

Yield: 8–10 servings (2¼ cups sauce)

RED SNAPPER
NEW ORLEANS STYLE

You might serve this dish with three-bean salad or garbanzo bean salad, grilled scallions, grilled large garlic cloves, and hot French bread. You may substitute sea bass or ocean perch for red snapper in this recipe.

NEW ORLEANS–STYLE SAUCE
2 tablespoons good-quality olive oil
3 cloves garlic, minced
1 medium-large onion, minced
2 cups chopped peeled tomatoes
1 teaspoon paprika
½ teaspoon dried thyme, crushed
2 large bay leaves
⅛ teaspoon freshly ground pepper
⅛ teaspoon red pepper flakes, crushed
1 teaspoon prepared mustard

FISH
8 8- to 10-ounce red snappers, scaled and
   cleaned, heads and tails left on
Olive oil for brushing fish and greasing
   grill
8 slices lemon or lime
½ cup crumbled bay leaves

1. *Make the sauce:* Heat the oil in a medium-sized pan; add the garlic and onion and sauté until tender. Add the remaining sauce ingredients and sauté for 2 minutes, stirring often. Discard the bay leaves.

2. *Grill the fish:* Brush fish with oil and place a lemon or lime slice in each fish cavity. Sprinkle the bay leaves over the hot coals. Place the fish on the prepared grill and cook for 4–8 minutes. Turn fish over carefully with a long-handled spatula and continue to grill until done to taste. Reheat the sauce while the fish is cooking.

4. Serve the fish hot, topped with the hot New Orleans–style sauce.

Yield: 8 servings (1¾–2¼ cups sauce)

RED SNAPPER WITH
PINEAPPLE SALSA

❧

Pineapple adds a new twist to an old southwestern treat. You may want to prepare extra to pass at the table. Also serve refried beans with Spanish rice or grilled corn with a strip of bacon wrapped around it. Black sea bass also works well in this recipe.

2 cups mesquite chips

PINEAPPLE SALSA
½ cup minced cilantro
1 green bell pepper, seeded and minced
1 yellow bell pepper, seeded and minced
1 medium-large onion, minced
2 cups minced fresh pineapple

FISH
2 tablespoons oil
2 tablespoons lime juice
Oil for greasing grill
3 pounds red snapper fillets, cut into
    8 serving pieces

1. Soak the mesquite chips in cold water to cover for 1 hour.
2. *Make the salsa:* Toss the cilantro, peppers, onion, and pineapple in a mixing bowl. Cover and chill until ready to serve.
3. *Grill the fish:* Drain the mesquite chips and scatter them over the hot coals; replace the grill. Combine the oil and lime juice and baste the red snapper with the mixture. Grill the snapper on the prepared grill for about 4–8 minutes. Turn the snapper using a long-handled spatula and continue grilling for 4–8 minutes, or until fish begins to flake when tested with a fork. Place the fish on individual plates and spoon the salsa over the middle section of the fish.

Yield: 8 servings (3¼ cups salsa)

ROCKFISH
This West Coast fish is medium firm with a mild flavor. Substitute snapper or monkfish when it is not available.

ROCKFISH WITH LEMON SAUCE

Sprinkling rosemary over the hot coals adds a gourmet touch.

LEMON SAUCE
1 clove garlic, minced
Juice of 2 lemons
¼ cup olive oil
¼ teaspoon white pepper
1 teaspoon Dijon mustard
1 tablespoon grated lemon zest

FISH
¼ cup olive oil
2 teaspoons leaf rosemary
¼ teaspoon white pepper
4 7-ounce rockfish fillets
1 lemon, sliced
Oil for greasing fish basket

1. *Make sauce:* Puree all sauce ingredients in a blender or a food processor fitted with a steel blade. Set sauce aside until ready to serve.

2. *Marinate rockfish:* Combine ¼ cup olive oil with 1 teaspoon of the rosemary and the pepper. Brush fillets with seasonings. Let marinate for 1 hour.

3. *Grill rockfish:* Put 1 lemon slice over each piece of fish. Place rockfish in a greased hinged fish basket. Sprinkle remaining rosemary over hot coals. Grill fish for 5 minutes. Turn basket and continue grilling 2–3 minutes, depending on thickness of fish, until fish begins to flake when tested with a fork. Arrange rockfish on individual plates, leaving the lemon slices in place. Drizzle with lemon sauce.

Yield: 4 servings

ROCKFISH WITH WHITE WINE SAUCE

❧

You might serve a tossed green salad topped with a slice of warm goat cheese and grilled asparagus with this dish. Rainbow trout and flounder also work well in this recipe.

WHITE WINE SAUCE
3 tablespoons butter or margarine
5 shallots, minced
½ cup dry white wine
1½ cups evaporated milk
½ teaspoon dried tarragon, crumbled
½ teaspoon dried chervil, crumbled
½ teaspoon salt

FISH
3 pounds rockfish fillets, cut into
*   8 serving pieces*
Good-quality olive oil for brushing fish
*   and greasing grill*
1 bunch chives, trimmed

1. *Make the sauce:* Melt the butter in a saucepan; add the shallots and sauté until tender. Add the wine and cook over medium-high heat until reduced to about 5–6 tablespoons of liquid. Strain and return the liquid to the pan. Blend in the half-and-half and season with tarragon, chervil, and salt. Simmer until the sauce is warm, stirring often. Set aside and serve warm.

2. *Grill the fish:* Brush the fish with the oil and arrange on the prepared grill. Grill the fish for about 3–5 minutes, turn carefully, and continue grilling until the fish begins to flake when tested with a fork.

3. Serve the fish hot on individual dishes with the white wine sauce. Garnish with chive strips.

Yield: 8 servings (1¾ cups sauce)

ROCKFISH FILLETS WITH SAFFRON BEURRE BLANC

🌿

Red snapper and black sea bass can also be used in this recipe. You might serve it with a green salad with arugula and French green beans.

SAFFRON BEURRE BLANC
2 large shallots, chopped
1 cup dry white wine
1 cup (½ pound) butter or margarine at
 room temperature
3 pinches saffron threads soaked in
 2 teaspoons hot water
Salt and freshly ground pepper to taste

FISH
3 pounds rockfish fillets, cut into
 8 serving pieces
Melted butter or margarine for brushing
 fish
Oil for greasing grill or fish basket
½ cup minced hazelnuts

1. *Make the sauce:* Heat the shallots with the wine in a saucepan, bringing the mixture to a boil over medium heat. Continue cooking until all but 5–6 tablespoons of liquid remain. Strain and return the liquid to the pan. Beat in the butter, about 2 tablespoons at a time, until all the butter has been added. Whisk in the saffron liquid. Season with salt and pepper.

2. *Grill the fish:* Brush the fillets with butter and press ¼ cup of the hazelnuts firmly into the fish. Cook on the prepared grill or in a fish basket for 3 minutes. Turn and continue grilling for about 3–5 minutes, until done to taste.

3. Spoon some of the warm sauce onto each plate, arrange a fish fillet over the sauce, and sprinkle with the remaining hazelnuts. Serve hot.

Yield: 8 servings

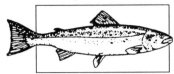

SALMON

Salmon is a universal fish, found in both the Atlantic and Pacific oceans as well as in many lakes, which lends itself to grilling. As a gourmet food it has an ancient history and continues today as a prized delicacy. Grouper and monkfish (whether fillets, steaks, or whole fish) can be substituted.

CHILLED SALMON WITH RED CAVIAR MAYONNAISE

This appetizer calls for bite-sized chunks of chilled salmon to be dipped into a homemade red caviar mayonnaise. The mayonnaise is made with Japanese rice vinegar because of its mildness, but plain white vinegar makes an acceptable substitute. You may use halibut or tuna instead of salmon.

This is a rich appetizer, so serve a spartan entree, such as a plain fillet marinated in our basic marinade (see Index), hot French bread, and a green salad.

CAVIAR MAYONNAISE

1 egg
1½ teaspoons fresh lemon juice
1 tablespoon sugar
1 tablespoon Japanese rice vinegar
¼ teaspoon salt
¼ teaspoon dry mustard
¼ teaspoon paprika
Pinch freshly ground white pepper
*⅔ cup imported mild, good-quality olive
    oil*
2 ounces red lumpfish caviar

FISH

*2 pounds salmon fillets, each cut ¾ inch
    thick*
Oil for brushing fish and greasing grill

1. *Make the mayonnaise:* Combine the egg, lemon juice, sugar, vinegar, salt, dry mustard, paprika, and white pepper in a blender or a food processor fitted with the steel blade, and process for a few seconds to combine.

2. Turn the processor on and with the motor running add the olive oil in a very thin, steady stream. When all the oil has been added, turn off the motor. Transfer the mayonnaise to serving bowl. Cover and refrigerate.

3. *Grill the fish:* Brush salmon fillets with oil. Place the fillets on the prepared grill and cook for about 4 minutes. Turn carefully with a spatula and cook for about 6 minutes. Transfer the fish to a large platter (do not use metal) and cover. Refrigerate the fish until well chilled.

4. Cut the chilled salmon into bite-sized chunks and place on a serving platter along with cocktail toothpicks. Mix the caviar into the mayonnaise and set the bowl in the center of the platter. Serve as an appetizer.

Yield: 8 appetizer servings (1 scant cup mayonnaise)

GRILLED SALMON WITH CORN RELISH

☙

This recipe comes from chef Maggie Wanglin. It also works with whitefish. Serve it with cornbread and a tossed green salad.

FISH

*4 5-inch wooden presoaked barbecue
   skewers*
*4 5-ounce center-cut skinless salmon
   fillets, cut in half, each half
   approximately 1½ inches by 5 inches,
   for a total of 8 pieces*
Good-quality olive oil for brushing fish
Oil for greasing grill

RELISH

2 strips bacon
1 cup fresh corn kernels
1 red bell pepper, seeded and diced
1 bunch chives, trimmed and minced

   1. *Grill the fish:* With the thick ends opposite each other, interlock two c-shaped fillets (ying/yang style) into a medallion. Brush salmon lightly with olive oil and cook on the prepared grill for 3–4 minutes on each side; the centers will be slightly translucent.

   2. *Make the relish:* Sauté bacon until crisp and drain it, discarding all but 1 tablespoon of the drippings. Let the bacon cool and crumble it. Sauté the corn in the tablespoon of bacon drippings. Add red pepper, chives, and crumbled bacon. Place in a small bowl and serve with the salmon.

Yield: 4 servings (1½ cups relish)

STUFFED SALMON WITH
WILD MUSHROOMS

Serve this dish with a mixed green salad and warm blueberry muffins. Trout or whitefish may be substituted for salmon.

WILD MUSHROOM STUFFING

2 tablespoons butter or margarine
1 large onion, minced
2 cups fresh shiitake mushrooms, trimmed
1 cup fresh oyster mushrooms, trimmed
  and chopped coarse
½ cup bread crumbs
1 carrot, grated
½ teaspoon dried dill
½ teaspoon dried tarragon, crumbled
¼ teaspoon salt
⅛ teaspoon freshly ground pepper

FISH

8 8- to 10-ounce salmon, cleaned and
  scaled, heads and tails left on
Good-quality olive oil for brushing fish
  and greasing grill
½ cup drained capers, for garnish

1. *Make the stuffing:* Melt the butter in a skillet, add the onion, and sauté about 2 minutes. Stir in the mushrooms and continue cooking until the mushrooms are soft. Toss with the bread crumbs, carrot, dill, tarragon, salt, and pepper.

2. Lightly stuff the salmon, using about 3–5 tablespoons of stuffing per salmon. Brush the salmon with olive oil.

3. *Grill the fish:* Arrange the salmon on the prepared grill and cook for 4–8 minutes on each side or until it begins to flake easily when tested with a fork.

4. Place one salmon on each plate and garnish with the capers.

Yield: 8 servings

SALMON PATTIES
ON THE GRILL

Canned mackerel or tuna will not do for this recipe. We recommend side dishes of french-fried potatoes and hearty coleslaw.

2 tablespoons butter or margarine
½ cup very finely chopped onions
1½ cups toasted bread crumbs
¼ cup evaporated milk
2 eggs, lightly beaten
2–3 tablespoons drained capers
2 tablespoons fresh lemon juice
1 teaspoon salt

½ teaspoon freshly ground pepper
⅛ teaspoon Tabasco sauce (to taste)
2 7¾-ounce cans salmon, drained
2 scallions, green part only
Oil for greasing grill
Melted butter or margarine for brushing patties
Dijon mustard

1. Melt the butter in a small saucepan. Add the onion and sauté for 10 minutes over low heat or until the onion is limp and translucent. Transfer to a mixing bowl and add the bread crumbs, evaporated milk, eggs, capers, lemon juice, salt, pepper, and Tabasco sauce.

2. Place the drained salmon in a strainer and press with the back of a wooden spoon to remove as much excess liquid as possible. Add the salmon to the onion–bread crumb mixture. Use scissors to snip the scallions into the mixture, cutting them into small pieces. Mix well, then measure. You should have 3 cups.

3. Measure out a slightly heaping ⅓ cup of the mixture and form into a 4-inch-long oval patty. Repeat with the remaining mixture until you have eight patties.

4. Carefully transfer the patties to the prepared grill and brush with melted butter. Cook for 5 minutes on each side, using a spatula to turn the patties and brushing again with melted butter. Serve immediately with Dijon mustard.

Yield: 8 servings

SALMON AU POIVRE
WITH LIME

This dish, for those who like "hot" food, can be made even hotter by using more crushed peppercorns. It is adapted from the classic French recipe Steak Au Poivre.

2½ tablespoons peppercorns
2 tablespoons each: melted butter and
    fresh lime juice
4 salmon steaks, each about 1 inch thick
8 slices fresh lime
Oil for greasing fish basket
Tartar sauce (see Index)
Lime wedges for garnish

1. Crush peppercorns using mortar and pestle. Or, if no mortar is available, put peppercorns in kitchen towel, then fold it to form envelope. Use a hammer to crush peppercorns coarsely.

2. Combine melted butter and lime juice and brush each salmon steak on one side with the mixture. Press crushed peppercorns thickly into salmon steaks with heel of hand. Turn and brush remaining side with melted butter and lime combination. Press crushed peppercorns thickly into remaining side of salmon steaks.

3. Arrange 4 slices of lime in prepared fish basket and set salmon steaks over lime slices. Top each salmon steak with another lime slice. Fasten top of basket. Grill over ashen coals for about 4 minutes on each side or until fish flakes easily with fork. Serve, with tartar sauce, immediately, garnished with lime wedges.

Yield: 4 servings

SALMON FILLETS WITH CHAMPAGNE SAUCE

CHAMPAGNE SAUCE
1 cup chicken stock
½ teaspoon crumbled dried thyme
1 shallot, minced
⅛ teaspoon ground nutmeg
1 cup champagne
1 cup heavy cream
2 tablespoons cold unsalted butter, cut
    into ½-inch pieces
Salt and white pepper to taste
1 tablespoon champagne vinegar
¼ cup champagne

FISH
4 7-ounce salmon fillets
Melted butter
Oil for greasing grill
Salmon roe for garnish

1. *Make sauce:* Place chicken stock in saucepan; mix in thyme, shallot, nutmeg, and 1 cup champagne. Bring sauce mixture to a boil over medium heat. Continue cooking until mixture is reduced to 2–3 tablespoons. Strain mixture and return to saucepan; stir in heavy cream. Place saucepan over low heat and simmer for 2–4 minutes. Remove from heat. Whisk in butter and season with salt and pepper to taste. Stir in vinegar. Just before serving, whisk in ¼ cup champagne. Serve warm.

2. *Grill salmon:* Brush salmon fillets with melted butter and place on prepared grill. Cook for 4–5 minutes, brush salmon with butter, and turn. Continue cooking 2–3 minutes until fish begins to flake when tested with a fork. Put salmon on individual plates and ladle warm sauce over top. Sprinkle with salmon roe.

Yield: 4 servings

WHOLE SALMON WITH LIME-GINGER SAUCE

Whole salmon is an old New England tradition, usually served during the 4th of July celebration. At that time of year beautiful salmon are plentiful. Using this easy recipe makes it simple to carry on the tradition.

LIME-GINGER SAUCE
6 ounces Neufchâtel cheese, room
    temperature
½ cup plain, nonfat yogurt
1 tablespoon chopped candied ginger
Grated zest of 1 lime

FISH
1 3- to 3½-pound whole salmon, cleaned
    and scaled, head and tail intact
Oil for brushing fish and greasing grill
Freshly ground pepper to taste
Ground gingerroot
1 lime, sliced

   1. *Make sauce:* Mix together cheese, yogurt, ginger, and lime zest in a small bowl. Serve at room temperature over the hot salmon.

   2. *Grill salmon:* Brush salmon, including the cavity, with oil. Sprinkle with pepper and ginger. Put sliced lime in the cavity of the salmon. Place fish on prepared grill or over a double thickness of greased aluminum foil with poked holes to allow the smoke to come through. Cook for 10 minutes. Brush salmon with oil and turn with spatula. Continue cooking for 8–10 minutes or until the fish begins to flake when tested with a fork. With a spatula, carefully transfer salmon to serving platter. Serve salmon with sauce.

Yield: 4–5 servings

SALMON STEAKS
WITH FENNEL

❧

Sprinkling fennel on the hot coals will make the fennel aroma delicately flavor the fish.

MARINADE
2 tablespoons minced fresh parsley
2 shallots, minced
1 tablespoon chopped fresh fennel or
  1 teaspoon dried fennel seeds
Pepper to taste
¼ cup salad oil
Juice of 2 limes

FISH
4 6- to 7-ounce salmon steaks
1 tablespoon chopped fresh fennel or
  1 teaspoon dried fennel seeds
Oil for greasing grill

1. *Marinate salmon steaks:* Combine parsley, shallots, 1 tablespoon fennel, pepper, oil, and lime juice in a shallow glass bowl or pie plate. Place fish in marinade and turn after 30 minutes. Leave fish to marinate for 15 minutes longer.

2. *Grill salmon steaks:* Sprinkle 1 tablespoon of the fennel over hot coals. Place fish on prepared grill and cook for 5 minutes. Brush salmon with remaining marinade and turn. Continue cooking 2–3 minutes, depending on thickness of the fish, until fish begins to flake when tested with a fork. Arrange the fish on individual plates and serve with a mixed salad and thinly sliced white or red onions.

Yield: 4 servings

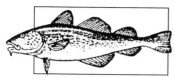

SCROD

Scrod is a low-fat delicate fish (it's actually young cod or haddock) that can be interchanged with flounder in recipes.

SCROD WITH ANISE BUTTER

We suggest you serve this dish with a mixed green salad, pumpernickel rolls, and grilled mushrooms.

ANISE BUTTER
1 teaspoon crushed aniseed
¼ cup (½ stick) butter or margarine, at
*   room temperature*
1 tablespoon chopped chives

FISH
Oil for greasing grill
3 pounds scrod fillets, cut into 8 serving
*   pieces*

1. *Make the anise butter:* Blend aniseed and butter in a food processor fitted with the steel blade or in a blender. Add the chives and combine.

2. Mound the butter in a small bowl, cover, and refrigerate. Remove from refrigerator 45 minutes before serving time so that the butter will be soft when served.

3. *Grill the fish:* Grill the scrod for 3–6 minutes. Turn and grill 2–3 minutes or until the fish is cooked to taste. Place the fillets on individual plates. Top each piece of fish with a dollop of anise butter.

Yield: 8 servings

SCROD FILLETS WITH APRICOT SAUCE

This Persian dish combines apricots, sugar, onions, and pomegranate seeds to form a colorful, unusual jamlike sauce with onion undertones. We suggest you serve it with cold rice salad or cracked wheat salad (tabbouleh) and hot French bread. Halibut or ono may be substituted for scrod.

FISH

½ cup imported mild, good-quality olive
   oil

3 tablespoons fresh lemon juice

3 pounds scrod or red snapper fillets, cut
   into 8 serving pieces

Salt and freshly ground pepper to taste

16 ¼-inch-thick slices lemon or onion for
   grilling fillets

APRICOT SAUCE

4 tablespoons butter or margarine

6 ounces dried apricots, quartered
   (about 36)

⅔ cup finely chopped onion (5 ounces)

1 heaping cup fresh pomegranate seeds

6 tablespoons fresh lemon juice

½ cup sugar

¼ teaspoon salt

1½ cups water (more if needed)

1. *Marinate the fish:* Combine the olive oil and 3 tablespoons lemon juice in a large plastic bag and place the bag in a bowl. Place the fillets in the bag, secure with a twister seal, and turn the bag several times to make certain all fish surfaces touch the marinade. Let sit at room temperature for 1 hour.

2. *Make the sauce:* Melt 2 tablespoons of the butter in a medium-sized frying pan, add the quartered apricots and sauté for 2–3 minutes. Transfer to

a blender or a food processor fitted with the steel blade and process until coarsely chopped.

3. Melt the remaining 2 tablespoons butter in the same frying pan, add the onion, and sauté for 10 minutes or until the onion is very limp. Add the pomegranate seeds and cook for an additional minute. Then add the coarsely chopped apricots, the 6 tablespoons lemon juice, sugar, salt, and water. Stir to combine. Heat to a boil, reduce the heat, and simmer for 15 minutes or until a thick but still liquid sauce results. Add more water if needed.

4. *Grill the fish:* Remove the fillets from the marinade. Lightly salt and pepper them on each side. Arrange the lemon or onion slices in pairs on the prepared grill. Then place the fillets on the lemon or onion slices. Grill the fillets for about 3–6 minutes, without turning, until the fillets are completely cooked through and have lost their translucence.

5. Use two spatulas to transfer each fillet carefully to a serving platter, discarding the onion or lemon slices. Serve immediately, spooning the hot apricot sauce over each fillet.

Yield: 8 servings (3 cups sauce)

SCROD FILLETS WITH POMEGRANATE SAUCE

❧

This unusual and delicious sweet-sour Persian sauce is dark brown because of its walnut base. The sauce is flavored with pomegranate syrup. Do not substitute grenadine for pomegranate syrup; grenadine used to be based on real pomegranates, but today it is usually made with artificial flavorings. If you cannot find the syrup, you can substitute pomegranate paste, but you must first thin it with water: mix 6 tablespoons pomegranate paste with 4 tablespoons water; use the resulting 10 tablespoons as pomegranate syrup. Ono or halibut may be substituted for the scrod. Serve this dish with rice and grilled vegetables.

FISH

½ cup imported mild, good-quality olive
 oil

3 tablespoons fresh lemon juice

3 pounds scrod or red snapper fillets, cut
 into 8 serving pieces

16 ¼-inch-thick slices lemon or orange for
 grilling fillets

Pomegranate seeds for garnish

POMEGRANATE SAUCE

10 ounces (2½ cups) finely ground
 walnuts

1½ cups water

5–10 tablespoons pomegranate syrup
 (to taste)

3 tablespoons sugar

¼ teaspoon salt

¼ teaspoon ground cinnamon

¼ teaspoon freshly grated nutmeg

¼ teaspoon freshly ground pepper

1½ teaspoons fresh lemon juice

1. *Marinate the fish:* Combine the olive oil and lemon juice in a large plastic bag and place the bag in a bowl. Place the scrod fillets in the bag, secure the bag with a twister seal, and turn the bag several times to make sure all fish surfaces touch the marinade. Let sit at room temperature for 1 hour.

2. *Meanwhile, make the sauce:* Combine the ground walnuts, water, and 5 tablespoons of the pomegranate syrup in a medium saucepan, heat to a boil, reduce the heat, and simmer over low heat for 5 minutes. Stir in the sugar, salt, cinnamon, nutmeg, black pepper, and lemon juice. Return to a simmer and cook 15 minutes. Now taste; if the dish is too sweet, and you want more of the faintly sour, pomegranate flavor, add pomegranate syrup, a tablespoon at a time, until you are satisfied with the sweet-and-sour quality. (We usually add 7 or 8 tablespoons of the syrup.)

3. *Grill the fish:* Remove the fillets from the marinade. Lay the lemon or orange slices in pairs on the prepared grill. Arrange a fillet on each pair of lemon or orange slices and cook the fillets for about 3–6 minutes, without turning, until the flesh has lost its translucence and is completely cooked.

4. Using two spatulas, carefully transfer the fillets, one at a time, to a serving platter. Serve a fillet to each guest, spooning warm pomegranate sauce over each. Garnish each serving with a spoonful of fresh pomegranate seeds.

Yield: 8 servings (3 cups sauce)

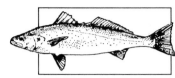

SEA BASS
A firm fish with a mild flavor, low fat content, and firm white meat. It is caught in Atlantic waters from New York to North Carolina. Redfish, striped sea bass, or monkfish will work in sea bass recipes. Red and black sea bass are comparable in flavor, texture and fat content.

RED SEA BASS IN A JAPANESE MARINADE

2 pounds red sea bass, cut into 4-inch-long fillets, skin on
1 teaspoon finely chopped fresh gingerroot
¾ teaspoon finely chopped garlic
¼ cup each: soy sauce, water, and sherry
2 teaspoons sugar
Oil for greasing grill

1. Lay fish in dish with raised sides.
2. In a separate bowl, mix gingerroot, garlic, soy sauce, water, sherry, and sugar.
3. Pour over fish, cover with plastic wrap, and refrigerate for 30 minutes.
4. Put fillets on well-oiled grill, skin side down, over ashen coals. Grill on one side only. Brush leftover marinade on fish 2 or 3 times during grilling. Serve immediately.

Yield: 4 servings

RED SEA BASS WITH REMOULADE SAUCE

REMOULADE SAUCE

1 egg
½ cup vegetable oil
2 tablespoons chopped fresh parsley
2 cloves garlic
2 green onions, cut into 1-inch pieces
1 teaspoon paprika
Dash Tabasco sauce, or to taste

FISH

4 7-ounce red sea bass, sea trout, or
 grouper fillets
Melted butter
White pepper to taste
Oil for greasing grill

   1. *Make sauce:* Using a food processor fitted with steel blade or a blender, process egg until light. With machine running, pour oil through feed tube in a slow, steady stream until it is incorporated. Add remaining sauce ingredients and puree. Place sauce in a covered container and refrigerate until ready to serve.

   2. *Grill bass:* Brush bass fillets with butter and sprinkle with pepper to taste. Place fish on prepared grill and cook for 4 minutes. Check fish and continue cooking about 2–3 minutes or until it begins to flake easily when tested with a fork. Place fish on individual plates. Ladle sauce over bass and serve.

Yield: 4 servings

ASIAN-STYLE SEA BASS

Red snapper and rockfish also work well in this recipe. Serve it with rice, stir-fried vegetables, and vanilla ice cream topped with minced sweet Oriental ginger, including syrup, for dessert.

MARINADE
4 tablespoons light soy sauce
5 tablespoons light brown sugar
1 teaspoon Oriental sesame oil
5 tablespoons fresh lime juice
3 cloves garlic, minced
3 quarter-sized slices fresh gingerroot,
    minced
¾ teaspoon red pepper flakes

FISH
8 8-ounce sea bass, scaled and cleaned,
    with heads and tails left on
2 limes, each cut into 8 slices
Oil for greasing grill
1 bunch scallions, trimmed

1. *Make the marinade:* Combine the marinade ingredients, and rub on both sides of the fish; let stand for 20 minutes.

2. *Grill the fish:* Place two lime slices in the cavity of each fish. Put the fish on the prepared grill and grill for 4–5 minutes. Turn with long-handled tongs and grill until done. At the same time, grill scallions 1–2 minutes on each side. Transfer the fish to individual plates and serve immediately with scallions.

Yield: 8 servings

SEA SCALLOPS

Scallops are mollusks dredged from the coastal waters. The edible muscle is a round, white, delicate, and delicious food. Sometimes the red roe is available. These bivalve mollusks are usually shelled by the time they come to market. If you do find some in the shell, you can put them on the grill to open, but since their shells are thin, set them on a layer of seaweed or leaves or put some other protective material on the grill. If you cannot get scallops fresh, the frozen are quite acceptable—even more so if they are marinated in our basic marinade (see Index).

Tiny bay scallops are sweeter and more delicious than are the larger sea scallops, but the larger ones are more fun to eat. In this chapter we include a skewered combination of bay scallops and large, marshmallow-size sea scallops that is guaranteed to delight your guests.

Remember that scallops are delicate and should be served only with delicate sauces and butters. Scallops also take well to marinades.

SEA SCALLOPS
WITH DRAWN BUTTER

2 pounds sea scallops
Oil for greasing fish basket or grill
Clarified butter (see Index)

2 lemons, quartered
Parsley or watercress sprigs for garnish
(optional)

1. *Grill scallops:* Brush scallops with oil and arrange them in a single layer in a fish basket or place them on the prepared grill. Cook for 2 to 3 minutes on each side or until scallops have lost their translucent appearance.

2. While scallops grill, prepare clarified butter. Serve scallops immediately, dividing them among guests. Garnish each serving with lemon wedges and a few sprigs of parsley or watercress if desired. Drizzle butter over scallops at the table.

Yield: 4 servings

SEA SCALLOP
ANTIPASTO KABOBS

The following grilled antipasto works beautifully as a main course too. To serve as an entree, double the ingredients, serving 2 skewers each.

1 2-ounce chunk prosciutto cut into 4
   skewer-size pieces
4 scallions, white parts only, each cut
   into 3 lengths
24 sea scallops
4 jarred pepperoncini
4 large pitted black olives
4 canned artichoke hearts, well drained
4 small, firm Italian tomatoes
1 2-ounce piece Genoa salami or
   cappicola, cut into 4 skewer-sized
   pieces
¼ cup extra-virgin olive oil
2 large cloves garlic, chopped fine
Oil for greasing grill

1. *Marinate kabobs:* Thread all ingredients except oil and garlic onto four skewers in alternating fashion. Lay skewers on platter. Mix olive oil and garlic and brush skewered ingredients liberally with mixture, making sure that canned artichoke hearts get a liberal dose of oil-garlic mixture inside. Let sit at room temperature for 20 minutes, brushing with mixture occasionally.

2. *Grill kabobs:* Lay skewers on prepared grill. Grill 3 to 4 minutes on each side, until scallops are done and remaining ingredients are charred on the edges.

Yield: 4 appetizer servings

SCALLOPS ON A BED OF PEPPERS WITH AVOCADO SAUCE

❦

AVOCADO SAUCE
1 large avocado, peeled and pitted
1 teaspoon fresh lemon juice
2 teaspoons mayonnaise
¼ teaspoon each: salt and cayenne pepper
1 hard-boiled egg, peeled and chopped
1 cup chopped pecans

SCALLOPS
2 green bell peppers, seeded and sliced
   thin
1 tablespoon olive oil
2 red bell peppers, seeded and sliced thin
1½ pounds sea scallops
Oil for greasing grill

1. *Make sauce:* Mash avocado pulp with lemon juice in a mixing bowl. Blend in mayonnaise, salt, cayenne, and egg. stir in chopped pecans.

2. *Prepare peppers:* Brush pepper slices with oil. Grill on both sides until slightly charred. Arrange pepper slices on heated serving platter.

3. *Grill scallops:* Place scallops in a prepared double-hinged fish basket. Brush scallops with oil. Grill scallops 3–4 minutes. Turn basket and continue cooking until scallops begin to turn opaque. Or thread scallops on skewers and turn every 3 minutes until done. Remove scallops and arrange on the bed of peppers. Serve scallops hot and pass avocado sauce at the table.

Yield: 4 servings

SEA SCALLOPS WITH
HOMEMADE TARTAR SAUCE

Be sure to use a grill basket because the scallops could fall through the grill.

TARTAR SAUCE

1 egg, room temperature
1 tablespoon fresh lemon juice
½ cup salad oil
1 teaspoon drained capers, dried with
   paper towels
4 pinches cayenne pepper
¼ teaspoon salt
2 tablespoons finely chopped fresh parsley
   (stems removed)
1 teaspoon finely chopped green onion,
   green part only
1 tablespoon finely chopped sweet pickle,
   squeezed in paper towel to extract the
   liquid

SCALLOPS

Oil for greasing fish basket
2 pounds sea scallops

1. *Make tartar sauce:* Put egg and lemon juice in food processor or blender container. Blend for 2–3 seconds.

2. Turn motor on again and begin adding oil, drop by drop. After ¼ cup has been added, begin adding oil in a very thin, steady stream, as slowly as possible, but still maintaining a flow of oil.

3. When oil has been added, mixture should be thick. Transfer to medium-sized bowl.

4. Stir in capers, cayenne pepper, salt, parsley, green onion, and sweet pickle. Mix well.

5. *Grill scallops:* Arrange scallops in a single layer in the bottom of a fish basket. Fasten top. Grill over ashen coals about 2 minutes on each side or until scallops are just done.

6. Remove from grill and transfer scallops to large, round, heated serving platter, leaving space in center for bowl of tartar sauce. Serve immediately.

Yield: 4 servings

SEA SCALLOPS WITH ORIENTAL VEGETABLES

1½–1¾ pounds sea scallops

Oil for brushing scallops and greasing fish basket

1 tablespoon peanut oil

½ teaspoon each: garlic powder and ground gingerroot

3 green onions, chopped

4 Chinese mushrooms (available at Oriental food markets), reconstituted for 10 minutes in hot water and drained

¼ cup canned sliced water chestnuts, drained

2 tablespoons soy sauce

1 teaspoon sesame oil

Salt and pepper to taste

1. Brush sea scallops with oil. Arrange scallops in prepared double-hinged fish basket. Grill scallops for 3–4 minutes. Turn over. Continue grilling until scallops become opaque. Place on a heated platter.

2. Heat the 1 tablespoon oil in a wok or a heavy skillet. Sprinkle oil with garlic and ginger. Stir-fry onions in the skillet until soft, about 1 minute. Mix in mushrooms and water chestnuts and stir-fry for 1 minute. Mix in remaining ingredients. Pour vegetables over sea scallops.

Yield: 4 servings

SKEWERED BAY AND
SEA SCALLOPS WITH
HONEY BUTTER

SHELLFISH

2 pounds sea scallops (about 48 large
scallops)
½ pound bay scallops (about 32 small
scallops)
6 10-inch wooden presoaked barbecue
skewers
1 recipe basic marinade (see Index)
Oil for greasing grill

HONEY BUTTER

4 tablespoons honey
10 tablespoons melted butter
1 tablespoon fresh lemon juice
2 tablespoons white wine

1. Arrange sea and bay scallops on skewers in alternating fashion as
follows: two big scallops, three small scallops, two big scallops, three small
scallops, etc. Use big scallops at ends of skewers.

2. *Marinate scallops:* Place skewers on a flat pan with raised sides and
pour marinade over top. Let sit for 1 hour at room temperature, basting
skewers and turning them in marinade often.

3. *Prepare honey butter:* Mix honey, melted butter, lemon juice, and wine
together.

4. *Grill scallops:* Remove skewers from marinade and place on prepared
grill. Cook about 4 minutes or just until scallops have lost their opaque look,
turning skewers once if desired. Serve immediately, passing honey butter to
spoon over scallops.

Yield: 6 servings

CURRIED MARINATED
SEA SCALLOPS

SHELLFISH
2 pounds sea scallops
Oil for greasing grill

MARINADE
1 cup plain yogurt
1 medium onion
6 cloves garlic
¼ cup sugar
2 tablespoons curry powder (Madras, if
*   possible)*
2 tablespoons fresh lemon juice
1 teaspoon cayenne pepper
1 teaspoon salt

GARNISH
Commercial sweetened flaked coconut
1 small jar (approximately 6 ounces)
*   chutney*

1. *Marinate scallops:* Place scallops in plastic bag and set bag in bowl.
Combine marinade ingredients in food processor container. Process until a
coarse puree results. Pour marinade into plastic bag and secure with twister
seal. Turn bag several times, making sure all scallop surfaces touch marinade.
Let sit at room temperature 2 hours or refrigerate 4 hours, turning
occasionally.

2. *Grill scallops:* At serving time, remove scallops from marinade. Place
scallops on prepared grill and cook 2 to 3 minutes on each side, watching
carefully. Transfer to serving platter and serve immediately. Pass bowls of
coconut and chutney for sprinkling.

Yield: 4 servings

SEA SCALLOPS IN AN ALMOND CRUST

1 egg
4 egg whites
2 tablespoons snipped fresh chives
½ teaspoon salt
¼ teaspoon cayenne pepper
8 ounces blanched almonds, chopped fine
   or ground into powder
2 pounds sea scallops
¼ cup sliced almonds
⅓ cup butter
Oil for greasing grill

1. Mix egg, egg whites, chives, salt, and cayenne in a small bowl. Sprinkle ground almonds into a large, flat platter in as thin a layer as possible.

2. Dry scallops on paper towels. Dip scallops into egg mixture, then roll them in ground almonds. Arrange coated scallops in a single layer on a plate and refrigerate for at least 30 minutes.

3. Meanwhile, sprinkle ¼ cup sliced almonds in a single layer on a baking sheet and place in a 350°F oven for about 6 to 8 minutes or until almonds are just beginning to turn golden. Remove from oven immediately and let cool.

4. Melt butter in a small saucepan. Stir in toasted almond slices. Let sit until ready to serve.

5. *Grill scallops:* Arrange scallops carefully on a well-oiled grill. Cook 2 to 3 minutes on each side, turning carefully. Scallops must be watched so the almond coating does not burn.

6. Transfer scallops to serving platter. Spoon melted butter and toasted almond slices into sauceboat. Serve immediately, passing sauce.

Yield: 4 servings

SEA SCALLOPS ON A
BED OF SPINACH

SPINACH

1 10-ounce package frozen spinach,
    chopped fine
3 ounces shallots, chopped fine
1 cup dry white wine
1 tablespoon butter
1 tablespoon flour
1 cup half-and-half
½ teaspoon salt
¼ teaspoon grated nutmeg

SHELLFISH

2 pounds sea scallops
4 10-inch wooden presoaked barbecue
    skewers
Vegetable oil for brushing scallops
Oil for greasing grill

1. Cook spinach according to package directions, then transfer to strainer. Press spinach with the back of a wooden spoon until most of the moisture has been extracted. Spinach should measure 1 scant cup.

2. Meanwhile, place shallots and wine in a small saucepan and simmer until both wine and shallots measure scant ½ cup.

3. Melt butter in a medium saucepan, then add flour and cook for a moment, stirring constantly with a wire whisk, until butter-flour mixture bubbles and is golden. Slowly add half-and-half, stirring constantly with whisk. Continue cooking, whisking frequently, until mixture is smooth and thickened and coats a spoon.

4. Add shallot-wine mixture and spinach to cream sauce. Stir to combine, then add salt and nutmeg. Continue cooking for about 5 minutes.

5. *Grill scallops:* Meanwhile, skewer scallops loosely, then brush with oil on both sides. Place skewers on a heated, well-oiled grill and cook 2 to 3 minutes on each side, or as long as necessary until scallops are cooked through and have lost their translucency.

6. Transfer hot spinach to a large serving platter with slightly raised sides. Unskewer scallops carefully onto spinach, arranging them in an attractive fashion. Serve immediately.

Yield: 4 servings

SEA SCALLOPS WRAPPED IN BACON AND GOAT CHEESE

You will need 2 teaspoons goat cheese and a half-slice of bacon for each scallop in the following dish. If desired, substitute cream cheese or mix equal parts of Roquefort and cream cheese to stuff bacon. Soft feta cheese and chive cream cheese are also good substitutes for goat cheese, although the feta and bacon together are somewhat salty. Half-cooked bacon pieces are also delicious wrapped around shrimp.

> *16 slices bacon*
> *1½–2 cups mild goat cheese, such as*
>   *Montrachet*
> *32 large sea scallops*
> *Round wooden toothpicks*
> *Oil for greasing grill*

1. *Cook bacon:* Place bacon in large frying pan and sauté over low heat 4 to 5 minutes or until half cooked. Drain bacon on paper towels, pressing on all sides to absorb fat. Cut bacon slices in half to yield 32 pieces.

2. *Wrap scallops:* Spread each bacon piece with 2 teaspoons goat cheese. Wrap one piece of bacon with goat cheese around each scallop, using toothpick to secure. Continue wrapping bacon and goat cheese around scallops until all are prepared.

3. *Grill scallops:* Place bacon-wrapped scallops in a single layer on an oiled grill and cook 2 to 3 minutes or until bacon is cooked. Turn and cook on remaining side if necessary. Serve immediately.

Yield: 4 servings

SEA SCALLOPS IN SZECHWAN SAUCE

❧

Use only Oriental sesame oil, as it has the stronger sesame flavor that is characteristic of many Oriental dishes. Do not use the Middle Eastern variety of sesame oil. It is much lighter in color and will not impart the appropriate flavor to Oriental dishes.

SHELLFISH
2 pounds sea scallops
1 recipe basic marinade (see Index)
8 10-inch wooden presoaked barbecue
    skewers,
Oil for greasing grill

SZECHWAN SAUCE
1 1-inch piece fresh gingerroot, peeled and
    quartered
4 large garlic cloves, quartered
2 green onions, cut into pieces
2 tablespoons vegetable oil
½ teaspoon crushed red pepper
3 tablespoons sugar
5 teaspoons Japanese soy sauce
3 tablespoons catsup
2 tablespoons dry white wine
1 teaspoon white vinegar
½ teaspoon Oriental sesame oil

1. *Marinate scallops:* Place scallops in large plastic bag set in bowl. Pour marinade over. Secure with twister seal and turn to make sure that all surfaces of scallops touch marinade. Let sit at room temperature 1 hour, turning occasionally.

2. Fifteen minutes before scallops are ready to be cooked, combine ginger, garlic, and green onion pieces in food processor container and coarsely chop.

3. Thread drained scallops on skewers.

4. *Prepare sauce:* Heat vegetable oil in heavy-bottomed skillet or wok. Then sauté chopped ginger, garlic, and green onion for about 1 minute.

5. Meanwhile combine red pepper, sugar, soy sauce, catsup, wine, vinegar, and sesame oil. Stir this into onion mixture. Simmer 1 more minute.

6. *Grill scallops:* Place scallops on prepared grill and cook about 2 to 3 minutes on each side or until scallops have lost their translucency. Remove from heat and transfer to serving platter. Serve guests 2 skewers each and drizzle a few spoonfuls of sauce over scallops.

Yield: 4 servings

SEA SCALLOPS WITH HOMEMADE JALAPEÑO MAYONNAISE

We suggest you serve this dish with heated French bread.

JALAPEÑO MAYONNAISE

1 large egg or *2 egg yolks, at room*
temperature
2 tablespoons white vinegar
1 teaspoon dry mustard
½ to ¾ cup good-quality olive oil
¼ teaspoon salt
¼ teaspoon white pepper
1 handful fresh parsley, washed, stems
removed
⅓ cup thawed and thoroughly drained
frozen chopped spinach
2 green onions, green part only, cut into
1-inch pieces
2 fresh or canned (packed in vinegar),
jalapeño peppers, seeded

SHELLFISH

2 pounds sea scallops
Oil for greasing fish basket

1. *Prepare jalapeño mayonnaise:* Rinse blender or food processor container and blade with hot water, dry quickly, and replace on motor unit. Place egg or yolks in warmed container, along with vinegar, dry mustard, olive oil, salt, and white pepper. Pulse twice or enough times to combine.

2. Add parsley, spinach, green onion pieces, and jalapeños to mixture. Carefully pulse a few times until mixture is finely chopped but has not dissolved into the mayonnaise. Green pieces should be very discernible.

Transfer to serving bowl and reserve until scallops are cooked.

3. *Grill scallops:* Brush scallops with oil and set on prepared grill in wire fish basket with a narrow grid. Grill scallops 2 to 3 minutes on each side or until they've lost their translucent appearance.

4. Transfer scallops to a heated serving platter. Serve immediately with mayonnaise at room temperature. Use mayonnaise as a dip.

Yield: 4 servings (with 1½ cups sauce)

SEA SCALLOPS WITH ROE, SERVED WITH CREME FRAICHE AND FRESHWATER CAVIAR

The caviar used in this recipe is available from Carolyn Collins Caviar (see Appendix). Serve with a light pasta. Ask your fishmonger for sea scallops with roe.

CREME FRAICHE
1 cup heavy cream
1½ tablespoons buttermilk

SHELLFISH
1½ pounds sea scallops with roe (it isn't necessary for all of the scallops to have the roe)
Melted butter for brushing scallops
Oil for greasing fish basket
12-ounces freshwater caviar

1. *Prepare crème fraîche:* Prepare the crème fraîche the day before it is needed in recipe. Combine heavy cream and buttermilk in a sterilized jar. Leave jar on kitchen counter in a warm area. Turn jar occasionally. Mixture will thicken in about 12 to 16 hours. Refrigerate until ready to use.

2. *Prepare sea scallops:* Gently wash scallops and pat dry with paper toweling. Brush scallops with melted butter.

3. Arrange in prepared fish basket: close basket. Grill scallops for 3 to 4 minutes over medium-hot heat (coals will be mostly ashen). Turn basket and continue cooking until scallops begin to turn opaque. Remember that scallops, like most fish and shellfish, are best slightly undercooked.

4. Remove scallops and arrange on four plates. Drizzle with crème fraîche and top with caviar.

Yield: 4 servings

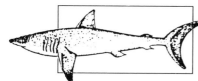

SHARK

Shark is a firm fish; it should be soaked in milk for 1 hour before cooking. Swordfish can be substituted in all shark recipes.

SHARK KABOBS WITH ORANGE AND THYME

Feel free to be creative. Add and change fruits and vegetables as desired. Serve with noodles. Thyme sprinkled on the hot coals adds extra aromatic flavoring.

ORANGE SAUCE
4 tablespoons (½ stick) butter
2 large shallots, minced
1 tablespoon grated orange zest
¼ cup fresh orange juice

KABOBS
2 pounds shark steaks, cut into 1½-inch
    pieces
Milk
2 medium zucchini, cut into 1½-inch
    pieces
12 pearl onions, blanched in boiling water
    for 2 minutes
2 oranges, quartered
Peanut oil
4 tablespoons crumbled dried thyme

1. *Make sauce:* Melt butter in a saucepan over medium heat. Sauté shallots in it until tender, stirring occasionally. Whisk in orange zest and juice. Bring mixture to a boil, stir, and remove from heat. Reheat sauce when ready to serve.

2. *Grill shark kabobs:* Soak shark cubes in milk for 1 hour before grilling. Drain fish and pat dry with paper toweling. Thread 4 10-inch skewers with fish, zucchini, onions, and orange quarters. Brush with peanut oil and sprinkle with 1 tablespoon of the thyme. Sprinkle remaining thyme over hot coals. Grill kabobs, rotating every 3 minutes until shark cubes begin to flake when tested with a fork. Serve on individual plates and allow guests to remove food from individual skewers. Pass warm orange sauce at table.

Yield: 4 servings

SHARK WITH
BARBECUE BUTTER

❧

Serve with warm flour tortillas, grilled red and green pepper slices, and grilled tomatillos or tomatoes. Halibut and tuna may also be used in this recipe.

BARBECUE BUTTER

*½ cup (¼ pound) butter or margarine, at
    room temperature*
1 scallion, minced
2 teaspoons prepared barbecue sauce
3 tablespoons minced cilantro

BARBECUE SAUCE

1½ cups catsup
¾ cup tomato sauce
½ cup cider vinegar
1 teaspoon soy sauce
2 cloves garlic, minced
2 teaspoons Worcestershire sauce
2 teaspoons prepared mustard
½ teaspoon salt
¼ teaspoon freshly ground pepper
2 teaspoons honey
¼ cup white wine (optional)

FISH

2 cups hickory chips
*3 pounds shark steaks, cut into 8 serving
    pieces, about ½–¾ inch thick*
Milk for soaking shark steaks
Oil for brushing fish and greasing grill

1. *Make the barbecue butter:* Soften the butter in a bowl with the back of a wooden spoon. Blend in the scallion, prepared barbecue sauce, and cilantro. Transfer to a 10-inch sheet of waxed paper. Spread the butter 1 inch thick

along the edge of the paper. Roll, jelly roll style, keeping the inch thickness but shaping into a roll. Secure the ends. Refrigerate or freeze until the butter is firm. When ready to serve, unroll, discard paper, and slice butter as necessary.

2. *Make the barbecue sauce:* Combine all barbecue sauce ingredients in a pan and bring to a boil. Reduce the heat to a simmer and continue cooking for 5 minutes, stirring occasionally. Taste and adjust seasonings. Cool, place in a bowl, cover, and refrigerate.

3. Meanwhile, soak the hickory chips in cold water to cover for 1 hour and soak the shark steaks in milk to cover in a shallow glass dish for 1 hour.

4. *Grill the fish:* Drain the fish and pat dry with paper toweling. Drain the hickory chips and sprinkle over the hot coals. Replace the grill. Brush the shark steaks with oil. Grill the fish on the prepared grill for 4–8 minutes. Turn and continue grilling until the fish is just fork-tender.

5. Serve each portion of fish hot with a ½-inch slice of barbecue butter. Pass the warm barbecue sauce and extra butter slices at the table.

Yield: 8 servings (2¾ cups sauce)

SHRIMP

Shrimp are graded according to size and weight by the seafood industry. There are about 30 different grades, which range from the very large (under 5 shrimp per pound) to the very small (72 to 100 per pound). Although large shrimp are sometimes called *prawns*, the American seafood industry frowns on this word, which is descriptive rather than precise.

Shrimp are available everywhere and sold in every possible form: both cooked and raw, both shelled and in the shell. Shrimp are cooked and ready to eat when they turn opaque; be careful not to overcook, for they will become tough.

SHRIMP SATE
WITH PEANUT SAUCE

This dish is very exciting. Serve it as an appetizer or entree. Use Japanese light soy sauce, if possible.

PEANUT SAUCE
1 tablespoon oil
2 tablespoons finely chopped onion
2 large garlic cloves, minced
1 teaspoon peeled and chopped fresh gingerroot
½ teaspoon cayenne pepper
¾ teaspoon salt
⅛ teaspoon ground cumin
2 tablespoons soy sauce
3 tablespoons dark corn syrup
3 tablespoons fresh lemon juice
½ cup peanut butter
6 ounces canned coconut milk

MARINADE
2 tablespoons oil
6 cloves garlic, minced
2 tablespoons finely chopped onion
2 teaspoons turmeric
¼ teaspoon cayenne pepper
1 teaspoon salt
4 tablespoons peanut butter
8 tablespoons fresh lemon juice

SHRIMP
4 dozen medium-sized shrimp, shelled and deveined
Oil for greasing grill
Lemon wedges for garnish

224

1. *Make sauce:* Heat 1 tablespoon oil in skillet. Add 2 tablespoons onion, 2 minced garlic cloves, and ginger and sauté for 3 minutes over low heat. Add ½ teaspoon cayenne, ¾ teaspoon salt, and the cumin. Sauté for 1 minute and transfer to bowl or food processor container.

2. Stir in soy sauce, corn syrup, 3 tablespoons lemon juice, ½ cup peanut butter, and the coconut milk. Mix very well. At serving time, if sauce is too thick, add additional coconut milk or lemon juice to thin to desired dipping consistency (serve at room temperature). Sauce will keep several days in the refrigerator if well covered.

3. *Marinate shrimp:* Thread shrimp onto 8 10-inch skewers and lay in bottom of a large pan with raised sides.

4. Heat oil in a medium-sized skillet. Add garlic, onion, turmeric, cayenne, and salt. Sauté over low heat for about 4 minutes.

5. Transfer to bowl or food processor container and mix with peanut butter and lemon juice. Spoon over skewered shrimp and marinate for 30–60 minutes.

6. *Grill shrimp:* Place shrimp on prepared grill and cook about 1 minute or until done on each side or until slightly charred.

7. Serve shrimp with ample lemon wedges. Pass peanut sauce.

Yield: 4 appetizer servings, with about 1¾ cups sauce

SHRIMP WITH KA'EK
AND ZA'TAR

❧

Ka'ek is a Middle Eastern bread that resembles French and Italian bread, except that it is baked in large, donutlike rings and sprinkled liberally with sesame seeds. In the Middle East, this bread is traditionally made by hand; so if you do not have a food processor, you can make ka'ek *by following any standard yeast bread directions for mixing yeast with water and sugar, then stirring in remaining ingredients and kneading until smooth and silky. The version we've worked out here uses the food processor, and the bread is mixed in half-recipe batches because it is hard for food processors to accommodate 4 cups of flour all at once. We have also added untraditional egg yolks because we like the added richness. If you are a strict traditionalist and wish to make the bread without the egg, simply add a few teaspoons of extra water to compensate. Remember, ingredients in the directions are given in half amounts for two batches.*

Middle Easterners eat their ka'ek *in a fascinating way. They break off a piece of the* ka'ek, *then dip the torn edge of the bread into two small dishes—first into a bowl of good-quality olive oil, then into a flat dish filled with a spice mixture called* za'tar. *Za'tar is a greenish herb mixture that combines thyme, marjoram, and oregano, along with salt. The commercially sold* za'tar *mixtures also contain sesame seeds. You can make* za'tar *at home by mixing 2 tablespoons each of these ground herbs, then adding salt to taste along with a teaspoon or two of sesame seeds. Or you can buy the* za'tar *at any local Middle Eastern market. There's a reddish herb mixture that is also called* za'tar, *but this reddish mixture of thyme and sumac is not nearly as palatable for Westerners as is the greenish* za'tar. *For information on where to order* za'tar *by mail, see the Appendix.*

We have added grilled shrimp to this charming ritual. Dip the shrimp in the za'tar *and oil along with the* ka'ek. *We also suggest serving this as an appetizer. If you wish to serve it as a main dish, add at least one more type of Middle Eastern dip to serve along with the* za'tar.

KA'EK (SESAME-TOPPED BREAD RINGS)

2 ¼-ounce packages dry yeast
1 tablespoon sugar
½ cup lukewarm water (just warm to the touch)
4 cups all-purpose flour
1 teaspoon salt
2 egg yolks
1 tablespoon oil
½ cup milk
¼ cup water

SHRIMP

3 pounds shrimp, shelled and deveined
1 recipe basic marinade (see Index)
1 bowl extra-virgin olive oil
1 large flat dish filled with za'tar
Oil for greasing grill

TOPPING

1 egg, lightly beaten
2–3 tablespoons sesame seeds

1. *Make* ka'ek: Pour 1 package dry yeast into small bowl, add 1½ teaspoons sugar, then add ¼ cup lukewarm water and stir to combine. Let sit 5 to 10 minutes or until yeast becomes active.

2. Place 2 cups flour and ½ teaspoon salt in food processor container and pulse once to combine. In a separate bowl, mix 1 egg yolk, 1½ teaspoons oil, ¼ cup milk, and 2 tablespoons water.

3. Add yeast mixture to flour. Pulse two or three times to combine. Then turn on motor and pour egg yolk/milk mixture through feed tube. Process until a smooth, silky dough is formed, then continue processing 45 seconds longer.

4. Remove dough from food processor container. Squeeze it a few times, then set aside for a moment.

5. Repeat steps, making a second batch of *ka'ek*. Squeeze both balls of dough together and knead a few times to combine.

6. Place ball of dough in a large, lightly oiled bowl. Cover loosely with a sheet of plastic wrap or place a dish towel over top of dough. Let rise in a warm place for about 45 minutes, until doubled in bulk.

7. Punch dough down, remove from bowl, and squeeze dough a few times. Divide dough into four equal portions (8 to 9 ounces each). Roll and squeeze each portion into a rope about 11 to 12 inches long. Form into a ring, overlapping the ends slightly. Use a few drops of water to act as glue between overlapped ends, pressing to seal. Cover dough loosely with dish towel or plastic wrap and place on a baking sheet that has been either well oiled or topped with a sheet of parchment paper.

8. Let rings sit in a warm place until doubled in bulk.

9. *Marinate shrimp:* Place shrimp in a plastic bag, pour marinade in to cover, and secure with twister seal. Turn bag several times to make sure that all shrimp surfaces touch the marinade. Place bag in a bowl and let sit at room temperature for 1 hour.

10. *While shrimp marinates, make* ka'ek *topping:* Beat egg and use an egg-dipped pastry brush to paint top and sides of one *ka'ek* ring. Sprinkle ring with 1½ teaspoons of sesame seeds or more if desired. Repeat with remaining dough rings, egg, and sesame seeds.

11. Place baking sheet in a 400°F oven and immediately turn heat down to 350°F. Bake *ka'ek* about 30 minutes or until tops of rings are golden brown and loaves sound hollow when tapped. Let cool on wire rack. Place *ka'ek*, olive oil, and *za'tar* on dinner table.

12. *Grill shrimp:* Remove shrimp from marinade and place on prepared grill. Grill shrimp 2 to 3 minutes on each side or until they have lost their translucency and have a cooked appearance. Transfer to serving platter and bring to table immediately.

13. Show guests how to dip both the shrimp and the hunks of *ka'ek* first in the olive oil, then in the *za'tar*.

Yield: 4 appetizer servings

CAJUN SHRIMP

1½ pounds large shrimp
1 tablespoon paprika
¼ teaspoon each: salt and freshly ground
   pepper
1 clove garlic, minced
4 tablespoons (½ stick) butter, melted
Oil for greasing grill
Lettuce leaves for garnish
Parsley sprigs for garnish

1. *Butterfly shrimp:* Leaving shell intact, slit underside of shrimp lengthwise, but don't cut all the way through. Remove legs.

2. *Marinate shrimp:* Combine paprika, salt, pepper, and garlic, and stir into melted butter. Pour mixture into a shallow dish. Add shrimp and stir to coat evenly. Marinate shrimp for 1 hour, turning once.

3. *Grill shrimp:* Shake off and reserve any extra marinade and arrange shrimp on prepared grill or in a double-hinged grill basket. Grill shrimp for 3–4 minutes, brush with reserved marinade, and continue cooking 1–2 minutes or until done. Arrange shrimp decoratively on a plate over lettuce leaves, garnish with parsley, and serve hot.

Yield: 4 servings

SHRIMP TOSTADAS WITH GUACAMOLE

＊

GUACAMOLE

2 large ripe avocados

2 teaspoons fresh lime juice

½ teaspoon salt

2 green onions, cut into rough 1-inch
lengths, both green and white parts

1 small tomato, peeled and quartered

1 clove garlic, halved

1 small fresh hot chili pepper, halved
lengthwise and seeded

SHRIMP AND TOSTADAS

Oil for frying tortillas

8 fresh corn tortillas

32 cleaned and deveined, medium-sized
shrimp

Oil for greasing grill

1 16-ounce can refried beans

2 tablespoons oil

1 recipe red salsa (see Index)

Small bowls of each of the following:
chopped lettuce, chopped onion,
chopped queso fresco (Mexican cheese),
and chopped fresh cilantro or parsley

1. *Make guacamole:* Cut avocados in half and remove pits. Scoop avocado out of shell and place in container of food processor. Add lime juice; process until pureed.

2. Add salt, onion, tomato, garlic, and small hot pepper to avocado mixture; process again until finely pureed. Transfer to small bowl. Add avocado pits to bowl (they will help retard discoloration). Remove pits before bringing bowl to table.

3. *Fry tortillas:* Heat 1 inch of oil in a shallow 8″ or 9″ skillet. Slide tortillas one by one into oil and fry on each side until just golden. Remove immediately; drain on paper towels.

4. *Grill shrimp and prepare beans:* Meanwhile, thread shrimp onto 8 10-inch skewers and grill over ashen coals. While shrimp cook, transfer refried beans from can to saucepan, add 2 tablespoons oil, stir well, and heat over low heat.

5. When shrimp are cooked, remove from skewers, transfer to small dish, and bring to table.

6. Guests should make their own tostadas: Spread refried beans on top of a fried tostada. Arrange shrimp over this. Spoon red salsa and guacamole over top of shrimp. Then add a little shredded lettuce, chopped onion, and grated fresh Mexican cheese over the top. Top with some chopped fresh cilantro or parsley.

Yield: 4 servings

SHRIMP FAJITAS

Tuna and marlin also work well in this recipe. Serve with grilled corn on the cob. To grill, pull husks back, remove silk, replace husks, brush with oil, and grill until done to taste (1–2 minutes per side).

FAJITA SAUCE

2 tablespoons oil
1 red onion, sliced thin
3 cloves garlic, minced
4 tablespoons dark brown sugar
2½ tablespoons cider vinegar
½ cup catsup
1 cup beer
⅛ teaspoon salt
1 teaspoon Worcestershire sauce

SHELLFISH

Oil for greasing fish basket
4 limes, sliced thin
1½ pounds large shrimp, peeled and
  deveined
½ teaspoon red pepper flakes
½ teaspoon paprika
4 large onions, sliced thin
Good-quality olive oil for brushing onions
Salt and freshly ground pepper to taste
8 flour tortillas

1. *Make the sauce:* Heat the bacon drippings in a saucepan. Add the red onion and garlic and sauté for 1 minute. Stir in the sugar, vinegar, catsup, beer, salt, and Worcestershire sauce; reduce the heat to a simmer and continue cooking for 10 minutes.

2. *Grill the shrimp:* Arrange the lime slices on one side of a prepared fish basket. Put shrimp over and around the lime and sprinkle with the red pepper flakes and paprika. Close the basket. Grill on each side for about 2–4 minutes, until the shrimp no longer look translucent. Don't overcook shrimp as they get tough. Brush the onions with oil and sprinkle with salt and pepper. Grill for about 2 minutes on each side or until done.

3. Place the grilled shrimp on a heated serving platter and drizzle with the sauce. Serve with the grilled onions and tortillas that have been warmed on the grill for 2–3 minutes.

4. Have each guest place a tortilla on his or her plate, arrange shrimp on left side of the tortilla, and cover with onion slices. Roll tortilla from left to right.

Yield: 8 servings (1½ cups sauce)

SESAME-COATED SHRIMP WITH HONEY

3 large eggs, well beaten
1½ cups sesame seeds
3 pounds shrimp, shelled and deveined
Oil for greasing grill
1 cup honey

1. Place eggs in bowl and beat well. Pour sesame seeds into a large heavy-bottomed frying pan and place over medium heat. Let seeds heat slightly, then watch carefully, stirring with wooden spoon until seeds start to take on a light brown color (you will smell this before you see it). Pour seeds into large, flat dish and allow to cool sufficiently to handle.

2. Dry shrimp well with paper towels. Dip shrimp in beaten egg, then in sesame seeds. Arrange sesame-coated shrimp on a large platter in a single layer and refrigerate for at least 30 minutes.

3. Place shrimp on hot, well-oiled grill and cook about 3 minutes on each side or until shrimp have lost their translucent appearance. Transfer to serving platter and serve immediately, passing honey. Spoon only a thin stream of honey over sesame shrimp.

Yield: 6 servings

MARINATED SHRIMP WITH FIVE-MINUTE TUNA DUNK

※

The following dip is made from ingredients that can be kept in the cupboard for use as a fast, last-minute sauce. Serve with heated French bread.

SHELLFISH
3 pounds shrimp, shelled and deveined
1 recipe basic marinade (see Index)
Oil for greasing grill

SAUCE
2 cloves garlic, peeled and quartered
3 tablespoons red wine vinegar
1 6½-ounce can white albacore tuna, drained
4 anchovy fillets
½ teaspoon drained capers
8 tablespoons good-quality olive oil
¼ cup water
2 tablespoons drained capers (or more if desired) for sprinkling on top of dip and serving at table

1. Place cleaned shrimp in plastic bag and set plastic bag in bowl. Pour marinade into plastic bag over shrimp and use a twister seal to close bag. Turn bag several times, making certain that all sides of shrimp touch marinade. Let sit at room temperature for 1 hour, turning occasionally.

2. *Prepare sauce:* Place garlic, vinegar, tuna, anchovies, ½ teaspoon capers, olive oil, and water in food processor container. Process until mixture is creamy. Transfer to serving bowl. Sprinkle with 2 tablespoons capers or use more if desired. Let sit until ready to serve.

3. *Grill shrimp:* Remove shrimp from marinade and arrange in a single layer on prepared grill. Cook 2 to 3 minutes on each side or until shrimp has lost its translucent appearance. Remove from heat and transfer to large serving platter. Serve immediately with tuna sauce as dip. Pass additional capers at table if desired.

Yield: 6 servings (with about 1½ cups tuna sauce)

SHRIMP IN A GARLIC MARINADE

❧

SHELLFISH
3 pounds shrimp, shelled and deveined
Oil for greasing fish basket

MARINADE
¾ cup imported good-quality mild olive oil
6 tablespoons fresh lemon juice
½ small onion, quartered
4 large cloves garlic, quartered
½ teaspoon salt
½ teaspoon freshly ground pepper

DRAWN BUTTER
1 recipe clarified butter (see Index)
4 garlic cloves, peeled and mashed
  (optional)

1. Place plastic bag in large bowl and fill bag with shrimp.
2. *Prepare marinade:* Place marinade ingredients in food processor container. Process until combined and onion and garlic are chopped fine. Pour into plastic bag over shrimp and secure with twister seal. Turn bag a few times, making sure that all surfaces of shrimp touch marinade. Let sit at room temperature for 1 hour, turning occasionally.
3. Prepare clarified butter. If desired, add a peeled, mashed garlic clove to each drawn butter serving as soon as it has been skimmed of the top foam. Remove garlic before serving.
4. Arrange drained shrimp in a single layer in prepared wire fish basket. Grill 3 to 4 minutes on each side or until shrimp appears cooked. Transfer to serving platter. Serve with drawn butter.

Yield: 6 servings

SHRIMP GRILLED ON A
BED OF TARRAGON

This dish is best prepared in the fall, when herbs are plentiful. Serve shrimp plain, tossed in your favorite pasta salad, or on a salad of Bibb lettuce and yellow cherry tomatoes.

MARINADE
½ cup good-quality olive oil
3 tablespoons fresh lime juice
1 bay leaf
1 clove garlic, minced

SHELLFISH
1½ pounds medium-large shrimp (21–25
*   per pound), peeled, deveined, and*
*   washed*
Oil for greasing grill
3 cups fresh tarragon
½ teaspoon fennel seeds

1. *Marinate shrimp:* Combine olive oil, lime juice, bay leaf, and garlic in a shallow glass bowl or pie plate. Pat shrimp dry, arrange in marinade, and marinate for 1 hour, turning after 30 minutes. Drain shrimp.

2. *Grill shrimp:* Arrange a bed of tarragon on prepared grill. Place shrimp on the tarragon. Sprinkle shrimp with fennel. Some of the leaves will fall into the grill on the hot coals, adding their own special essence to the shrimp. Turn shrimp after 2 minutes. Continue grilling for 2 minutes or until shrimp are cooked to taste.

Yield: 4–5 servings

SHRIMP IN A KOREAN-STYLE MARINADE

SHELLFISH

3 pounds shrimp, shelled and deveined
Oil for greasing fish basket

KOREAN MARINADE

⅓ cup Japanese soy sauce
⅓ cup water
⅓ cup Oriental dark sesame oil
2 tablespoons sugar
5 garlic cloves, peeled and halved
1 2-inch-long piece fresh gingerroot, peeled and quartered
2 teaspoons sesame seeds

1. Place shrimp in a large plastic bag and set bag in a large bowl.

2. *Prepare marinade:* Put soy sauce, water, sesame oil, sugar, garlic, and ginger in food processor or blender container and process until garlic and ginger are chopped fine. (If you do not own a food processor, put garlic through press and chop ginger fine by hand).

3. Pour mixture into plastic bag over shrimp and close bag with twister seal. Turn bag a few times so all surfaces of shrimp are exposed to marinade. Let sit at room temperature 30 minutes, turning bag often.

4. Sprinkle sesame seeds in a single layer in a small frying pan and place over medium heat. Watch carefully. In a moment or two, seeds will start to brown (you will smell this as it starts to happen). Stir seeds with a wooden spoon and remove pan from heat. Allow seeds to cool in pan, then transfer to tiny serving bowl.

5. *Grill shrimp:* Arrange drained shrimp in a single layer in prepared fish basket and fasten top as tightly as possible. Place on hot grill and cook about 3 to 4 minutes on each side or until shrimp have turned red and the meat is no longer translucent.

6. Transfer shrimp from basket to serving platter. Sprinkle toasted sesame seeds over top of shrimp. Serve immediately.

Yield: 6 servings

SHRIMP IN AN INDONESIAN MARINADE

❧

This recipe calls for shrimp paste, an inexpensive Oriental shrimp concentrate that comes in a small jar with a screw top and stores in the refrigerator. Shrimp paste is similar to anchovy paste, except that it is much less strongly flavored. It does add an important quality to the flavor of certain dishes. If you have an Indonesian or Oriental market nearby, buy your shrimp paste there. If not, you'll find mail-order sources of shrimp paste in the Appendix.

SHELLFISH
3 pounds shrimp, peeled and deveined
Oil for greasing fish basket

INDONESIAN MARINADE
3 tablespoons fresh lemon juice
6 tablespoons water
1 tablespoon sugar
½ teaspoon salt
*3 small fresh hot chilies, peeled, seeded,
    and quartered*
¾ teaspoon shrimp paste
6 cloves garlic, peeled and quartered

1. Place shrimp in plastic bag and set bag in bowl.

2. *Prepare marinade:* Mix marinade ingredients in food processor or blender container. Process until a coarse paste results. (If you have no food processor, chop everything as fine as possible and shake together in a small jar with a lid.)

3. Pour marinade into plastic bag over shrimp and secure with twister seal. Shake and turn bag until all surfaces of shrimp have come in contact with the marinade. Let sit at room temperature 30 minutes, turning bag occasionally.

4. *Grill shrimp:* Empty plastic bag into bowl and arrange shrimp in a single layer in prepared fish basket with top. Grill about 5 minutes on one side or until shrimp are no longer translucent and they have a grilled appearance. While shrimp grill, baste at least once with marinade remaining in bottom of bowl. Turn basket and grill 3 to 4 minutes or until other side also has a slightly grilled look. Transfer shrimp from wire basket to large serving plate with raised sides. Serve immediately.

Yield: 6 servings

SHRIMP WITH FONDUE

❧

Serve with thick slices of crusty French bread.

FONDUE
1 pound Swiss cheese
1 clove garlic, minced
¼ teaspoon grated nutmeg
2 tablespoons dry white wine (or to taste)
1 tablespoon kirschwasser
4 fondue forks

SHELLFISH
4 pounds large shrimp, shelled and
  deveined
Oil for greasing grill or fish basket

1. *Make fondue:* Grate cheese. Combine cheese, garlic, and nutmeg in top of a double boiler over simmering water or in a fondue pot over heat. Cook, stirring often, until smooth. Stir in white wine and kirschwasser. Keep warm until ready to serve. Transfer to serving bowl.

2. *Grill shrimp:* Grill shrimp on prepared grill or in a double-hinged fish basket for 2 to 3 minutes, turn, and continue cooking 1 to 2 minutes or until done.

3. Arrange shrimp on a large serving platter at the table with the cheese fondue in the center, within easy reach of guests. Using fondue forks, dip the grilled shrimp into the fondue.

Yield: 8 servings

SHRIMP WITH BAGNA CAUDA

Bagna cauda *is a traditional Italian sauce and ritual in which cold sliced vegetables are dipped into a hot anchovy sauce. The vegetables usually served in Italy are cardoons, celery, peppers, fennel, cabbage, cauliflower, and small Italian tomatoes. The dip is traditionally made of crushed garlic, anchovies, butter, and olive oil, but local variations include cream, wine, or truffles. Our version is made with sour cream, but you can substitute sour half-and-half, if desired. If you wish, serve a platter of vegetables for dipping along with the shrimp and pass heated French bread.*

SHELLFISH
3 pounds shrimp, shelled and deveined
1 recipe basic marinade (see Index)
Oil for greasing grill or fish basket

SAUCE
4 tablespoons butter
4 tablespoons extra-virgin olive oil
6 large cloves garlic, peeled and smashed
1 2-ounce can flat anchovy fillets, drained
    and chopped very fine
1 cup sour cream at room temperature

1. Place cleaned shrimp in a plastic bag. Pour marinade over shrimp and secure bag with twister seal. Let sit at room temperature for 1 hour.

2. *Prepare sauce:* Heat butter, oil, garlic, and anchovies together in a small saucepan over medium heat until butter is melted and mixture is just about to simmer.

3. Spoon mixture into blender or food processor container. Add sour cream. Process until smooth. Keep warm until ready to serve; then transfer to one large dipping bowl or individual dipping bowls.

4. *Grill shrimp:* Remove shrimp from marinade and arrange on grill or in a fish basket in a single layer. Grill shrimp 2 to 3 minutes on each side or until they have lost their translucent quality. Transfer shrimp to heated serving platter and serve immediately, using warm bagna cauda as a dip.

Yield: 4 servings (with 1½ cups sauce)

PRAWNS ON THE BARBI

❧

Despite what you might think, Australians do not put shrimp on the barbi. They put prawns on the barbi, which is what large shrimp are called down under. Giant, five-inch prawns—the ones most commonly put on Australian barbis—are called king prawns. *Australian barbecues too, are different from American-style barbecues; in Australia, most barbecues are not grids, but are instead solid plates of metal set over a wood fire. According to Ann Mickelson, Information Assistant at the Australian Consulate General's office in Chicago, "Most Australians would use a dipping sauce with prawns on the barbi. This might be something like sour cream or yogurt flavored with dill and cucumber; or it might be an Indonesian-style dipping sauce—one with hot peppers added to make it hot. Australians are very innovative cooks and not only cook dishes from many different cuisines (particularly the surrounding ones, such as Indonesia and Malaysia), but also tend to use whatever is fresh and in season." Some Aussies forgo the sauce entirely, though, and just marinate the shrimp in honey before putting it on the barbi. Although we have included a recipe for Indonesian shrimp with a peanut dipping sauce in this book, we couldn't resist adding this one, which is hotter and entirely different from the other recipe.*

SHELLFISH
3 pounds largest shrimp
Oil for brushing shrimp and greasing grill

HOT INDONESIAN PEANUT
DIPPING SAUCE
¾ cup peanut butter
4 cloves garlic, peeled and quartered
3 tablespoons Japanese soy sauce
3 tablespoons fresh lemon juice
1 2-inch piece fresh gingerroot, peeled and
  quartered
2 teaspoons sugar
1 teaspoon crushed red pepper
1 fresh jalapeño pepper, peeled, seeded,
  and quartered
6 tablespoons water

1. With a sharp knife, split shrimp shells along the back and remove the dark vein under running water. Do not remove shells. Place shrimp in large plastic bag and set bag in large bowl.

2. *Prepare dipping sauce:* Place sauce ingredients in a food processor or blender container and process until coarsely pureed. Transfer to a serving bowl or use four individual dipping bowls.

3. *Grill shrimp:* Brush shrimp with oil and place on prepared grill. Cook giant shrimp about 4 minutes on each side, watching very carefully so shrimp are removed from grill at exact point of doneness. Transfer to serving platter and serve immediately with dipping sauce.

Yield: 6 servings (with 1½ cups sauce)

GARLIC·STUFFED SHRIMP, THAI STYLE

Three different ethnic cuisines use the commercial bottled fish sauce called for in this recipe. It is known as nam pla *in Thai food stores,* nuoc mam *in Vietnamese food stores and* tuk trey *in Cambodian food stores (or see Appendix). Although bottled fish sauce sounds like it would taste and smell just awful, it is actually very mild in scent and flavor and adds substantially to the final taste of the dish.*

FILLING

6 tablespoons very finely chopped fresh garlic (chop by hand; do not use a blender or food processor)

1 cup firmly packed fresh bread crumbs (made in blender)

6 teaspoons nam pla

1½ teaspoons freshly ground pepper

⅛ teaspoon salt

¼ cup vegetable oil

SHELLFISH

3 pounds large shrimp, shelled, deveined, and butterflied

Oil for brushing shrimp and greasing grill

1. *Prepare filling:* Combine finely chopped garlic, bread crumbs, *nam pla*, pepper, and salt in a small bowl and mix together well.

2. Heat ¼ cup oil in a small skillet over very low heat and fry *nam pla* mixture very slowly, stirring often with a wooden spoon until it turns golden brown; this should take about 15 minutes.

3. Stuff each shrimp with a small amount of mixture, securing with toothpick, if necessary. Reserve extra filling.

4. *Grill shrimp:* Brush stuffed shrimp with oil lightly on both sides, using a pastry brush, and arrange on prepared grill. Cook shrimp 2 to 3 minutes on each side or until shrimp have lost their translucent appearance and are slightly browned on the edges.

5. Meanwhile, heat remaining filling and transfer to serving bowl. Remove shrimp from grill and transfer to serving platter. Serve immediately, passing bowl of filling to sprinkle over shrimp.

Yield: 6 servings

EAST INDIAN SHRIMP
IN A TANDOORI MARINADE

*4 pounds medium-sized shrimp, shelled
   and deveined*
*16 ounces (2 8-ounce cartons) plain
   yogurt*
6 tablespoons fresh lemon juice
*1¼ teaspoons each: cayenne pepper,
   turmeric, and curry powder*
4 teaspoons paprika
½ teaspoon salt
2 teaspoons finely minced or pressed garlic
*2 teaspoons peeled and finely minced fresh
   gingerroot*
Oil for greasing grill
*Lemon wedges and chopped onions for
   garnish*

1. Thread shrimp on 8 10-inch skewers and lay skewers on a jelly roll
sheet or any pan that will hold them in one layer.

2. *Marinate shrimp:* In a small bowl, mix yogurt, lemon juice, cayenne
pepper, turmeric, curry powder, paprika, salt, garlic, and ginger. Spoon
yogurt mixture over skewered shrimp, covering completely. Slip into a plastic
bag and refrigerate at least 6 hours.

3. *Grill shrimp:* Grill skewered shrimp over ashen coals for 3–4 minutes.
Turn and continue cooking, about 3 minutes, until done. Serve immediately
with lemon wedges and chopped onion.

Yield: 8 servings

MARINATED SHRIMP WITH THREE MIDDLE EASTERN DIPS

🌿

The combination of three Middle Eastern dips and marinated shrimp makes an interesting Middle Eastern menu. Sesame seed paste is available at Middle Eastern shops (or see Appendix for mail-order sources).

YOGURT CHEESE DIP
2 cups plain yogurt
1 clove garlic, quartered
1 tablespoon olive oil
¼ teaspoon salt
¼ teaspoon freshly ground pepper
1 cucumber, peeled, seeded, chopped, then wrung out in a kitchen towel to extract as much liquid as possible
1 teaspoon fresh lemon juice
6 walnut halves for garnish

SHRIMP
3 pounds large shrimp, shelled and deveined
1 recipe basic marinade (see Index)
Oil for greasing grill

BABA GHANOUJ (EGGPLANT PUREE DIP)
1 medium eggplant, peeled with vegetable peeler and cut into thin slices
Salt
4 cloves garlic, quartered
2 tablespoons good-quality mild olive oil
¼ cup fresh lemon juice
¼ cup tahini (sesame seed paste)
1 small handful parsley sprigs, stems removed
Fresh pomegranate seeds for garnish

TAHINI DIPPING SAUCE (SESAME SEED PASTE DIP)
½ cup tahini
⅓–½ cup fresh lemon juice (depending on degree of tartness desired)
2 cloves garlic, quartered
1 cup water
1 teaspoon sugar
1 whole bunch parsley, stems removed
4–5 Calamata olives (or similar salted Mediterranean-style black olives) for garnish

1. *Prepare yogurt:* Lay a double thickness of cheesecloth or a thin piece of muslin in a colander so that the edges overlap and spoon yogurt into cheesecloth. Cover top of yogurt with edges of cloth. Set colander in a flat pan with raised sides and refrigerate for 6 to 24 hours. Yogurt will drain as it

sits, getting thicker and thicker. (After 24 hours it will have shrunk to approximately half its original volume. Six hours of draining time will yield 1⅔ cups yogurt.)

2. *Marinate shrimp:* Place shrimp in a plastic bag in a large bowl. Pour basic marinade over shrimp and close bag with twister seal. Turn bag several times, making certain that all sides of shrimp touch marinade. Let sit at room temperature for 1 hour.

3. *Prepare baba ghanouj:* Salt eggplant slices lightly on both sides and arrange in a single layer on paper towels. Let sit 30 minutes or until enough bitter juices have run out to discolor towels. Transfer eggplant slices to a foil-covered baking sheet in a single layer. Bake 20 to 30 minutes at 350°F, until eggplant has softened and has a cooked appearance.

4. Quarter eggplant slices and put into food processor container. Add garlic, olive oil, lemon juice, tahini, and parsley sprigs. Process to combine, making a coarse puree. Transfer to an attractive serving bowl and sprinkle with pomegranate seeds. (If you have no food processor, simply chop everything fine and combine.) This will yield 1¾ cups baba ghanouj.

5. *Prepare tahini dipping sauce:* Place tahini, lemon juice, garlic, water, and sugar in food processor. Process until a coarse puree results, adding more water if needed to make a coarse paste that is fluid enough for dipping. Add parsley and process only enough to combine so green flecks of parsley remain in dish. (If you don't have a food processor, chop everything fine and combine.)

6. Transfer tahini dipping sauce to an attractive serving dish and arrange 4 or 5 Calamata olives on top for garnish. This dish can also be garnished with toasted sesame seeds. This will yield 1½ cups tahini dipping sauce.

7. *Make yogurt cheese dip:* Discard liquid in pan under colander. Place garlic, olive oil, salt, pepper, cucumber, and lemon juice in food processor and process until pureed. Remove from processor and stir in drained yogurt, mixing well. (If you have no food processor, chop everything and stir into drained yogurt.) Transfer to serving bowl and garnish with walnut halves.

8. *Grill shrimp:* Arrange shrimp in a single layer on prepared grill or in a grill basket. Grill 2 to 3 minutes on each side or until shrimp appear done. Serve immediately with the three Middle Eastern dips.

Yield: 6 servings

CHICAGO-STYLE SHRIMP

Also serve rolls, romaine lettuce with French dressing, and fresh pineapple chunks.

GARLIC CRUMB TOPPING
*¼ cup (½ stick) butter or a combination
  of butter and margarine
¼ teaspoon salt
⅛ teaspoon cayenne pepper
¼ teaspoon paprika
2 cloves garlic, minced
½ cup fresh bread crumbs, ground fine
3 tablespoons minced fresh parsley
1 tablespoons dry sherry*

SHELLFISH
*Oil for greasing fish basket
4 large lemons or limes, sliced thin
3 pounds large or jumbo shrimp, peeled
  and deveined*

1. *Make the topping:* Melt the butter in a heavy skillet over medium heat. Mix in salt, cayenne, paprika, and garlic. Toss with bread crumbs, parsley, and sherry. Cook only until ingredients are combined; reserve.

2. *Grill the shrimp:* Use a prepared fish basket or grill rack or soaked and drained wooden barbecue skewers. Arrange the lemon or lime slices on one side of the basket. Place shrimp over lime and secure the basket shut. If using a grill screen, arrange shrimp randomly with lime slices over screen, turning occasionally as you grill. Or thread lemon or lime slices with shrimp on skewers, turning as you grill. Cook only until the shrimp are done, approximately 4 minutes; do not overcook as shrimp tend to get tough. To serve, place the shrimp on a heated serving dish and top with the garlic crumb mixture; serve immediately.

Yield: 8 servings

SHRIMP WITH LOW-CALORIE SPICY TOMATO DRESSING

Also serve oatmeal muffins or bread, grilled corn, fresh fruit for dessert.

LOW-CALORIE SPICY
TOMATO DRESSING
4 large tomatoes, peeled and chopped,
*   including juice*
1 teaspoon (or to taste) prepared white
*   horseradish*
1 small onion, minced

SHELLFISH
Oil for greasing grill
3 pounds large shrimp
8 10-inch wooden presoaked barbecue
*   skewers*
2 large oranges, sliced thin
Low-calorie margarine at room
*   temperature*

1. *Make the dressing:* In a bowl, combine the tomatoes, horseradish, and onion. Chill until ready to serve.

2. *Grill the shrimp:* Thread the shrimp on skewers with orange slices arranged randomly. Brush with margarine. Cook on the prepared grill, turning occasionally, until shrimp are done to taste, approximately 4 minutes. Serve immediately with tomato dressing.

Yield: 6 servings (2½ cups sauce)

SOLE

Dover sole is characterized by a delicate flavor and subtle, fine texture. It lends itself easily to accompanying many flavors. Substitutes include flounder and orange roughy.

SOLE WITH TARRAGON

❧

This recipe is particularly simple and quick—yet impressive.

> *4 7-ounce sole fillets*
> *Oil for greasing grill*
> *Melted butter*
> *White pepper*
> *Crumbled, dried tarragon*
> *Carrot curls for garnish*
> *Cherry tomatoes for garnish*
> *½ pound green grapes for garnish*

Arrange sole fillets on a prepared double-hinged grill basket or on a sheet of aluminum foil with some air holes. Brush with melted butter. Sprinkle fish with white pepper and tarragon. Sprinkle 2 tablespoons of tarragon directly on hot coals. Place fish on prepared grill and cook about 4 minutes, until it begins to flake when tested with a fork. Brush with butter during grilling. Place fish on individual dishes and garnish with carrot curls, cherry tomatoes, and small clusters of green grapes.

Yield: 4 servings

GRILLED DOVER SOLE WITH HERBS AND MINT BUTTER

As the fish grills, some of the herbs will fall into the coals and add their own aroma as they burn. Brill also works well in this recipe. Serve it with spinach or egg linguine and grilled artichoke hearts.

FISH
1 recipe basic marinade (see Index)
3 pounds Dover sole fillets, washed and patted dry, cut into 8 serving pieces
1 cup trimmed fresh thyme sprigs
¾ cup trimmed fresh mint sprigs
1 cup trimmed fresh parsley sprigs
Melted butter or margarine for brushing fillets
Oil for greasing grill or fish basket

MINT BUTTER
¾ cup (1½ sticks) butter or margarine, cut into small pieces
¼ cup trimmed fresh mint sprigs
1 tablespoon crème de menthe liqueur

1. *Marinate the fish:* Pour the marinade into a large plastic bag and add the Dover sole fillets. Secure with a twister seal and turn the bag several times to make sure all fish surfaces touch the marinade. Place the bag in a bowl and let sit at room temperature for 1 hour.

2. *Meanwhile, make the mint butter:* Put the butter into a blender or a food processor fitted with the steel blade. Add the mint sprigs and the crème de menthe. Process until the ingredients are well blended. Spread in a bowl, cover, and refrigerate until needed.

3. *Grill the fish:* Arrange the thyme, ¾ cup mint, and parsley over the prepared grill or in a prepared fish basket. Remove the fish from the marinade, brush with butter, and place the sole fillets on the herbs. Grill without turning 2–6 minutes, or until the fillets have lost their translucence and are cooked to taste. Remove the mint butter from the refrigerator while the fillets are grilling so that the butter is soft when served. Serve the fillets hot with the mint butter.

Yield: 8 servings (¾ cup mint butter)

DOVER SOLE WITH NORMANDY SAUCE

NORMANDY SAUCE
3 tablespoons butter
1 small onion, sliced thin
2 large apples, cored and sliced thin
½ cup apple cider or juice
Salt and white pepper to taste
1 cup evaporated milk

FISH
6 7-ounce Dover sole fillets
Melted butter
Oil for greasing fish basket
1 apple, cored and sliced, for garnish

1. *Make sauce:* Melt 3 tablespoons butter in a saucepan. Sauté onion in it until tender. Add the 2 sliced apples and cook for 1 minute, stirring occasionally. Blend in cider and salt and pepper to taste. Cook until mixture has been reduced by half. Stir in milk and simmer until sauce is warm. Remove saucepan from heat and reheat when ready to serve.

2. *Grill Dover sole:* Brush Dover sole fillets with melted butter and arrange in a prepared double-hinged fish basket. Secure basket and cook fillets about 3–4 minutes. Continue grilling about 2–3 minutes, depending on thickness of fish, until sole begins to flake when tested with a fork. Arrange fillets on individual plates and drizzle sauce around fish. Garnish with a sliced apple.

Yield: 6 servings

SOLE AND SALMON BUNDLES

This dish can be called chinois—a combination of French style (sole stuffed with salmon) and Oriental presentation.

> *½ pound salmon fillet, skinned and cut
>   into ½-by-2½-inch pieces*
> *4 green onions, 2 halved horizontally and
>   remaining 2 cut lengthwise into thirds*
> *4 7-ounce sole fillets*
> *Crumbled dried tarragon*
> *Melted butter*
> *Oil for greasing grill*
> *1 lime, cut into wedges, for garnish*

With a pair of tweezers reserved for kitchen use, remove all visible bones from salmon. Place one piece of salmon and a green onion half on the end of each sole fillet. Sprinkle with tarragon to taste. Roll the sole, jelly-roll style, forming a bundle. Tie each bundle securely with a long green onion strip. Brush sole with melted butter and place on prepared grill. Cook for 4–6 minutes. Brush and turn and continue grilling 2–3 minutes, depending on thickness of fish, until fish begins to flake when tested with a fork. Place seafood bundles on individual plates and serve with lime wedges and cooked fresh asparagus.

Yield: 4 servings

SOLE WITH CIDER AND GRILLED PEAR SLICES

This dish works well with new potatoes boiled in skins and tossed with butter and chopped chives and hot French bread. You may substitute plaice for sole.

MARINADE

1½ cups apple cider
1 teaspoon prepared mustard
½ teaspoon ground allspice
¼ teaspoon freshly grated nutmeg
Salt and freshly ground white pepper to taste

FISH

3 pounds sole fillets, cut into 8 serving pieces
Oil for greasing fish basket
2 cups trimmed fresh parsley
1 large onion, sliced thin
4 firm pears, cored, and sliced horizontally into rings
Melted butter or margarine for brushing pears

1. *Make the marinade:* Combine the marinade ingredients and pour the marinade into a large plastic bag. Add the sole and secure the bag with a twister seal. Turn the bag several times to make sure all fish surfaces touch the marinade. Place the bag in a bowl and let sit at room temperature for 1 hour.

2. *Grill the fish:* Spread the parsley over one side of a prepared fish basket and place the onion slices over the parsley. Place the sole on the bed of parsley and onion slices and close the basket. Grill the fish for 2–6 minutes, without turning, until done to taste. While the fish is cooking, brush the pear slices with melted butter and grill lightly on both sides.

3. Serve the fish and pear slices hot with parsley and onions, discarding the very burned sprigs.

Yield: 8 servings

GRILLED SOLE FILLETS
WITH HERBS

Serve this dish with a salad of endive and watercress and tomato soup with sage. Plaice can be used in place of sole.

COATING
2 cups uncooked fine-grained oatmeal
4 tablespoons chopped fresh parsley
½ teaspoon dried rosemary, crumbled
Salt and freshly ground pepper to taste
2 egg whites, lightly beaten

FISH
3 pounds sole fillets, cut into 8 serving
*   pieces*
Oil for greasing fish basket
Lemon wedges

1. *Make the coating:* Combine the oatmeal, parsley, rosemary, salt, and pepper and place on a sheet of waxed paper. Put the egg whites into a shallow bowl.

2. Brush each fillet with the egg whites and roll in the oatmeal coating, patting the oats firmly onto the fish fillets.

3. *Grill the fish:* Arrange the fillets in a prepared fish basket and cook on the prepared grill for 2–6 minutes. Turn the basket and grill until the fish tests done with a fork.

4. Place the fillets on individual plates and serve with lemon wedges.

Yield: 8 servings

SOLE WITH PINE NUT SAUCE

❧

This Middle Eastern sauce, like so many nut- and seed-based sauces, needs no cooking. Simply process the ingredients in the food processor or blender and heat before serving. This sauce can also be served at room temperature. Scrod may be substituted for sole in this recipe. We suggest you serve it with a tart green salad and hot French bread.

FISH
Salt and freshly ground pepper to taste
3 pounds sole fillets, cut into 8 serving
  pieces
½ cup fresh lemon juice
16 ¼-inch-thick slices lemon for grilling
  fillets
Lemon wedges

PINE NUT SAUCE
1 cup pine nuts
⅔ cup toasted bread crumbs
4 cloves garlic, peeled and quartered
5 tablespoons fresh lemon juice
2 tablespoons imported mild, good-quality
  olive oil
1¼ cups water (more if needed)

1. *Marinate the fish:* Generously salt and pepper the fillets. Then pour the lemon juice into a plastic bag and set in a large bowl. Add the sole fillets to the bag and secure the bag with a twister seal. Turn the bag to be sure all fish surfaces touch the lemon juice. Let sit at room temperature for 15–30 minutes.

2. *Meanwhile, make the sauce:* Preheat the oven to 350°F to toast the pine nuts. Arrange the pine nuts in a single layer on a baking sheet and put them in oven for about 10 minutes, watching them carefully. After the first 5 minutes, check them every minute or so to make sure they don't burn. Remove from the oven as soon as they are lightly browned.

3. Reserve 1 tablespoon of the toasted pine nuts to use as garnish. Put the remaining nuts in a food processor fitted with the steel blade or in a blender along with the bread crumbs, garlic, lemon juice, olive oil, and water. Process, pulsing on and off for a minute or so, until a coarse sauce results. If you wish to serve the sauce at room temperature, set it aside. If you plan to serve it hot, transfer it to a saucepan.

4. *Grill the fish:* Arrange the lemon slices in pairs on the prepared grill. Place the fillets on the lemon slices and cook for 2–6 minutes, without turning, or until they are completely cooked through and have lost their translucence. If you are serving the sauce hot, heat it in the saucepan while the fish is grilling.

5. Using two spatulas, carefully transfer the fillets to a serving platter. Spoon the room-temperature or hot pine nut sauce over the fillets and garnish with the reserved pine nuts. Pass lemon wedges at the table.

Yield: 8 servings (2½ cups sauce)

SNAILS

The snail has a mild flavor and is usually served with sauces.

These univalve mollusks are usually not available fresh. We feel this is just as well. The enormous amount of work needed to coax them out of their shells (according to some books, the process takes more than two days) and prepare them makes them less attractive in the fresh state. Hopefully, they'll be widely available to the general public as squid is now—cleaned and frozen—in a few more years. Meanwhile, canned snails, which we use in the following recipes, can be found in specialty food shops or ordered by mail (see Appendix). The canned flavor can be eliminated entirely by using any seafood marinade. Remember that canned snails are precooked and only have to be warmed before serving. To prepare canned snails for grilling, remove snails from the can and place in a bowl, cover with water, allow to stand for one to two minutes, and drain.

GRILLED SNAILS WITH WHITE WINE MARINADE

MARINADE
1 cup dry white wine
2 teaspoons crumbled dried basil
6 cloves garlic, minced
¼ teaspoon salt
¼ teaspoon freshly ground pepper
1 tablespoon melted butter

SHELLFISH
2 7.5-ounce cans snails (about 36 snails
    per can), drained and rinsed
6 10-inch wooden presoaked barbecue skewers
Oil for greasing grill

1. *Prepare marinade:* Combine marinade ingredients in a medium saucepan; add snails. Simmer 10 minutes, stirring often.

2. Divide snails among skewers.

3. Arrange skewers on prepared grill over ashen coals. Grill for 2 minutes, turn, and grill for 2 minutes longer. Brush with remaining marinade during grilling.

Yield: 6 servings

SNAILS MARINATED IN RED WINE WITH HERBES DE PROVENCE

Serve on a bed of buttered spinach noodles.

MARINADE
1 cup dry red wine
2 teaspoons herbes de Provence
⅛ teaspoon salt
⅛ teaspoon freshly ground pepper
1 tablespoon butter, melted

SHELLFISH
2 7½-ounce cans snails (about 36 snails
per can), drained and rinsed
6 10-inch wooden presoaked barbecue
skewers
Oil for greasing grill

1. *Prepare marinade:* Combine marinade ingredients in a medium saucepan. Bring marinade to a boil over medium heat, reduce heat to low, and simmer for 3 to 4 minutes. Add snails. Simmer 10 minutes, stirring often. Liquid will reduce until snails are just covered with marinade.

2. Divide snails among skewers.

3. *Grill snails:* Place on prepared grill over ashen coals. Grill for 2 minutes, turn, and grill for 2 minutes longer. Brush with remaining marinade during grilling.

Yield: 6 servings

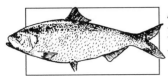

SHAD ROE
Handle shad roe, available in the spring, carefully, as the skin tears easily.

GRILLED SHAD ROE ON TOAST WITH CAPERS

We suggest you serve a mixed green salad tossed with candied almonds and orange slices and grilled tomato halves.

4 12-ounce pieces shad roe
Melted butter or margarine for brushing
   roe
Oil for greasing fish basket or grill
2 cups trimmed fresh parsley
8 slices buttered toast, trimmed
2 2-ounce cans flat anchovies, drained
1 3½-ounce jar large capers, drained

1. Brush shad roe with melted butter. Spread parsley sprigs on a prepared fish basket or the prepared grill. Place the roe on the parsley. Grill the roe for 3 minutes, turn using a long-handled spatula, and continue grilling for 3–4 minutes or until done to taste.

2. To serve, arrange hot toast on individual plates and place half of a roe piece on each slice of toast. Drizzle lightly with more melted butter. Cross 2 anchovies decoratively over the roe and sprinkle with capers.

Yield: 8 servings

SQUID

Except for baby squid, which are available fresh in most large cities, this univalve mollusk is largely available frozen. Luckily, frozen squid is absolutely delicious, especially when marinated before being grilled, and both frozen medium-sized mantles and frozen steaks are fine for our recipes.

To use squid steaks, simply defrost and with a sharp knife or scissors cut into serving squares of equal size.

To use frozen squid mantles, rinse under cold running water, then run your finger inside to make sure mantle is absolutely clean. Although our recipes call for medium-sized squid mantles, you can substitute fresh baby squid mantles, which are often available. None of our stuffed squid mantle recipes make use of the tentacles, but if you wish to substitute fresh baby squid and clean them yourself, see Index for directions for cleaning shellfish.

SQUID STEAKS WITH TAPENADE

SEAFOOD
2 pounds squid steaks
Oil for brushing fish and greasing grill
Black olives and capers for garnish
  (optional)

TAPENADE
1 6½-ounce can oil-packed tuna, well drained
1 2-ounce can flat anchovies, well drained
⅓ cup capers
⅔ cup medium pitted black olives
6 tablespoons fresh lemon juice
1 teaspoon freshly ground pepper
⅓ cup good-quality olive oil

1. *Prepare tapenade:* Place tuna, anchovies, capers, black olives, lemon juice, pepper, and olive oil in food processor container. Process to a coarse puree. Transfer to serving bowl.

2. *Grill squid:* Brush squid with oil and place on prepared grill. Cook 3 to 4 minutes on each side. Transfer to serving platter and top each squid steak amply with tapenade. Garnish with additional olives and capers, if desired.

Yield: 6 servings

SQUID STUFFED WITH GARLIC CRUMBS

❧

This recipe calls for cleaned baby squid mantles, each about 4 inches long. Many fish stores thoroughly clean the mantles before selling. If your store does not, buy baby squid and follow the directions for cleaning them in Part I (see Index). In this recipe, the squid tentacles are not used.

SEAFOOD
32 4-inch-long squid mantles, cleaned and
  tentacles discarded
Juice of 1 fresh lemon
¼ cup water

STUFFING
1½ cups unseasoned commercial bread
  crumbs
3 cloves garlic, minced very fine
½ cup finely minced fresh parsley
½ cup (1 stick) butter, softened
¾ teaspoon salt
¾ teaspoon freshly ground pepper
Round wooden toothpicks for closing squid
  mantle openings
Oil for brushing squid and greasing grill
Lime or lemon wedges for sprinkling on
  grilled squid

1. Open squid mantles and check to be sure insides are clean, using fingers. Mix lemon juice and water. Place squid in bowl and pour lemon juice mixture over squid, making sure that a little gets inside each mantle. Toss to combine and let sit.

2. *Prepare stuffing:* Combine crumbs, minced garlic, minced parsley, melted butter, salt, and pepper together in a bowl. Stuff squid mantles sparsely with crumb mixture, using a scant tablespoon of stuffing per squid mantle and taking care not to stuff any mantle too full.

3. Close mantle openings with round wooden toothpicks. If you are going to grill squid mantles immediately, brush with oil. Otherwise, place stuffed squid mantles on a plate, slip into a plastic bag, refrigerate for a few hours before serving, and then brush with oil.

4. *Grill squid:* Place squid on prepared grill and cook on each side for about 2 minutes, turning carefully with spatula. Serve immediately with lime or lemon wedges.

Yield: 8 appetizers

SQUID STEAKS WITH BESSARA (MIDDLE EASTERN BEAN DIP WITH TA'LEYA TOPPING)

❧

The following recipe uses a Middle Eastern bean puree called bessara *as a dip for chunks of grilled skewered squid. Bessara is made from broad fava beans (fava beans come in several sizes; use only the large, flat beans for this dish), which need 2 hours of preliminary simmering and 4 hours of soaking. The puree is garnished with thinly sliced onion rings and spoonfuls of a mixture of minced garlic and crushed coriander seed called* ta'leya, *which is sautéed for a few moments in olive oil. Fava beans are available at Middle Eastern markets or by mail order (see Appendix).*

SEAFOOD
2 pounds squid steaks
Oil for brushing squid and greasing grill

BESSARA
½ pound (8 ounces) broad fava beans
1 small onion, quartered
2 cloves garlic, peeled and quartered
2 tablespoons chopped fresh cilantro
1 teaspoon ground cumin
½ teaspoon salt
½ teaspoon dried mint
¼ teaspoon cayenne pepper
6 tablespoons cold water (or more if needed)
¼ cup good-quality olive oil

GARNISH
1 small onion, cut into paper-thin slices and separated into rings

TA'LEYA
2 tablespoons good-quality olive oil
3 cloves garlic, minced very fine
3 teaspoons ground coriander

1. *Prepare beans:* Soak fava beans in water to cover overnight. Then pick off any beans or debris floating on the surface of the water. Drain beans and place in a saucepan. Cover with water, heat to boil, and simmer 1½ to 2 hours, adding more water occasionally, until beans are fork-tender.

2. *Prepare* bessara: Place *bessara* ingredients in food processor. Process for a moment. Then add drained beans and process again, pulsing several times,

adding more water if necessary. Continue pulsing until a coarse puree results. Check consistency; the puree should be liquid enough to be scooped up on a piece of bread. If not, add water. Transfer puree to a flat serving dish with a lot of top surface and arrange onion rings decoratively over the top.

3. *Prepare* ta'leya: Heat oil in a small frying pan. Sauté garlic and coriander in oil for a few moments over low heat, stirring constantly with a wooden spoon and taking care that mixture does not burn. Use a rubber spatula to remove all *ta'leya* from pan and sprinkle over top of onion rings and *bessara*.

4. *Grill squid:* Brush squid steaks with oil and place on prepared grill. Grill about 3 to 4 minutes on each side. Serve immediately, topped with *bessara* and onion rings.

Yield: 4 servings

SQUID STEAKS AND GRILLED
POTATO SKINS NACHOS

SEAFOOD
2 pounds squid steaks
Oil for brushing squid and greasing grill

NACHOS
4 whole baked Idaho potatoes, cooled and
   halved lengthwise
Melted butter to brush potatoes
Garlic salt to taste
½ pound sharp cheddar cheese, grated
¾ cup evaporated milk
4 fresh or canned jalapeño peppers, seeds
   removed, cut into thin strips

1. Scoop out potato pulp from potato halves, leaving about ¼ to ½ inch of potato in skin. Paint inside of potatoes with melted butter, then sprinkle them liberally with garlic salt.

2. Place cheddar and evaporated milk in the top of a double boiler over simmering water and allow to melt. Place strips of jalapeño peppers in a small serving bowl.

3. *Grill potato skins and squid:* Place potato skins, skin side down, on grill for 4 minutes. Turn and cook another 4 minutes. Brush squid with oil. Place squid on grill and cook 3 to 4 minutes on each side. Transfer to serving platter and serve quickly, spooning cheese over potatoes and squid, then sprinkling cheese liberally with jalapeño strips.

Yield: 4 servings

SQUID CANNELLONI
WITH TOMATO SAUCE

SEAFOOD
28 4-inch-long squid mantles, cleaned and
    tentacles discarded
Juice of 1 fresh lemon
¼ cup water

STUFFING
1 cup (8 ounces) ricotta cheese
6 tablespoons (3 ounces) finely chopped
    prosciutto
½ cup grated Parmesan cheese
¼ cup finely chopped fresh parsley
1 clove garlic, minced fine
¼ teaspoon salt
¼ teaspoon freshly ground pepper
Round wooden toothpicks for closing squid
    mantle openings

TOMATO SAUCE
2 tablespoons good-quality olive oil
6 large ripe tomatoes, peeled, seeded, and
    chopped
½ teaspoon salt
¼ teaspoon freshly ground pepper
1 bay leaf
Pinch dried basil
Oil for brushing squid and greasing grill

1. Check squid mantles with fingers (see Index) to be sure that insides of mantles are clean. Place mantles in bowl and cover with lemon juice mixed with water. Let sit while you make the filling.

2. *Prepare stuffing:* Combine stuffing ingredients, mixing well. Stuff each squid mantle loosely with mixture, using only a scant tablespoon per mantle. Close openings with round wooden toothpicks.

3. *Prepare tomato sauce:* Heat oil in large heavy-bottomed frying pan. Add tomatoes, salt, pepper, bay leaf, and basil. Simmer 15 to 20 minutes over low heat, stirring occasionally with a wooden spoon.

4. *Grill squid:* When tomato sauce is done, brush stuffed squid mantles with oil and place on prepared grill. Cook about 2 to 3 minutes on each side. Serve immediately with hot tomato sauce.

Yield: 4 servings

SQUID STEAKS
WITH CAPONATA

Caponata is a delicious Sicilian vegetable stew based on sweet and sour eggplant. It is traditionally served cold or at room temperature. But it's also delicious hot, as this recipe illustrates.

SEAFOOD
2 pounds squid steaks
Oil for brushing squid and greasing grill

CAPONATA
½ cup good-quality mild olive oil
1 pound eggplant (use baby eggplant if possible), cut into ¼-inch dice
1 large onion, minced fine
2 stalks celery, peeled thoroughly with vegetable peeler (make sure that all veins are removed) and chopped fine
1 green pepper, seeded, deveined, and chopped fine
1 red pepper, seeded, deveined, and chopped fine
1 1-pound can Italian tomatoes with liquid
2 tablespoons brown sugar
¼ cup red wine vinegar
½ teaspoon salt
1½ teaspoons freshly ground pepper
½ cup raisins
2 tablespoons capers
⅓ cup pitted green olives, quartered (pimiento-stuffed, if desired)
⅓ cup quartered pitted black olives
¼ cup pine nuts

1. *Prepare caponata:* Heat oil in large, heavy-bottomed frying pan. Sauté eggplant, onion, celery, green and red peppers, and canned tomatoes with liquid for a moment, turning with wooden spoon. Then add brown sugar, wine vinegar, salt, pepper, raisins, capers, and green and black olives. Stir to combine. Simmer over low heat 20 minutes, stirring often.

2. *While caponata simmers, toast pine nuts:* Place pine nuts in a small frying pan and place over medium heat. Watch carefully, stirring occasionally with wooden spoon. As soon as nuts begin browning, stir constantly until they have been exposed to the heat on all sides. Then remove frying pan from heat. Spoon caponata into serving bowl. Sprinkle with toasted pine nuts for garnish.

3. *Grill squid:* Brush squid steaks with oil and place on prepared grill. Grill steaks 2 to 3 minutes on each side. Transfer to heated serving platter. Serve each steak topped with a liberal portion of caponata and pass additional caponata.

Yield: 4 servings

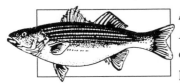

STRIPED BASS
A medium-firm fish with a mild flavor and low fat content. Black sea bass, orange roughy, and ocean perch taste great in striped bass recipes.

STRIPED BASS MARINATED IN THE KOREAN MANNER

MARINADE
¼ cup soy sauce
2 tablespoons sugar
1 tablespoon finely minced garlic
1 tablespoon finely minced green onions,
*   green part only*
2 tablespoons oil
2 tablespoons sesame seeds

FISH
4 striped bass fillets (about 2 pounds),
*   each cut into 2 pieces, skin on*
Oil for greasing grill

1. *Prepare marinade:* Combine soy sauce, sugar, garlic, green onion, and oil. Put sesame seeds in a medium-sized frying pan and set over medium heat. Stir for a moment or until they begin to brown. Add to soy sauce mixture.

2. *Marinate striped bass:* Lay fillets skin side down in a single layer in a pan with raised sides. Pour soy mixture over fillets. Let sit for a moment, then turn fillets flesh side down. Refrigerate, covered, for 30 minutes.

3. *Grill striped bass:* At serving time, remove bass from marinade and place on prepared grill over ashen coals, skin side touching grill, for 3–4 minutes on one side only. (Do not turn fillets or they will fall apart.) Baste fillet with marinade every minute or so until done. Use a greased spatula to transfer fish to serving platter.

Yield: 4 servings

WHOLE STRIPED BASS IN THE STYLE OF SOLONIKA

This fish is served on a bed of chopped parsley and onions in a classic Greek style.

SOLONIKA DRESSING
¼ cup olive oil
1 cup firmly packed chopped fresh parsley
   sprigs
1 medium onion, sliced thin

FISH
2 tablespoons olive oil
2 tablespoons fresh lemon juice
¼ teaspoon each: salt and freshly ground
   black pepper
1 teaspoon crumbled dried oregano
4 small striped bass or snapper fillets,
   head and tail intact
Grapevine pieces (optional), available in
   Greek food stores or backyard if you
   have grapevines
Oil for greasing fish basket
Greek olives for garnish

1. *Make dressing:* Toss dressing ingredients together in small bowl. Cover and refrigerate until ready to serve.

2. *Grill striped bass:* Combine 2 tablespoons olive oil, lemon juice, and seasonings. Rub the outside and cavity of the fish with seasoning mixture. Place 2 foot-long pieces of grapevine over the hot coals. Arrange fish in a prepared double-hinged fish basket. Place basket over grill and cook for 5–7 minutes. Baste with remaining seasoning mixture and continue cooking 2–3 minutes, depending on thickness of fish, until fish begins to flake when tested with a fork. Place dressing on bottom of serving platter and arrange fish over it. Sprinkle fish with olives.

Yield: 4 servings

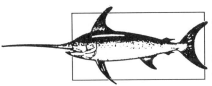

SWORDFISH
A favorite for grilling. It is a firm, mildly distinct fish. Substitute shark or tuna; recipes will work but taste will be different.

SWORDFISH KABOBS WITH MIDDLE EASTERN DIPPING SAUCES

Serve with warm pita bread. Sesame seed paste is available at specialty food stores.

TARAMOSALATA
1 small onion, quartered
3 slices white bread, crusts removed
½ cup water
½ cup (4 ounces) tarama (salted carp roe, available at specialty food stores)
1½ tablespoons fresh lemon juice
½ cup olive oil

HUMMUS
2 cloves garlic
1 small onion, quartered
1 19-ounce can chick-peas, drained
½ cup tahini (sesame seed paste)
2 tablespoons fresh lemon juice
3 tablespoons olive oil
Salt to taste

FISH
1½ pounds swordfish cut into 1-inch chunks
12 cherry tomatoes
Oil for greasing grill

1. *Make taramosalata:* Using a blender or a food processor fitted with a steel blade, puree quartered onion. Soak bread in water for 4–5 minutes. Squeeze bread dry and discard water. Add bread to machine and puree. Place tarama and 1½ tablespoons lemon juice in work bowl with onion and bread and puree. With the machine running, pour in ½ cup olive oil through the feed tube in a slow steady stream until it is incorporated. Taste taramosalata and adjust seasonings. Store in a covered container and chill until ready to serve.

2. *Make hummus:* Using a food processor fitted with a steel blade, mince garlic and quartered onion. Add remaining hummus ingredients and puree. Taste and adjust seasonings. Store hummus in a covered container and chill until ready to serve.

3. *Grill swordfish:* Thread 4 10-inch skewers alternately with swordfish and cherry tomatoes. Cook, turning every 3 minutes until done. Serve immediately and pass dipping sauces (room temperature) at the table.

Yield: 4 servings

SWORDFISH IN A TABASCO-BUTTERMILK MARINADE

4 cups buttermilk
1 tablespoon Tabasco sauce
6 swordfish steaks, cut 1 inch thick
Oil for greasing grill
Salt

1. *Marinate swordfish:* Mix buttermilk and Tabasco sauce together. Cut skin off swordfish steaks and pierce each in several places on both sides with the tines of a fork.

2. Lay a large plastic bag inside a bowl and open the top. Pour marinade into plastic bag, then add steaks. Close bag with twister seal and place in refrigerator for 3 hours.

3. *Grill swordfish:* At serving time, remove from marinade and place swordfish on prepared grill over ashen coals. Cook about 5 minutes on each side or until swordfish begins to flake when tested with a fork. Salt lightly and serve immediately.

Yield: 6 servings

GRILLED SWORDFISH ON GRAPE LEAVES

Placing dried grapevine pieces over the hot coals adds a slightly smoky flavor to this fish. You might also serve a cucumber and onion salad or Greek salad, a dish of olives, and crusty bread. Ono also works well in this recipe.

BASTING MIXTURE
3 tablespoons good-quality olive oil
3 tablespoons fresh lemon juice
1 teaspoon dried oregano, crumbled
¼ teaspoon salt
⅛ teaspoon freshly ground pepper

FISH
Oil for greasing fish basket
4–6 pieces grapevine (optional; available
    in Greek food stores or in backyard if
    you have a grapevine)
Enough large fresh pesticide- and
    herbicide-free grape leaves to arrange a
    double layer on grill basket or on grill
3 pounds swordfish steaks, cut into 8
    serving pieces about ½ inch thick
2 lemons, sliced paper-thin
2 lemons, cut into wedges

1. *Make the basting mixture:* Whisk together the basting mixture ingredients in a shallow bowl. Brush fish generously with the mixture.

2. *Grill the fish:* Arrange grapevine pieces over the hot coals and replace the grill. Make a double layer of grape leaves in prepared fish basket, on both top and bottom. Place the fish in the basket with lemon slices on top and secure shut. Grill for 4–8 minutes, turn the basket, and continue grilling until done.

3. Put the swordfish pieces on individual plates. Serve with lemon wedges.

Yield: 8 servings

SERPENTINE
SWORDFISH STRIPS

This dish is easy and fun to serve with a tart green salad and sweet potatoes.

16 8-inch-long wooden presoaked barbecue
    skewers

MARINADE
½ cup sour cream or sour half-and-half
½ cup fresh lemon juice
½ teaspoon salt
¼ teaspoon freshly ground white pepper

FISH
3 pounds swordfish fillets, cut ¾ inch
    thick and as long as possible
Oil for greasing grill

SAUCE
2 cups sour cream or sour half-and-half
2 tablespoons fresh lemon juice
¼ teaspoon salt (more to taste)
Few grinds black pepper

1. *Make the marinade:* Mix the marinade ingredients together, pour into a large plastic bag, and set the bag in a bowl.

2. Add the swordfish strips to the marinade in the bag and secure with a twister seal. Turn the bag several times to make certain all the surfaces of the fish touch the marinade. Let sit at room temperature for 1 hour, turning occasionally.

3. *While the fish marinates, make the sauce:* Mix the sauce ingredients together in a small saucepan and set aside.

4. Remove the swordfish strips from the marinade and remove the skewers from the water. Thread the swordfish strips onto the skewers by weaving the strips over and under the skewers at 3-inch intervals.

5. *Grill the fish:* Place the skewered swordfish on the prepared grill and cook for about 4 minutes on each side or until the swordfish is completely cooked through and has lost its opacity.

6. While the fish cooks, heat the sour cream sauce slowly over low heat. When the sauce is warmed, transfer it to a serving bowl and bring it to the table.

7. When the swordfish is cooked, transfer the skewers to a serving platter and bring the platter to the table. Present the skewers topped with the sour cream sauce.

Yield: 8 servings (2 cups sauce)

SWORDFISH WITH HOMEMADE LEMON MAYONNAISE

LEMON MAYONNAISE
1 egg plus 1 egg yolk, room temperature
3 tablespoons fresh lemon juice
⅔ cup salad oil
½ teaspoon salt
Big pinch cayenne pepper
Finely grated zest of 1 lemon

FISH
Oil for brushing fish and greasing grill
8 swordfish steaks, each 1 inch thick

1. *Make mayonnaise:* Put egg and yolk in container of food processor or blender along with lemon juice, 2 tablespoons of the oil, the salt, cayenne pepper, and lemon zest. Blend for a few seconds. With machine on, add remaining oil as slowly as possible in a very thin (less than ⅛ inch thick) but steady stream. When all oil has been added, mayonnaise will be thickened. Transfer to serving bowl.

2. *Grill swordfish steaks:* Oil swordfish steaks liberally on both sides. Place swordfish steaks on prepared grill for about 5 minutes on each side or until fish flesh has turned white. Watch carefully and do not overcook. Serve steaks with lemon mayonnaise.

Yield: 8 servings

SWORDFISH STEAKS WITH BARBECUE SAUCE

❧

Swordfish will convince even the die-hard meat-eater that fish can be an immensely satisfying dish. There is not a bone or sinew in sight, just thick, meaty eating.

BARBECUE SAUCE
2 tablespoons oil
1 cup very finely chopped onion
4 garlic cloves, minced fine or pressed
1–2 small fresh hot peppers, seeded and chopped fine
1 cup canned tomato sauce
⅓ cup each: Worcestershire sauce and brown sugar
⅔ cup red wine vinegar
¼ teaspoon salt
2 pinches dried rosemary
1 pinch dried thyme
⅛ teaspoon Liquid Smoke
Tabasco sauce to taste (optional)

FISH
Oil for brushing fish and greasing grill
4 swordfish steaks, each 1 inch thick

1. *Make sauce:* Heat 2 tablespoons oil in large frying pan. Sauté onion, garlic, and peppers in it for about 10 minutes over moderate heat, stirring often. Add tomato sauce, Worcestershire sauce, brown sugar, red wine vinegar, salt, rosemary, and thyme. Heat to boil, reduce heat, and simmer for about 5 minutes. Stir in Liquid Smoke. Taste and adjust seasoning, adding Tabasco if a hotter flavor is desired.

2. *Grill swordfish steaks:* Meanwhile, oil swordfish steaks on both sides. Then oil grill. Set fish on grill over ashen coals. Cook for 5–6 minutes on each side or until fish just flakes when tested with a fork. Serve immediately with barbecue sauce spooned over the top. Pass remaining barbecue sauce.

Yield: 4 servings

SWORDFISH WITH CANTONESE SAUCE

❧

CANTONESE SAUCE
¼ cup dry white wine
½ teaspoon black soy sauce
1 teaspoon sesame oil

FISH
1 teaspoon minced fresh gingerroot
Grated zest of 1 orange
4 green onions, minced
4 7-ounce swordfish steaks
Peanut oil for brushing fish and greasing
   grill
2 medium cucumbers, sliced horizontally,
   for garnish
¼ cup minced fresh cilantro (coriander),
   for garnish
4 green onions, cut into 1½-inch slivers,
   for garnish
Grated zest of 1 orange, for garnish

1. *Make sauce:* Mix together wine, soy sauce, and sesame oil in a small bowl. Cover sauce and set aside.

2. *Grill swordfish:* Mix together ginger, zest of 1 orange, and green onions. Brush fish with oil and sprinkle with ginger mixture. Arrange swordfish steaks on prepared grill. Cook for 5–6 minutes. Turn fish over with a spatula and continue cooking 2–3 minutes, depending on thickness of fish, until fish begins to flake when tested with a fork. Place swordfish on platter and drizzle sauce over fish. Decoratively arrange cucumbers, cilantro, onions, and zest of 1 orange over fish. Serve hot or cold.

Yield: 4 servings

TROUT
Brook trout, lake trout, and rainbow trout are medium-firm fish, medium flavored and high in fat content. Each can be substituted for the other.

WHOLE TROUT WITH ROSEMARY AND SAGE

Double flavor, inside and out, with lime slices and rosemary sprinkled over the hot coals in the French style. We suggest you serve it with a pasta salad.

1 tablespoon dried leaf rosemary
1 tablespoon rubbed sage
½ teaspoon freshly ground pepper
¼ cup olive oil
1 3½-pound lake trout or four individual
    rainbow trout, 8–10 ounces each,
    cleaned, head and tail intact
1 large lime, sliced
1 tablespoon dried leaf rosemary
Oil for greasing grill

1. Combine 1 tablespoon rosemary, the sage, and the pepper with olive oil. Rub the trout, including the cavity, with the herb mixture. Place lime slices in the cavity.

2. Sprinkle remaining rosemary over coals. Place trout on prepared grill or on a double layer of greased aluminum foil with a few holes poked in it. Grill for 5–6 minutes on each side or until the fish begins to flake when tested with a fork. Baste fish during cooking. With a greased spatula, carefully transfer trout to platter.

Yield: 4 servings

INDIVIDUAL TROUTS WITH ARMENIAN STUFFING

FISH

4 whole fresh trout, about 8–10 ounces
   each, boned, scaled, fins removed,
   heads and tails intact
White wine to cover trout
Oil for brushing fish and greasing fish
   basket

STUFFING

4 tablespoons (½ stick) butter
4 medium onions, chopped fine
⅔ cup each: pine nuts and currants
Scant ½ teaspoon each: cinnamon,
   allspice, and salt
1 tablespoon chopped fresh parsley
2½ teaspoons fresh lemon juice
Large pinch cayenne pepper

1. *Marinate trout:* Lay trout in a shallow nonmetallic dish with raised sides. Cover with dry white wine (jug wine is perfectly acceptable). Let sit for 30 minutes.

2. *Make stuffing:* Melt butter in a medium frying pan over low heat. Sauté onions for 10 minutes, stirring often. Then stir in pine nuts, currants, cinnamon, allspice, salt, parsley, lemon juice, and cayenne pepper. Mix well and cook for another minute. Remove from heat and allow to cool, about 10 minutes.

3. *Stuff fish:* Remove fish from white wine, shake to remove excess, and oil them well on both sides. Divide stuffing evenly among fish, patting it into center of fish.

4. *Grill trout:* Lay all four fish in well-oiled fish basket (or lay them on well-oiled grill) and fasten top of basket. Cook fish for 6–7 minutes on each side or until fish has turned white and is beginning to flake. Serve immediately.

Yield: 4 servings

GRILLED TROUT WITH
TWO CHEESES

❧

You may substitute walleye pike for the trout in this recipe. We suggest you serve it with garlic mashed potatoes, a mixed endive salad, sliced beets, and green olives.

MARINADE
¼ cup good-quality olive oil
4 tablespoons fresh lemon juice
1½ cups Portuguese or other white wine
3 cloves garlic, minced
4 tablespoons minced fresh parsley

FISH
8 8- to 10-ounce trout, cleaned and
    scaled, heads and tails left on
1 onion, sliced thin
Salt and freshly ground pepper to taste
Oil for greasing foil
¼ pound Parmesan cheese, grated
¼ pound Romano cheese, grated

1. *Make the marinade:* Combine the olive oil, lemon juice, wine, garlic, and parsley and divide between two large plastic bags; place the bags in a large bowl. Place 4 trout in each bag and divide the onion slices between the bags. Secure the bags with twister seals. Turn the bags a few times to make sure all fish surfaces touch the marinade. Let sit at room temperature for 1 hour.

2. Remove the fish from the marinade and salt and pepper each liberally inside and outside.

3. *Grill the fish:* Arrange the fish on oiled foil placed on the prepared grill. Sprinkle with cheese, adhering cheese to the fish. Cook for about 4–8 minutes, until done.

4. Serve the fish on hot plates immediately.

Yield: 8 servings

TROUT WITH
SESAME SEED SAUCE

This Middle Eastern sauce is based on tahini (sesame seed paste) and tastes like a liquid form of that Middle Eastern sweet called halvah, which is also tahini-based. Tahini is available at Middle Eastern grocery stores or by mail (see Appendix for sources). The sauce is made slightly piquant by the addition of a Middle Eastern hot pepper sauce called shatta (hot sauce), also available by mail. If shatta is unavailable, just substitute any picante sauce. Sesame seed sauce can be served warm, at room temperature, or even cold with cold fillets. Serve it with a cracked wheat salad (tabbouleh) and salad of peeled, seeded, and chopped cucumber, plain yogurt, a little finely chopped garlic, and salt. This dish is traditionally prepared with Mousht, but we have substituted trout for the Mousht, which is unavailable in the United States. You may substitute 8 12- to 16-ounce scaled and gutted black sea bass.

SESAME SEED SAUCE
2 tablespoons vegetable oil
6 cloves garlic, minced
¼ cup chopped fresh parsley
1 teaspoon salt
¼ teaspoon ground coriander
1 cup tahini
1 cup cold water
¼ cup fresh lemon juice
1½ teaspoons shatta or other hot pepper
  sauce
Salt and freshly ground pepper to taste

FISH
8 10- to 12-ounce rainbow trout, scaled
  and gutted, heads and tails intact
Oil for brushing fish and greasing fish
  basket

GARNISHES
3 tablespoons sesame seeds
3–4 tablespoons shatta or other hot
  pepper sauce
3 tablespoons finely chopped fresh parsley
Lemon wedges

1. *Make the sauce:* Heat oil in a small saucepan over medium heat. Add the garlic, parsley, salt, and coriander and sauté for about 5 minutes, watching carefully so the mixture does not burn. Allow to cool slightly.

2. Scrape the garlic mixture into a food processor fitted with the steel blade or into a blender. Add the tahini along with the cold water, lemon juice, and *shatta.* Process until a smooth paste results.

3. *Grill the fish:* Brush the fish with oil. Place the fish in a prepared fish basket and cook for 4–8 minutes until one side has browned. Then turn the basket and grill until the second side has browned. Transfer the fish carefully to a serving platter.

4. *Meanwhile, toast the sesame seeds:* Place the seeds in a single layer in a small saucepan and set over medium heat. Watch carefully and have a wooden spoon handy. They should start to brown in a minute or two. As soon as they begin to brown, stir them with the wooden spoon, cook another minute, until they're golden, then remove from heat. Transfer to a small bowl and set on the table along with the shatta, chopped parsley, and lemon wedges.

5. Transfer the sesame seed sauce to a saucepan and heat, stirring often and watching carefully so it does not burn. Then spoon the warmed sauce into a serving bowl and place on the table. If desired, this sauce may be served at room temperature.

6. To serve, transfer each fish carefully to a dinner plate. Spoon a mound of sesame seed sauce to one side of the fish on each plate. Instruct your guests to top the sesame seed sauce with a large spoonful of shatta, a sprinkle of sesame seeds, and some chopped parsley. Pass the lemon wedges.

Yield: 8 servings

ST. PETER'S
FISH ON THE GRILL

This dish is based on a fish with the scientific name Telapia galilaea, *which is abundantly available in the Sea of Galilee. Although the fish is served primarily by Hebrews—it's known in Israel as* Mushat b'Shalem—*and by Moslems—it's known in Arab countries as* Mousht—*Christians have nicknamed it St. Peter's fish for biblical reasons.*

According to John 21:6, St. Peter and his friends went fishing one day but came home empty-handed. Learning that the fishing trip had been fruitless, Jesus intervened, instructing the fishermen to "cast the net on the right side of the boat, and you will find some."

According to the story, the net was cast and immediately grew so heavy with 153 Telapia galilaea *inside that it could not be hauled in. Jesus then told St. Peter to try hauling the net in, and following Jesus's instruction, St. Peter was able to bring the whole net ashore by himself.*

Telapia galilaea *is also thought to be the fish that Jesus advised St. Peter to pull out of the water in Matthew 17:27—the one that contained the shekel needed by St. Peter for taxes.*

Telapia galilaea, *a very flat fish, also figures in Jewish legend: it is said to have flattened when its ancestors were split in two lengthwise, during the parting of the Red Sea.*

Whatever you believe, you'll probably want to prepare the fish as it is served all over the Middle East. The most common preparation, made on the shores of the Sea of Galilee, involves stuffing the fish with onions and parsley, adding salt and pepper, and grilling it over glowing coals. Serve it with potato salad or homemade baked beans and coleslaw.

Since you will have difficulty getting this breamlike fish in the U.S., we suggest substituting rainbow trout. Eight 12- to 16-ounce dressed black sea bass will also work.

Oil for brushing onions and fish and
  greasing grill and fish basket
2 pounds medium-sized onions, cut into
  ¼-inch-thick slices
Salt and freshly ground pepper to taste
8 10- to 12-ounce gutted and scaled
  rainbow trout, heads and tails left on
2 cups finely chopped fresh parsley
Lemon wedges

1. *Grill the onions:* Brush onion slices with oil and salt and pepper them lightly. Place the onions on the prepared grill and cook for about 6 minutes, watching carefully and turning the onions with a spatula as soon as one side has browned. Remove them from the grill.

2. Brush fish with oil and salt and pepper each liberally inside. Sprinkle 2 tablespoons of the chopped parsley on the inside of each fish, then arrange the onion slices on the parsley. Sprinkle 2 tablespoons of the parsley over the onion slices in each fish. Skewer each fish to close it.

3. Place the fish in an oiled fish basket and set on the prepared grill. Cook the fish for 4–8 minutes or until it is browned on one side. Transfer the fish to a serving platter and serve immediately. Pass a platter of lemon wedges.

Yield: 8 servings

LAKE TROUT
ON ROSE LEAVES
SERVED WITH ROSE BUTTER

Rose petals and leaves grown for the express purpose of being used as food should be free of herbicides and pesticides. Rose water is available from Maid of Scandinavia; see Appendix. Serve this dish with wild and white rice, cruditées, and a hearts of palm salad.

ROSE BUTTER

½ teaspoon rose water
½ cup (¼ pound) butter or margarine, at room temperature, cut into ½-inch chunks
2 tablespoons minced fresh parsley

FISH

Oil for greasing fish basket or grill
Enough well-washed rose leaves on completely clean short stems to arrange in a double layer in a grill basket
8 8- to 10-ounce lake trout, cleaned, head discarded
2 large oranges, cut into 16 thin slices
Melted butter or margarine for brushing fish
1 teaspoon dried tarragon, crumbled
½ cup pesticide- and herbicide-free rose petals, completely clean, for garnish (optional)

1. *Make the rose butter:* Blend rose water and butter in a food processor fitted with the steel blade. Add parsley and combine. Mound the butter in a small bowl, cover, and refrigerate. Remove from refrigerator 45 minutes before serving time so that the butter will be at room temperature.

2. *Grill the fish:* Arrange a double layer of rose leaves on one side of a prepared fish basket or on the prepared grill. Place 2 orange slices inside each fish. Brush the fish with melted butter and arrange the fish on the rose leaves. Sprinkle the fish with the tarragon. Grill for 4–8 minutes, depending on the thickness of the fish. Turn over and continue grilling until done to taste or test with a fork to see if fish is just beginning to flake.

3. Put the fish on individual plates and top each with a dollop of rose butter. Sprinkle with rose petals if desired.

Yield: 8 servings

TROUT IN A BACON BLANKET

This is a Mormon specialty from Utah. You might serve it with potato salad or homemade baked beans and coleslaw. You may substitute 8 12- to 16-ounce dressed black sea bass for the trout in this recipe.

> 8 12-ounce trout, scaled and gutted, heads
>   and tails left on
> Oil for brushing fish
> Salt and freshly ground pepper to taste
> 16 slices bacon, half-cooked
> Lemon wedges

1. Brush the fish with oil. Salt and pepper the insides of the fish heavily.

2. *Grill the fish:* Wrap each fish completely in half-cooked bacon, using 2 slices per fish. Fasten the bacon with toothpicks. Arrange the fish in a fish basket.

3. Place the fish basket on the prepared grill and cook for about 5 minutes on each side or until brown. The bacon should be crisp.

4. Transfer the fish to a serving platter and serve. Pass a plate of lemon wedges.

Yield: 8 servings

LAKE TROUT WITH
GRILLED TOMATO SLICES

4 10-ounce lake trout
Melted butter
2 lemons, sliced thin
Oil for greasing fish basket
4 tablespoons minced fresh parsley for
*   garnish*
2–3 large, firm fresh tomatoes, sliced into
*   ½-inch slices*

1. *Grill trout:* Brush individual trout with melted butter and put lemon slices in cavities. Arrange fish in a prepared double-hinged fish basket and grill trout for 3–4 minutes. Brush fish with butter, turn, and grill 2–3 minutes depending on thickness of fish, until it begins to flake when tested with a fork. Arrange trout on individual plates.

2. *Prepare tomato slices:* Brush tomatoes with oil. Place on prepared grill. Cook 1–2 minutes on each side. Do not overcook. Serve with fish and garnish with minced parsley.

Yield: 4 servings

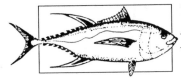

TUNA
A firm fish high in fat content. Substitute swordfish when tuna is not available.

TUNA WITH GREEN SALSA

Green husk tomatoes are available in Mexican food stores. Serve this dish with warm flour tortillas that have been wrapped in aluminum foil and stacked in a 350°F oven for 15 minutes. Eat tortillas as you would bread, spread with butter.

GREEN SALSA
1 10-ounce can tomatillos (green husk
    tomatoes), including juice
1 medium onion, quartered
1 clove garlic
2 mild chili peppers, seeded and chopped
¼ cup chopped fresh cilantro (coriander)
1 small hot pepper, or to taste, seeded
    and chopped (optional)

FISH
4 7-ounce tuna fillets
Peanut oil for brushing fish and greasing
    fish basket
1 cup chopped fresh cilantro (coriander)

1. *Make salsa:* Puree all salsa ingredients in a food processor fitted with a steel blade or in a blender. Cover and refrigerate until ready to serve.
2. *Grill tuna:* Brush tuna with peanut oil. Arrange half of the cilantro in prepared fish basket and place fish on top. Cover with remaining cilantro. Secure basket. Grill for 5 minutes. Turn basket and continue cooking until fish begins to flake when tested with a fork. Slightly undercook tuna. Transfer to individual plates. Pass green salsa at the table.

Yield: 4 servings

TUNA WITH ORIENTAL BARBECUE SAUCE

Hoisin sauce is available at Oriental food markets.

BARBECUE SAUCE
¼ cup hoisin sauce
1 teaspoon sugar
½ teaspoon sesame oil
2 cloves garlic, minced

FISH
4 7-ounce tuna steaks
Oil for greasing fish basket or grill
1 cup snow peas (fresh, if possible),
  trimmed, for garnish

1. *Make sauce:* Combine hoisin sauce, sugar, sesame oil, and garlic in a small saucepan. Simmer, stirring often over low heat, for 2 minutes. Remove saucepan from heat and cool sauce.

2. *Grill tuna:* Brush tuna steaks with barbecue sauce and place in a prepared double-hinged wire fish basket or cook directly on prepared grill. Cook tuna for 5–6 minutes. Brush steaks with sauce and turn. Continue grilling 2–3 minutes or until fish begins to flake when tested with a fork. Tuna should be cooked like roast beef, only until slightly pink in the center. Place tuna on individual dishes and sprinkle with snow peas for garnish.

Yield: 4 servings

GRILLED TUNA SALAD NICOISE

Once you've had grilled tuna, you'll never want to open a can again. Try this delectable salad with simple garlic bread.

VINAIGRETTE
⅔ cup good-quality imported olive oil
⅓ cup red wine vinegar
2 teaspoons Dijon mustard
2 teaspoons snipped fresh chives
¾ teaspoon each: dried tarragon and salt

SALAD
1½ pounds small round boiling potatoes
2 large heads Boston lettuce, washed, dried, leaves separated
12 ounces green beans, cooked and chilled
6 medium eggs, hard-boiled and quartered lengthwise
12 firm fresh plum tomatoes, quartered lengthwise
Oil for brushing tuna and greasing grill
18 ounces fresh tuna
12 flat anchovy fillets, drained
½ cup jumbo pitted black olives, drained
3 tablespoons finely chopped fresh parsley

1. *Make vinaigrette:* Combine ⅔ cup oil, the vinegar, mustard, chives, tarragon, and salt in a medium-sized bowl.

2. *Marinate potatoes:* Put potatoes in a saucepan and add water to cover. Heat to boiling, lower heat to simmer, and cook until soft enough to be pierced with a fork. When potatoes are cooked, drain and peel. Carefully add hot potatoes to bowl in which vinaigrette has been sitting and spoon some vinaigrette over potatoes. Let sit in vinaigrette until ready to use.

3. *Prepare vegetables:* Use Boston lettuce leaves to line a glass bowl. Then arrange green beans, eggs, and tomatoes in individual piles over lettuce. Carefully remove potatoes from vinaigrette and arrange them in a pile on lettuce.

4. *Grill tuna:* Oil tuna on both sides and cook on prepared grill over ashen coals for about 4 minutes on each side or until tuna is almost cooked. Do not cook tuna all the way through; it should be served rare, like roast beef. Separate cooled tuna into small chunks with a fork and arrange in a pile on lettuce.

5. *Dress and garnish:* Lay anchovy fillets and black olives over top of entire salad. Then pour remaining vinaigrette over salad. Sprinkle with parsley and serve immediately.

Yield: 6 servings

GRILLED TUNA SALAD
WITH CAPERS AND
HOMEMADE MAYONNAISE

❧

Leftover homemade mayonnaise, if covered, will keep at least 2 days in refrigerator.

MAYONNAISE
1 egg
3 tablespoons cider vinegar
½ teaspoon salt
Large pinch cayenne pepper
⅔ cup oil

SALAD
Oil for lubricating fish and greasing grill
16 ounces fresh tuna
3 tablespoons drained capers
¼ cup finely chopped fresh parsley

1. *Make mayonnaise:* Put egg in food processor or blender container along with vinegar, salt, cayenne pepper, and 2 tablespoons of the oil. Process for about 6 seconds as necessary.

2. Turn on motor and begin adding remaining oil. Add oil in a very thin (no more than ⅛ inch thick), steady stream. Keep motor running until all oil is added, then turn off motor. Let sit at room temperature for 5 minutes.

3. *Grill tuna:* Oil tuna on both sides and place on prepared grill for about 4 minutes on each side or until tuna is almost cooked. Tuna should always be cooked slightly rare like roast beef, so watch carefully.

4. *Assemble salad:* Let tuna cool to room temperature or until just warm. Separate tuna into small, irregular chunks with a fork and place in a glass bowl. Add ⅔ cup of the mayonnaise and mix well. Then mix in capers. Top with parsley. Serve at room temperature.

Yield: 8 servings

GRILLED TUNA SANDWICHES

You might serve dill pickles, potato chips, grilled potato skins with sour cream, and creamy coleslaw with this dish. You may also prepare it using marlin.

3 cups mesquite chips

ROLLS
½ cup (¼ pound) butter or margarine
½ teaspoon minced garlic
8 seeded kaiser rolls, split

FISH
8 ½-inch-thick slices tuna
Oil for brushing tuna and greasing grill
1 large red onion, sliced thin
8 crisp, trimmed lettuce leaves
2 large tomatoes, sliced
Coarsely ground mustard (optional)

1. Soak the mesquite chips in cold water to cover for 1 hour.

2. *Prepare the rolls:* Melt the butter in small saucepan over low heat, mixing in the garlic as the butter melts. Remove from the heat. Brush the cut sides of the rolls with the garlic butter. Grill the rolls slightly, cut side down, on the prepared grill. Put the rolls on a tray and cover with aluminum foil.

3. *Grill the fish:* Brush the tuna slices with oil. Drain the mesquite chips and sprinkle them over the ashen coals. Grill the onions briefly on both sides or place under the tuna and grill together. Grill the tuna for 4–5 minutes, turn, and continue grilling on the other side until done to taste. Transfer the tuna slices to a platter and assemble the sandwiches immediately.

4. Place a lettuce leaf on the bottom half of each roll, then arrange an onion slice and a tuna slice over the lettuce. Top with a tomato slice and brush with mustard if desired.

Yield: 8 servings

GRILLED TUNA WITH RED PEPPER SAUCE

We suggest you serve lettuce with avocado and mango, warm muffins, and grilled red onion slices with this dish. You may substitute marlin or shark for the tuna.

RED PEPPER SAUCE
Oil for greasing grill
3 large red bell peppers
3 tablespoons fresh lemon juice
1 cup (½ pound) butter or margarine, cut into 1-inch pieces
¾ teaspoon dried tarragon, crumbled
½ teaspoon dried thyme, crumbled
¼ teaspoon salt
⅛ teaspoon freshly ground white pepper

FISH
½ cup dried thyme for sprinkling on hot coals
3 pounds tuna, cut into 8 steaks
Good-quality olive oil for brushing tuna

1. *Make the sauce:* Grill the peppers on the prepared grill, turning frequently using long-handled tongs. This will take about 8–10 minutes; all sides should be charred and blistered. Immediately place the peppers in a large plastic bag, and secure shut with a twister seal. Let stand for 10–12 minutes.

2. Remove the peppers from the bag, cut off the tops, and remove the skins by rubbing gently under cold water. Discard the seeds. Slice the peppers and puree in a food processor fitted with the steel blade or in a blender.

3. Blend together the lemon juice and pepper puree in a saucepan. Cook over medium heat for 5 minutes and remove from the heat. Using a wire whisk, incorporate the butter. Whisk in the tarragon, thyme, salt, and

pepper. The sauce should be served immediately, so grill the fish while completing the sauce.

4. *Grill the fish:* Sprinkle the dried thyme over the hot coals and replace the grill. Brush the tuna with oil on both sides and cook on the prepared grill over ashen coals for about 4 minutes on each side, depending on the thickness of the tuna. Do not cook the tuna all the way through; it should be served medium-rare or to taste. To serve, place the tuna on a plate and spoon the sauce down the center.

Yield: 8 servings (2½ cups sauce)

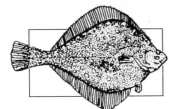

TURBOT
Turbot is a lean fish with a rich, delicate flavor.

TURBOT FILLETS WITH
TURKISH HAZELNUT SAUCE

This hazelnut sauce is a Turkish version of the nut-based sauces served all over the Middle East. Like all of those sauces, it is made quickly and needs only to be heated, not cooked.

Orange roughy, ono, scrod, and ocean perch work well in this recipe. Serve it with sweet potatoes and a tart green salad.

TURKISH HAZELNUT SAUCE
1 cup blanched hazelnuts
1 cup fresh bread crumbs
7 cloves garlic
½ cup white vinegar
½ cup mild, good-quality olive oil
2 large handfuls parsley, stems removed
1 teaspoon salt
1¼ cups water

FISH
16 ¼-inch-thick slices lemon for grilling
   fillets
3 pounds turbot fillets, cut into 8 serving
   pieces

1. *Make the sauce:* To toast the hazelnuts, preheat the oven to 350°F. Place the hazelnuts in a single layer on a baking sheet and place in the oven for 5 minutes. Check to see if they've begun to brown. If not, toast them a few minutes longer, checking often. As soon as they begin to brown lightly, remove them from the oven. They will continue browning slightly once

they're away from the heat. Then measure out 3 tablespoons, chop coarsely, and reserve for garnish.

2. Place the remaining toasted hazelnuts, bread crumbs, garlic, vinegar, olive oil, parsley, salt, and 1 cup of the water in a blender or a food processor fitted with the steel blade. Process until a coarse puree results. The puree should be thick but liquid enough to pour. If it is not, add the remaining ¼ cup water and process again.

3. *Grill the fish:* Place the lemon slices in pairs on the prepared grill and arrange the turbot fillets over the lemon slices. Grill the fillets 3–6 minutes, without turning, or until the fillets have lost their translucence and are cooked through.

4. Meanwhile, transfer the sauce to a small, heavy-bottomed saucepan and heat, stirring occasionally. Check sauce consistency. If too thick, add a little water. When hot, spoon the sauce into a serving bowl and garnish with the reserved chopped hazelnuts.

5. Using two spatulas, carefully transfer the turbot fillets to a serving platter, discarding the lemon slices. Serve the fillets topped with a few spoonfuls of sauce.

Yield: 8 servings (3 cups sauce)

TURBOT WITH CUMIN

❧

This dish is based on a Moroccan preparation in which a whole fish is spread, inside and out, with a cumin-garlic paste topping. Our version for the grill uses a meaty fillet that is spread with the paste. Since the fillet is not turned, the paste stays intact on top and is attractive when served. This easy, delicious dish is as good cold as it is hot, and scrod, ono, and orange roughy also work well. Serve it with noodles tossed with a small amount of butter or margarine and a green salad.

1 tablespoon plus ¾ teaspoon ground
    cumin
1 tablespoon plus 1½ teaspoons paprika
9 cloves garlic, peeled and quartered
¼ teaspoon salt
¼ teaspoon freshly ground pepper
3 large handfuls parsley, stems removed
6 tablespoons imported mild, good-quality
    olive oil
16 ¼-inch-thick slices lemon for grilling
    fish
3 pounds turbot fillets, cut into 8 serving
    pieces

1. Combine the cumin, paprika, garlic, salt, pepper, parsley, and oil in a food processor fitted with the steel blade. Process until an oily puree results.

2. Spread the top of each fillet lightly with the cumin-garlic paste. Arrange the lemon slices in pairs on the prepared grill. Arrange the fillets on the lemon slices and grill without turning for about 6 minutes or until the fish has lost its translucence and is just cooked through. Using two spatulas, carefully transfer the fillets to a serving platter. Discard the lemon slices. Serve immediately.

Yield: 8 servings

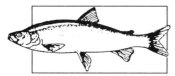

WHITEFISH
A medium-flavored fish that can be substituted with salmon or haddock. Both fillets and whole fish work well on the grill.

WHITEFISH DE JONGHE

STUFFING

4 tablespoons butter, softened
½ teaspoon each: finely chopped garlic, finely chopped onion, and finely chopped fresh hot pepper
¼ teaspoon salt
1 pinch dried thyme
1 tablespoon finely chopped fresh parlsey (stems removed)
2–3 tablespoons sherry
1½ cups bread crumbs
4 tablespoons finely chopped blanched almonds

FISH

Oil for brushing fish and greasing fish basket
1 3-pound whole whitefish, scaled and boned
4 slices lemon

1. *Stuff whitefish:* Mix butter with garlic, onion, hot pepper, salt, thyme, and parsley. Add sherry, bread crumbs, and chopped almonds, stirring well. Stuff whitefish with the mixture.

2. *Grill whitefish:* Oil whitefish on both sides, then oil inside of fish basket. Arrange 2 slices of lemon on fish basket bottom. Arrange fish over lemon slices. Top fish with remaining 2 lemon slices and fasten top of fish basket. Place on grill over ashen coals and grill 6–7 minutes on each side, or until fish begins to flake easily when tested with a fork. Serve immediately.

Yield: 4 servings

SKEWERED FISH SAUSAGE
APPETIZER

❧

Take care not to overcook these sausages. The mixture is intentionally dry, as it has to stay on the skewers, but if it is overcooked, it will be even drier. Be sure to serve lemon wedges; the sausages need the moisture. Any dry fish—orange roughy, redfish, or walleye pike—may be substituted for the whitefish. Since this appetizer is spartan, follow it with a richer entree and noodles that have been tossed lightly with butter or margarine.

16 8-inch wooden presoaked barbecue
   skewers
18 ounces whitefish fillets, skinned
4 garlic cloves, peeled and quartered
2 scallions, cut into 1-inch lengths
½ cup fresh bread crumbs, ground fine
2 tablespoons evaporated milk

1 teaspoon salt
1 teaspoon fresh lemon juice
6 dashes Tabasco sauce
Oil for brushing sausages and greasing
   grill
Lemon wedges

1. Examine the fillets carefully, rubbing your fingers up and down their surfaces to check for bones. If you find any, pull them out with tweezers. Cut the fish into chunks and place in a food processor fitted with the steel blade. Add garlic, scallion lengths, bread crumbs, evaporated milk, salt, lemon juice, and Tabasco sauce and process until the mixture is finely pureed.

2. Scoop out 2 tablespoons of the mixture and form into a 2-inch-long sausage at the end of a skewer. Repeat with the remaining mixture. You will end up with 16 sausages, each on its own skewer.

3. Brush each sausage lightly with oil and carefully place on the prepared grill. Grill for about 3 minutes on one side, then use a spatula to turn the sausages carefully. Grill for 3 minutes. Transfer the skewers to a serving platter and garnish with lemon wedges. Serve immediately.

Yield: 8 appetizer servings (2 sausages per person)

BUTTERFLIED WHITEFISH
IN A CRUMB CRUST

Serve with baked beans.

MARINADE

2 tablespoons oil
1 tablespoon fresh lemon juice
¼ teaspoon Tabasco sauce

FISH

1 2½- to 3-pound whole whitefish, boned
and butterflied

COATING

½ cup each: chopped cashews and bread
crumbs
⅓ cup grated Parmesan cheese
2 cloves garlic, minced fine
¼ teaspoon salt
Oil for greasing fish basket
8 slices lemon

1. *Marinate whitefish:* Mix 2 tablespoons oil, the lemon juice, and Tabasco sauce in small bowl. Open fish butterfly fashion and lay in a flat dish with raised sides. Pour marinade over fish. Let sit, covered, for 30 minutes in refrigerator.

2. *Stuff whitefish:* Meanwhile, mix cashews, bread crumbs, Parmesan cheese, garlic, and salt in a small bowl.

3. When fish has marinated for 30 minutes, remove from marinade and lay, butterfly fashion, on a flat plate. Pat half of cashew mixture over top of fish. Turn fish, brush with marinade if it needs lubrication, and pat remaining half of cashew mixture over other side of fish.

4. *Grill whitefish:* Oil a fish basket and lay 4 lemon slices on bottom. Arrange fish, butterfly fashion, on lemon slices. Top with remaining 4 lemon slices. Attach top of fish basket. Put on grill over ashen coals. Cook for 3–4 minutes on each side or until crumbs are lightly browned and fish flakes easily when tested with a fork. Serve immediately.

Yield: 4 servings

WHITEFISH FILLETS WITH BEURRE BLANC SAUCE AND LIME

❦

This is an all white entree: fish and sauce are both white. Serve it on colored plates with colorful accompaniments such as radicchio in the salad, broccoli or asparagus or a side dish of roasted red peppers.

BEURRE BLANC SAUCE
3 large shallots, minced
1 cup dry white wine
2 tablespoons fresh lime juice or white wine vinegar
16 tablespoons (2 sticks) butter, cut into ½-inch pieces

FISH
4 7-ounce whitefish fillets
Melted butter
Freshly ground white pepper
Oil for greasing grill
1 tablespoon grated lime zest
2 limes, quartered, for garnish

1. *Make sauce:* Combine shallots, wine, and lime juice in a heavy nonaluminum saucepan and cook until mixture is reduced to 2–3 tablespoons. Remove saucepan from heat, add 2 pieces of the butter, and whisk until incorporated. Whisk in remaining butter, 2 pieces at a time, being careful not to allow the sauce to separate. If sauce separates, whisk quickly and try to emulsify. Keep sauce warm over simmering water or serve immediately.

2. *Grill whitefish:* Brush whitefish fillets with melted butter and sprinkle with pepper. Arrange fish on prepared grill. If using the tail section, tuck tail under fish to help even the thickness. Cook for 4 minutes, brush with butter, and turn fish. Continue cooking 3 minutes or until done, depending on thickness of fish. Place on individual dishes and ladle sauce over fish. Sprinkle with lime zest. Serve whitefish fillets garnished with lime wedges.

Yield: 4 servings

WHITEFISH STUFFED WITH SHRIMP

Great for that special VIP dinner.

STUFFING
2 tablespoons butter
½ cup finely chopped onion
2 pinches cayenne pepper
¼ teaspoon each: salt and dried tarragon
12 medium-sized cooked shrimp, peeled,
deveined, and chopped coarse
1 cup bread crumbs

FISH
1 3-pound whole whitefish, scaled and
boned
Oil for brushing fish and greasing fish
basket
4 slices lemon

1. *Stuff whitefish:* Melt butter in medium saucepan. Add onion and sauté for about 10 minutes over medium heat. Stir in cayenne pepper, salt, and tarragon and cook for another minute. Remove from heat and stir in shrimp and bread crumbs. Mix well, then use to fill whitefish cavity.

2. *Grill whitefish:* Oil fish well on both sides and oil inside of fish basket. Lay 2 lemon slices on bottom of basket. Lay fish in basket over lemon slices. Top fish with 2 more lemon slices. Fasten top of basket and put on grill over ashen coals. Cook 8–9 minutes on each side or until fish flakes easily when tested with a fork. Serve immediately.

Yield: 4 servings

WHITEFISH WITH GARLIC AND BLACK BEAN SAUCE

This recipe is good hot or cold. Serve fish with rice. Salted black beans are available at Oriental food markets.

BLACK BEAN SAUCE

2 tablespoons peanut oil

1 tablespoon salted black beans, washed, drained, and mashed

2 cloves garlic, minced

3 green onions, minced

1 teaspoon minced fresh gingerroot

3 tablespoons light soy sauce

3 tablespoons dry white wine

½ teaspoon sugar

6 tablespoons water

¼ teaspoon salt

1 teaspoon cornstarch, mixed with
   1 teaspoon water

FISH

1 3½-pound whole whitefish or trout, scaled, head and tail intact

Peanut oil for brushing fish and greasing grill

1. *Make sauce:* Heat 2 tablespoons oil in a small saucepan. Stir in black beans, garlic, onions, and ginger. Combine remaining sauce ingredients, except cornstarch mixture, in a small bowl. Stir sauce into black beans. Blend in cornstarch mixture and continue cooking until sauce begins to thicken, stirring often. Set sauce aside.

2. *Grill whitefish:* Brush whitefish with peanut oil. Place fish on prepared grill or on a double layer of aluminum foil, poked with a few air holes. Grill for 6–7 minutes on each side. Arrange fish on heated platter and drizzle warm sauce over fish.

Yield: 4–6 servings

ORANGE WHITEFISH

We suggest you serve this dish with a large green salad.

MARINADE
¼ cup peanut oil
2 tablespoons minced fresh parlsey
1 tablespoon fresh lemon juice
Juice of 1 orange

FISH
4 7-ounce whitefish fillets
2 tablespoons grated orange zest
Oil for greasing grill
2 large oranges, sliced

1. *Marinate whitefish:* Combine all marinade ingredients and place in a shallow glass dish. Marinate whitefish fillets for 1 hour, turning once. Drain whitefish and reserve marinade.

2. *Grill whitefish:* Sprinkle fillets with orange zest and place on prepared grill. Cook for 4–5 minutes. Turn fish and continue grilling for 2–3 minutes, depending on thickness of fish, or until it begins to flake easily when tested with a fork. Place orange slices on grill and cook on both sides for 2–4 minutes. Place fish on individual serving plates and top with orange slices.

Yield: 4 servings

WHITEFISH FILLETS WITH PISTACHIO, GARNISHED WITH SKEWERED FRUIT

This elegant dish is Moroccan in origin, but we have changed it considerably, while retaining the original flavors, in adapting it for the grill. The original recipe calls for a large shad to be stuffed with dates, figs, prunes, and apricots, each of which has been previously stuffed with a pistachio nut mixture. Since large fish do not fit into standard-sized fish baskets and can't be turned on the grill, we use whitefish fillets that are spread with the pistachio mixture, then grilled without turning. The dried fruits also are stuffed with the mixture, then brushed with honey and placed on the grill for just a moment or until they are warm. Each guest is served one pistachio-topped fillet and one skewer of stuffed dried fruits. Also serve chilled marinated fresh asparagus spears and hot French bread. You may substitute scrod.

8 8-inch wooden presoaked barbecue
   skewers

MARINADE
¾ cup imported, mild, good-quality olive
   oil
¼ cup fresh lemon juice
¾ teaspoon salt

FISH
3 pounds whitefish fillets, cut into
   8 serving pieces
16 ¼-inch-thick slices lemon for grilling
   fillets

PISTACHIO PASTE
¾ cup cooked rice
6 ounces pistachio nuts, chopped fine
   (1½ cups)
6 tablespoons butter or margarine
1½ teaspoons sugar
⅜ teaspoon ground cinnamon
⅜ teaspoon ground allspice
⅛ teaspoon ground ginger
Few drops water to make paste spreadable
   (if needed)

FRUIT
8 large pitted dates
8 large dried apricots
8 large pitted prunes
8 large figs with hard stems snipped off
Honey for brushing skewered fruit

1. *Make the marinade:* Mix the olive oil, lemon juice, and salt in a large plastic bag. Set the bag in a bowl and add the whitefish fillets. Secure the bag with a twister seal and turn the bag several times to make sure all fish surfaces touch the marinade. Let sit at room temperature for 1 hour, turning the bag occasionally.

2. *Meanwhile, make the pistachio paste:* Combine the rice, pistachios, butter, sugar, cinnamon, allspice, ginger, and if needed, a few drops of water. Mix well to make a spreadable paste. Place the dates, apricots, prunes, and figs in a saucepan, cover with water, and heat to a boil. Immediately drain the fruit and allow to cool. When cool, stuff the fruit with the pistachio mixture, using ½–1 teaspoon stuffing per piece. Remove the skewers from the water and thread four pieces of fruit (one date, one apricot, one fig, and one prune) on each skewer. Brush with honey on all sides and reserve.

3. *Grill the fish:* Remove the fillets from the marinade and lay them flat on a large tray. Blot the tops of each fillet slightly with paper towels, then press 2–3 tablespoons of pistachio paste onto the top of each fillet, covering it as completely as possible. Arrange the lemon slices in pairs on the prepared grill. Place one fillet on each pair of lemon slices. Grill for 4–8 minutes without turning.

4. About 2 minutes before the fillets have finished cooking, place the skewered fruit on the grill and grill for a minute on each side.

5. Using two spatulas, carefully transfer the fillets to a serving platter. Arrange the fruit skewers attractively on the platter. Serve each guest a pistachio-topped fillet and a skewer of stuffed dried fruit.

Yield: 8 servings

WHITEFISH FILLETS WITH BLACK CAVIAR BUTTER

❧

The elegant butter served with this dish is made from whipping cream in a food processor or blender. The delicate, newborn butter is then mixed with black lumpfish caviar—the kind that's available in supermarkets and relatively inexpensive—and served at room temperature, melting over the hot fillets. Although the dish can be made successfully with commercial butter, the homemade variety is extra-delicate and makes for interesting dinner conversation ("What? You made your own butter?") as well. We suggest you serve this dish with baked potatoes, split and topped with a small amount of the caviar butter if desired.

Rainbow trout, lake trout, and sunfish are all suitable substitutes for the whitefish in this recipe.

FISH
1 recipe basic marinade (see Index)
3 pounds whitefish fillets, cut into
  8 serving pieces
16 ¼-inch-thick slices lemon for grilling
  fish
Lemon wedges

HOMEMADE BUTTER
2 cups whipping cream, at least 1 day old
1½ cups ice water, containing some small
  ice chunks
1 2-ounce jar black lumpfish caviar

1. *Marinate the fish:* Pour the marinade into a large plastic bag and add the whitefish. Secure with a twister seal and turn the bag several times to make sure all fish surfaces touch the marinade. Place the bag in a bowl and let sit at room temperature for 1 hour.

2. *Meanwhile, make the homemade butter:* Place the whipping cream in a food processor and turn on for a few seconds or until the cream is stiffly whipped. Turn on the motor again and pour in ¾ cup of the ice water. Let the

motor run for 3 minutes. Add the remaining ¾ cup ice water and let the motor run for another minute or 2 and listen for the sound of the motor groaning slightly. When you hear it, turn the processor off and look at the cream. If it has a curdled, spoiled appearance, the butter has "come," as our great-grandmothers used to say to describe the cream-into-butter process. It will not look like butter at all, but have faith; this is the first step. It may take even longer than the 5 or 6 minutes it usually takes. If so, relax. Just let the motor continue to run and check the container contents occasionally. The cream will turn to butter eventually. (Beats churning by hand, doesn't it?) As soon as the cream has a curdled, spoiled appearance, transfer it to a strainer and gently press out all the water, using either your fingers or the back of a wooden spoon. After a minute or so of gentle pressure, the mixture will begin to look and feel like butter.

3. Transfer the butter to a small serving bowl and reserve for a minute at room temperature. You will have a scant cup of butter. Dump the contents of the lumpfish caviar jar into a strainer and hold it under gently running tap water for a minute or two or until the black dye washes off and the water runs clear. Mix 2 tablespoons of the caviar into the soft butter. Taste and add more caviar if desired.

4. *Grill the fish:* Arrange the lemon slices in pairs on the prepared grill. Place one whitefish fillet on each pair of lemon slices. Grill for 8 minutes, without turning, or until the fillets have lost their translucence and are slightly browned on the edges.

5. When the fillets are cooked, transfer them to a serving platter. Spoon 1–2 tablespoons of the caviar butter onto each hot fillet and serve with lemon wedges.

Yield: 12 servings (1 cup butter)

WHITEFISH FILLETS WITH DARK RAISIN SAUCE

We suggest you also serve boiled new potatoes and steamed broccoli. Scrod and catfish make fine substitutes for the whitefish.

DARK RAISIN SAUCE

2 tablespoons butter or margarine

4 teaspoons flour

1 cup beef broth (canned broth can be
    used, but do not use beef bouillon)

1¼ cups dry white wine

1½ ounces commercial gingersnaps
    (6 2-inch cookies), crumbled

½ cup dark raisins

¼ cup sugar

1 tablespoon fresh lemon juice

¼ teaspoon salt

¾ cup water

FISH

3 pounds whitefish fillets, cut into
    8 serving pieces

16 ¼-inch-thick slices orange, for grilling
    fish

1. *Make the sauce:* Melt the butter in a large saucepan over medium heat. Add the flour and stir with a wooden spoon until the mixture turns golden brown. Stir in the beef broth and white wine and simmer over low heat, stirring often, until the mixture thickens slightly. Add the gingersnaps, raisins, sugar, lemon juice, and salt. Return to a simmer and cook for about 5 minutes, stirring often to make sure the mixture does not burn. Add ½ cup of the water and stir. Remove from heat.

2. *Grill the fish:* Place the orange slices in pairs on the prepared grill. Carefully arrange the whitefish fillets on the orange slices, skin side down.

Cook for about 4–8 minutes, without turning, or until the fish is cooked through and opaque.

3. While the fillets are cooking, reheat the sauce to a simmer and check the consistency. If necessary, add the remaining ¼ cup water and return to a simmer. Transfer to a serving bowl.

4. Carefully remove the fillets from the grill, discarding the orange slices, and place on a serving platter. Serve immediately, topping each fillet with a liberal spoonful of raisin sauce. Pass additional raisin sauce.

Yield: 8 servings (3 cups sauce)

WHITEFISH WITH CHICAGO SAUCE

❧

The word Chicago is really a corruption of an Indian word Checagou, which meant "great" or "powerful" and which the Illinois Indians used alternately to refer to a large fort or to the wild onions that grew along the banks of what became the Chicago River. Since wild onions are in shorter supply today than they once were, we suggest you substitute small, tender leeks for the once plentiful young, green, odoriferous shoots. You may substitute trout for the whitefish.

We suggest you serve this dish with a tossed spinach and orange salad and grilled sweet potatoes.

CHICAGO SAUCE
1 tablespoon olive oil
3 tablespoons butter or margarine
1 large shallot or 2 small shallots, minced
¾ cup chopped wild onion or small leek,
    both white and green parts
1 tablespoon flour
½ teaspoon dried tarragon, crumbled
¼ teaspoon salt
1 cup evaporated milk

FISH
3 pounds whitefish fillets, cut into
    8 serving pieces
Melted butter or margarine for brushing
    fillets
16 ¼-inch-thick slices orange for grilling
    fish
8 wild onions or scallions, trimmed, for
    garnish

1. *Make the sauce:* Heat the oil and butter in a skillet. Add shallots and wild onions and simmer for 2 minutes or until tender. Whisk in the flour and cook until it is absorbed. Season with tarragon and salt. Stir in the milk and reduce the heat. Simmer until slightly thickened and warm.

2. *Grill the fish:* Brush the fish with melted butter. Arrange the orange slices in pairs on the prepared grill. Place a whitefish fillet on each pair of orange slices and grill for 4–8 minutes, without turning, or until the fillets have lost their translucence and are slightly browned on the edges.

3. When the fillets are cooked, transfer them to a serving platter and spoon the warm sauce over the fish. Arrange the wild onions across the fish as a garnish.

Yield: 8 servings (1½ cups sauce)

WHITEFISH WITH LICHEES AND SHIITAKE MUSHROOMS

Brook trout also works well in this recipe. Serve it with wonton soup, grilled leeks, and stir-fried green bell pepper strips.

MARINADE
2 cloves garlic, minced
1½ cups dry white wine
¼ cup soy sauce
1 teaspoon brown sugar
4 scallions, minced
½ teaspoon Oriental sesame oil

FISH
3 pounds whitefish fillets with skin, cut into 8 serving pieces
3 oranges, sliced thin (you'll need 16 slices altogether)
¾ pound fresh shiitake mushrooms or white button mushrooms, trimmed
Oil for brushing mushrooms
1 16-ounce can lichee nuts, drained
Orange slices for garnish

1. *Make the marinade:* Combine the marinade ingredients. Pour the marinade into a large plastic bag and add the whitefish. Secure with a twister seal and turn the bag several times to make sure all fish surfaces touch the marinade. Place the bag in a bowl and let sit at room temperature for 1 hour.

2. *Grill the fish:* Arrange the orange slices in pairs on the prepared grill. Place one whitefish fillet on each pair of orange slices. Grill for 4–8 minutes, without turning, or until the fish has lost its translucence and is slightly browned on the edges.

3. *Grill the mushrooms:* Brush the mushroom caps with oil and grill for about 1 minute or until done to taste.

4. Transfer the whitefish to a serving platter. Sprinkle with the drained lichees and grilled mushrooms and garnish with extra orange slices.

Yield: 8 servings

APPENDIX:
MAIL-ORDER SOURCES OF INGREDIENTS

The Chef's Catalog
3215 Commercial Ave.
Northbrook, IL 60062
(708) 480-9400
Grill basket.

Carolyn Collins Caviar
925 W. Jackson Blvd., 3rd Fl.
Chicago, IL 60607
(312) 226-0342
Fax (312) 226-2114
Freshwater caviar.

Food Stuffs
338 Park Ave.
Glencoe, IL 60022
(708) 835-5105
Canned snails.

Gamatech
1275 Lincoln Ave., Suite 10
San Jose, CA 95125
(408) 291-5220
Double-pronged skewers, grill wok.

Holy Land Grocery, Inc.
4806 N. Kedzie Ave.
Chicago, IL 60659
(312) 588-3306
Tahini, za'tar (specify green, not red),
and broad fava beans.

Maid of Scandinavia
3244 Raleigh Ave.
Minneapolis, MN 55415
(800) 328-6722
Rosewater

People's Gourmet Woods
75 Mill St.
Cumberland, RI 02864
(800) 729-5800
Pure hardwood charcoal,
smoking/cooking woods.

The Oriental Food Market
2801 W. Howard St.
Chicago, IL 60645
(312) 274-2826
Black beans, Oriental wooden barbecue
skewers, Oriental sesame oil, shrimp
paste, and nam pla (Thai bottled
fish sauce).

Star Market
3349 N. Clark St.
Chicago, IL 60659
(312) 472-0599
Japanese soy sauce.

Wild Game, Inc.
1941 W. Division St.
Chicago, IL 60622
(312) 278-1661
Shiitake mushrooms.

INDEX